THE
ANATOMY OF THE
ZULU ARMY

THE
ANATOMY OF THE
ZULU ARMY

From Shaka to Cetshwayo
1818–1879

IAN KNIGHT

Frontline Books

Greenhill
Books

First published in 1995 by Greenhill Books, Lionel Leventhal Limited
www.greenhillbooks.com

This revised paperback edition published in 2015 by Frontline Books

an imprint of Pen & Sword Books Ltd,
47 Church Street, Barnsley, S. Yorkshire, S70 2AS
For more information on our books, please visit
www.frontline-books.com, email info@frontline-books.com
or write to us at the above address.

ISBN: 978-1-84832-910-2

CIP data records for this title are available from the British Library

Printed and bound by CPI Group (UK) Ltd, Croydon, CR0 4YY

Contents

List of Illustrations

Pages 65–80

1. Zulu man with weapons
2. Married Zulu man wearing the *isicoco*
3. Warriors in King Mpande's army
4. Zulu *induna*
5. Zulu warriors of the 1830s
6. Zulu 'chief' and his wife
7. Zulu 'chief' with attendants
8. Zulu warrior in traditional costume
9. The *inkosi* Ngoza kaLudaba
10. Ngoza with unmarried warriors
11. Ngoza with his senior men
12. *Amabutho* of the 1860s
13. *Amabutho* of the 1860s
14. Zulu with stabbing spear and knobkerrie
15. *Induna* wearing headdress and necklace
16. The *umqele*
17. The *amabutho* in ceremony
18. Warrior in full regalia
19. Warrior in full regalia
20. Ceremonial costume of the younger *amabutho*
21. Ceremonial costume of the senior *amabutho*

Pages 129–144

22. Warrior in war-dress, with *umbumbuluzo* type shield
23. Girls carrying food
24. Ceremonial costume within an *ibutho*
25. Zulu blacksmith at work
26. King Dingane's *komkhulu*, eMgungundlovu
27. King Dingane's uKhangela homestead
28. Life in the *amakhanda*
29. An *umyango*, to house regimental war-shields
30. Model of King Cetshwayo's quarters at the oNdini homestead
31. Girls carry food to the occupants of an *ikhanda*

List of Maps

Maps drawn by Ian Castle, 1995

Foreword

Throughout the histories of nations, mention may be found of groups or formations of fighting men which have left their names deeply inscribed in the annals of military legend and endeavour. Some reach back to the dim and distant past: the Spartans, the hoplites of Greece, the janissaries of the Ottoman empire, the praetorian guard of the Emperor Augustus. Most, if not all, were special groupings or formations of an existing larger army. In this book the author, Ian Knight, deals with such a military force, which was not part of an army, but an army in its own right, and which became a legend in its own time – the *impi* of King Shaka Zulu.

As such, the Zulu army was a monument – presumably an unintentional one – to Shaka himself. Shaka, the brilliant tactician and leader of men in the field. The training of his *impi*, the discipline he instilled and maintained, his evolution of the short stabbing spear and the shield as an aid to attack, the creation of a formal military institution, his war policy – fighting to annihilate and adopting scorched earth tactics – all filled his adversaries with fear and awe. It gave his soldiers from the outset a psychological ascendancy. The cry 'Hannibal ad portas!' which reverberated from the walls of ancient Rome had its echo over two thousand years later on the vastness of the African veld: *'Namp'amaZulu!'* – the Zulus are here!

There is something special and unique about the Zulu army. In the few instances quoted above, the élite formations were products of an already centuries-old tradition. Shaka and his Zulu army, on the other hand, gave substance to the oft-cited adage 'ex Africa semper aliquid novi' – always something new out of Africa. Shaka's army may have been rooted in the culture of his people, but as a military force it was a new creation, and within a few years it had developed such a capability that it was able to confront the far greater technological power of the army of the British Empire. Even though the Zulus were foot-soldiers, the British general officer commanding felt compelled to order his officers, when planning action against them, to plan as if for cavalry.

The other aspect which singles out the Zulu warriors is the intense pride they had in being members, not only of the Zulu *impi* as such, but in particular of the regiment into which they had been mustered. The pride in their regimental name was even greater than the pride in their personal

13

name, so that many soldiers would prefer to be known by their regimental, rather than their family name.

Membership of a regiment was the epitome of being a Zulu. The spirit of *ubuZulu* – of Zuluness – has transcended time and changed circumstances and still, in the 1990s, imbues hundreds of thousands of Zulu.

In congratulating the author on his choice of subject matter – this book will fill a definite gap in the available literature on the Zulu – one must also give credit to his painstaking research and presentation of, to my knowledge, the first all-embracing and detailed history and analysis of the Zulu army as such – the *impi yesizwe* – which, if not physically, is spiritually alive among abakwaZulu even today.

Cmdt S. Bourquin, DWD
Westville
KwaZulu-Natal
1995

Introduction and Acknowledgements

It was that great poet of the British empire, Rudyard Kipling, who, cataloguing the various peoples around the world who had recently given the British a bloody nose, noted that 'a Zulu *impi* dished us up in style'. Indeed they did; on 22 January 1879, the army of the independent kingdom of Zululand overran a British camp at the foot of Mount Isandlwana and slaughtered 1300 of its defenders. It was an incident that reverberated around the world at the time, and its echoes still haunt the emergence of the fledgling democracy in South Africa today. Furthermore, it has captured the imagination of generations of authors and film-makers, and the events of the Anglo-Zulu War exert a hold on the popular imagination which outweigh even their not inconsiderable historical importance.

It is only more recently, however, that historians have chosen to look beyond the rhetoric of the imperial politicians who made the war, and the red-coat soldiers who fought it, and consider the view from the other side of the river. This shift of attention began almost exactly a century after the last shots of the war were fired, and since the pioneering work of Jeff Guy, John Laband and others, more attention has been focused on the Zulu perspective than on any other aspect of the campaign. Yet gaps have remained. *The Anatomy of the Zulu Army* does not pretend to be a history of the Zulu army in the nineteenth century – that would take several volumes – nor even of its role in 1879, which John Laband has covered in his masterly *Kingdom in Crisis*. Instead, I have attempted to examine the way the army actually worked; and whereas it is almost a cliché to point out that it was not a full-time professional body in the manner of its British counterpart, it nonetheless did function as a military force, and it is necessary, therefore, to consider how. I have tried to look at the way in which the *amabutho* were formed, how the warriors were maintained in barracks, what they ate, what their duties were, and what rewards they might have expected. To some extent I have tried to do this 'from the bottom up', but it has been neither possible nor desirable to remove the military institution from the context of its social function, and I hope those whose interest is not primarily anthropological will forgive the necessary digressions. Most of all, however, I have tried to look at the way the army operated in the field – how it was armed, dressed and provisioned, its spiritual preparation, its tactics, and the shock of battle itself.

Although I have tried to make this material appropriate to the army's history from King Shaka to King Cetshwayo, there is, perhaps inevitably, a bias towards the Anglo-Zulu War, if only because there is far more information available for this period than for others. Many of the cultural attitudes, traditions and institutions that framed Zulu military life remained largely constant between 1818 and 1879; despite obvious modifications, King Cetshwayo's army was recognisably the same organisation as King Shaka's. Nevertheless, the army clearly did not exist in a historical vacuum, and I have tried to suggest some of the historical and economic factors that influenced those modifications over the years. I have also deliberately drawn on early European accounts of the army, not merely for the descriptive material they contain, but also in an attempt to conjure up something of the atmosphere of time and place, and explore the way the Zulu kingdom was perceived by outsiders, since such a perception ultimately played no small part in its fate. Where possible, however, I have also endeavoured to allow the Zulus themselves to describe the system from within, so far as is possible across the gulfs of time and culture. Here I must acknowledge my debt to that remarkable collection of Zulu evidence, *The James Stuart Archive*, translated and edited by Colin Webb and John Wright and published by the University of Natal, which, allowing for an occasional and inevitable distortion by Stuart's own preoccupations, still remains an astonishing and invaluable collection of source material, without which no serious work in the field could be undertaken.

Several debts are of a more personal nature. I could never have attempted a work such as this without the help over the years of the great expert on Zulu history, culture and language, S.B. Bourquin of Westville. The trips I undertook in Zululand with S.B. during the early years of my interest have had a profound effect on me; they made Zululand's past come alive, and the memory of them continues to be an inspiration, particularly when I am working in my office on a dreary, grey English winter's day. Ian Castle has proved a consistently reliable and amusing travelling companion – we have stumbled, staggered and tripped together across most of Zululand's historic sites, in baking heat and pouring rain, falling into rivers or getting stuck in ditches, and somehow survived – and has always shared the fruits of his own researches most willingly. In the UK, Keith Reeves has been similarly generous with his magnificent collection of Zulu War memorabilia, as has Rai England with his collection of contemporary newspapers. In South Africa, Professor John Laband has tolerated my invasion of his academic field with customary charm, and Graham Dominy has not only allowed me unrestricted access to the collections of the Natal Museum, but proved the most imperturbable of hosts. I have the fondest memories, too, of warm, quiet evenings spent on the veranda of Graeme Smythe's home on the battlefield of Rorke's Drift, sipping cool beers and watching the sun go down over this most famous of battlefields. Gillian Berning and George Foster at the Local History Museum in Durban, and the staff of the Killie Campbell collection, together with the various regimental and other military museums in the UK, have always been most helpful and encouraging. Doctors Barry Marshall and John Vincent, of the former KwaZulu Monuments Council and Natal Museums Services respectively, have always allowed me unfettered access to the sites under their charge, and Dave Rattray has spun me many a spell-binding yarn of bygone battles around the fire at his beautiful Fugitives' Drift Lodge. Ken Gillings, another valued travelling companion, allowed me unstinting access to his office facilities during the final corrections of the manuscript.

Most of all, however, my thanks are due to my wife Carolyn, who has embarked willingly on this long adventure, which has already taken her down strange and exotic roads, and who has accepted the sacrifices she has been called upon to make on behalf of my other passion without complaint.

Ian Knight
1995

Schematic breakdown of a Zulu Ibutho (Regiment)

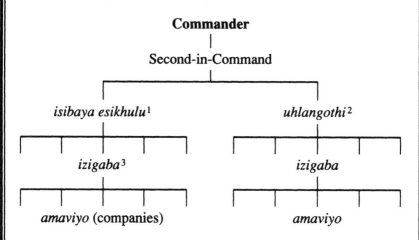

Commander

|

Second-in-Command

isibaya esikhulu[1]

izigaba[3]

amaviyo (companies)

uhlangothi[2]

izigaba

amaviyo

[1] The term *isibaya esihkulu* has a complex meaning. Literally 'the great enclosure', it refers either to the 'great house' (i.e., the senior wives and children, including the heir) of a royal homestead, or that part of an *ikhanda* – and its inhabitants – who were particularly associated with the royal household. In this sense it therefore represents one half of an *ibutho*, which was housed together in the huts down one side of an *ikhanda*, and which was considered the senior section.

[2] Literally 'flank', the arc of huts on one side of an *ikhanda* distinct from the *isibaya esikhulu*. Therefore, in this context, the subordinate section of an *ibutho*.

[3] Sections who *kleza'd* at the same *ikhanda*. The number of *izigaba* varied from regiment to regiment, as did the number of *amaviyo*, and the number of men in each *iviyo*.

CHAPTER 1

Breaking the Rope

There is an old story told in Zululand, even today,[1] about the rivalry between the British empire and the independent Zulu kingdom on the eve of the 1879 Anglo-Zulu War. Like all good stories, it is almost certainly apocryphal, and it seems to have gained its greatest currency in the last years of the nineteenth century, when the full impact of the Zulu military defeat had become obvious to all levels of society. The story refers to a time before the war, which even then was assuming all the mythic status of a vanished golden age; King Cetshwayo kaMpande was on the throne, and the kingdom had never seemed richer or more powerful. Yet the true situation was very different, for in fact the balance of regional power had already shifted south across the Thukela river, to the neighbouring territory of Natal, where the British had ruled since 1843. The British and the Zulus were being propelled into conflict by deep political and economic rivalries, the full implications of which were scarcely recognised in the Zulu heartland. When the first tensions arose, so the story has it, King Cetshwayo sent a container of millet, *uphoko*, to Natal's Secretary for Native Affairs, Theophilus Shepstone. It was a gesture which implied both a boast and a veiled threat, a warning not to interfere in the affairs of a strong nation: 'If you can count the number of grains in this *uphoko*', the king's message ran, 'then you will have counted the number of the Zulu people.' Shepstone, who was never one to shirk a theatrical gesture himself, immediately sent back to the king a bullock hide. 'Ah,' he is said to have replied, 'but if you can count the hairs on this hide, then you will know how many are the English.'

It is, of course, a story that is only poignant with hindsight, for by the time it became widely believed, the bitter underlying truth of the parable was all too apparent. Tension had given way to military confrontation, and the Zulus, whose military prowess had been renowned across southern Africa, had been broken and humiliated. On no less than three occasions, their army had defeated the British in the field: once, at Isandlwana, that defeat had been as spectacular as any endured by the imperial power in the nineteenth century.[2] Yet in the end, the courage of the Zulu people had proved an ineffective armour against the might of European industrial technology. The grand heroic charges of the massed *amabutho*, the king's regiments, had withered before the storm of shot and shell, and the inva-

19

ders, thrusting right into the heart of the Zulu country, had defeated the king on the very threshold of his royal homestead. The great settlements which embodied the power of the Zulu royal house were razed to the ground, and Cetshwayo himself captured and sent into exile. Few Zulu families escaped without a father, brother or son being struck down or wounded in the struggle. In the bitter years that followed, the country fell apart into civil war, and the people were drawn increasingly into a colonial system which dismissed their culture and traditions and valued them only as a source of cheap labour. King Cetshwayo's container of millet was indeed spilt upon the ground, and the hairs on the hide of European ascendancy grew more luxuriant than ever.

The coming of the whites

Ironically, early relations between the British and the Zulu kingdom had been good. European settlement in the sub-continent dated back to 1652, when the Dutch East India Company had occupied the Cape peninsula, establishing a victualling station for their ships on the long haul from Europe to the profitable markets of the Indies. Although the company proved reluctant to expand into the hinterland, it was unable to contain its own settler population, that mixture of Dutch, German and French religious refugees who came in time to think of themselves as Afrikaners – white Africans – or, with simple pride, Boers – farmers. As the settler community expanded slowly eastward, so it clashed with the robust African societies who inhabited the rolling downland of the eastern Cape. In 1806, as part of the fall-out from the wide-ranging conflicts in post-Revolutionary Europe, Britain took over control of the Cape from the Dutch, inheriting a complex and tense situation which deteriorated still further over the next half-century.

By the 1870s, a deep-rooted antagonism had sprung up between the Afrikaners, who had established two independent republics in the interior, the Orange Free State and the Transvaal, and the British, who held the Cape and Natal on the eastern seaboard. Sandwiched in between, their political and economic independence steadily eroding, lay the remains of the original black groups. The constant friction between all of these people was increasingly resolved at the expense of the blood of the British red-coat, and by a constant drain on the exchequer. Not until diamonds were discovered at Kimberley in 1867 did the region offer any potential return on Britain's investment, and the politically fractured state of the region hampered the introduction of an effective infrastructure to exploit the mineral wealth. Grasping the nettle, the Colonial Office in London hit upon a scheme, tried with some success in Canada, which it called Confederation. The idea was to bring all of the disparate parties together under British rule, ostensibly for their own good. Ironically, the Transvaal was the first to be absorbed, since its fragile economy and chaotic administration made annexation an easy British option. In 1877, after the most cursory and selective sampling of Boer opinion, British troops raised the Union Flag in Pretoria.

With the Transvaal, however, came a festering border dispute with the Zulus. The two states abutted each other along the foothills of the inland mountain range known to the Africans as *Kahlamba*, 'the barrier of upturned spears', and to the Boers as the *Drakensberg* – the Dragon Mountains. When the first Boers had trekked away from British rule at the Cape in the 1830s, and settled the Transvaal, the border had remained largely undefined, but by the 1870s population pressure on both sides had thrown the issue into relief, and on several occasions it had threatened to erupt into violence. It was at this point that a new British High Commissioner, Sir Henry Bartle Frere, arrived in the Cape, with a brief to push through the Confederation policy as swiftly as possible.

Frere and Confederation

Ironically, it was Frere, who wished to see the Zulu kingdom destroyed, who was largely responsible for focusing outside attention on one of its major institutions, its army. Advised by expansionists within the settler community, who saw in Zululand a block to Natal's economic development, and by missionaries frustrated at their lack of success in Zululand, Frere came to believe that the Zulus were a potential threat to the Confederation scheme; he saw the Zulu monarch as the 'head and moving spirit' behind a wave of unrest that swept through the black population across the region as Britain tightened its grip. Furthermore, Zulu intransigence offered an ideal opportunity for a little judicious wielding of British military might, which would serve as a useful example to any other groups who might be inclined to oppose Confederation.[3]

Frere began a propaganda campaign with the aim of mobilising opinion, both among the settlers of British southern Africa and inside the Colonial Office in London, behind the cause of armed intervention. Fuelling his arguments with imagery borrowed from the missionary community in Zululand, he characterised the Zulu kingdom as a ruthless and godless despotism, which exercised unnatural restraint over its army, and kept its own civilian population in check by the unsubtle use of naked force. 'I would not for an instant question,' he wrote to the Colonial Secretary, Sir Michael Hicks Beach, in December 1878,[4]

> our responsibility for putting an end to a system which locks up all the manhood of the country in a compulsory celibacy, considered by the despot necessary for the efficiency of his army, that army having no possible use but

to threaten us or other friendly people who surround him, a system which massacres hundreds of young women who refuse at his bidding to become the wives of elderly soldiers to whom they are sold off, a system which destroys all private property and industry, which forbids all improvements by civilisation or education, and relies solely on a regular course of murder and plunder by armed bands of the King's soldiers for the replenishment of the royal exchequer.

This image, of course, reveals more about the preoccupations of Victorian Britain than it does about the Zulu kingdom, based as it is on the virtues of the Christian marriage contract, the ennobling power of labour, and the sanctity of private property. Yet Frere had couched his message well; in England, the picture of the swaggering and truculent Zulu bully was sure to be decidedly unappealing to the public school-educated élite which controlled the government and civil service, while the implied threat of hordes of young black warriors, seething with a sexual frustration somehow transmuted to bloodlust and poised to sweep down upon helpless white families, must have had genteel young ladies swooning clear across the Home Counties. In South Africa, too, Frere's vision of the 'faithless and cruel' King Cetshwayo and his army, 'forty to sixty thousand strong, well armed, unconquered, insolent, burning to clear out the white man', struck a chord, for the history of colonial Natal and its northern neighbour had been inextricably entwined, and for a generation many white settlers had been living under the shadow of the Zulu threat.

Zululand and Natal

The Zulu kingdom had emerged early in the nineteenth century, expanding from a heartland along the middle reaches of the White Mfolozi, until it exerted control over considerable tracts of country south of the Thukela river, the area known to the European world as Natal. When the first British traders had arrived in 1824, the Zulu king, Shaka kaSenzangakhona, had granted them land around the bay of Port Natal – the region's only viable harbour – and from this tiny anarchic settlement all British claims in the region had stemmed. Within a few years the Zulus had abandoned their claims to Natal, and the British colony had slowly developed, but those early years had been marked by occasional ruptures in the good relations between the two states which had been so spectacular that they were seared into the folk memory of the settler community. When in 1838 the first Boers crossed the Drakensberg mountains into Natal, a particularly brutal war had broken out between them and King Dingane, Shaka's successor. In the ensuing campaigns, the Zulu army had swept into Natal twice, once massacring Boer civilians in the foothills of the inland mountains, and once sacking the settlement at Port Natal itself. Although there were no further clashes between Natal and the Zulu kingdom in the years between 1840 and 1879, occasional discontent within Natal's black population, and political friction inside Zululand, were enough to keep alive the feeling of vulnerability among Natal's whites. In 1878 a local newspaper articulated this insecurity:

> Hitherto we have lived in a species of phantasmagoria of Zulu scares. We have been all our lifetime subject to bondage, our Colonists may well say, by reason of this black shadow across the Tugela ... it is believed that an effective demonstration of British power will be required before the Zulu power shall cease to be such a disquieting element in South-East Africa.... Such a nation must of necessity form a constant menace to the peaceable European communities beyond their borders.... Civilisation cannot co-exist with such a condition of things beyond its outskirts.[5]

Frere's highly charged rhetoric intensified these fears, but it did beg a number of interesting questions. It assumed, for one thing, that the Zulu army was indeed a threat (of course it was only so if the Zulu monarch chose to unleash it) and that the Zulu people felt themselves to be oppressed by their own political system. Yet these issues were not Frere's primary concerns, and neither was he being entirely honest in his depiction of the Zulu danger. Had he been asked he might, like Shepstone, have pointed to the bullock skin as an indication of how the balance of power really lay. Although Frere enjoyed only tepid support for a forward policy among Colonial Office officials in London, the military resources of the British empire world-wide were almost limitless, and it was inconceivable that Britain, once committed, would allow itself to be defeated by the Zulus. Frere was keen to break the independent power of the Zulu kingdom, in keeping with the Confederation scheme and its broader aims: the fact that he was prepared to embark on a war at all was indication enough that he did not expect to lose. In short, whatever real or imagined threat the Zulu army posed to Natal, it was of the greatest value to Frere as a scapegoat.

Nor was Frere short of issues with which to provoke a confrontation. In 1873 a party of Natal officials had attended the installation of Cetshwayo kaMpande as Zulu king, and during the vaguely farcical proceedings, they had proclaimed a number of ambiguous conditions upon which Frere was to claim Natal's support for Cetshwayo rested. Although there is evidence that the Zulu regarded these 'laws' in a very different light, Frere was later able to cite incidents of their apparent infringement to justify his aggressive posturing. A commission was also appointed to look into the disputed Transvaal border, and Frere confidently expected it to refute the Zulu claims. He was somewhat disappointed, therefore, when in fact it upheld them, but a minor border transgression of July 1878 played into his hands. Citing it as proof of the Zulu king's hostile intentions, Frere's representatives presented an ultimatum to Cetshwayo's envoys on the banks of the Thukela river in December 1878. Frere demanded that the Zulus comply with all its demands within thirty days; among these were two clauses relating directly to the Zulu army:

  − That the Zulu army should be disbanded and only brought together with the permission of the Great Council of the nation assembled, and with the consent also of the British government.
  − That every Zulu on arriving at man's estate should be free to marry, the King's permission be no longer required.[6]

To make such demands on an independent monarch betrayed a finely honed degree of imperial arrogance; Frere knew King Cetshwayo could not afford to comply. He understood that the Zulu army was inextricably entwined with the apparatus of the Zulu state, and that the king could not abandon it without undermining the very mechanisms of his own power-base. It was, indeed, a fundamentally different organisation from the British equivalent of the time. The Zulu soldier was not a full-time professional like his British counterpart and the Zulu army was no self-contained institution, separate from civilian life and governed by its own laws, custom and tradition; it was rather a citizen army which placed an obligation of service on every Zulu man for part of his life, but which was deeply rooted in the customs and practices of his culture.[7]

The Zulu way of life

African settlement of the area now known as Zululand and Natal predated the formation of the Zulu kingdom by several thousand years. Archaeologists have discovered evidence of African Bronze Age settlement in the Thukela valley which dates back to the sixth century. By the sixteenth and seventeenth centuries, the north-eastern coastal belt was evenly settled by black groups who belonged broadly to the same culture and spoke recognisably the same language. To give a label and a name to this culture presents problems of terminological exactitude which have tormented academics for nearly a century: because of the enormous impact the later history of the Zulu kingdom has had upon public consciousness throughout the world, it is conveniently referred to by the term Zulu. In fact, the true Zulu were merely the ruling élite which dominated the kingdom from the nineteenth century, and just a small part of the culture which has become associated with their name. Many groups belonging to the same culture lived in areas never conquered by the Zulu kings, and never gave their allegiance to them, although their lifestyle was largely the same.

It was a lifestyle which revolved around a dependency on cattle that framed the human relationship with the natural environment. Cattle were not only an important source of food – they were only eaten for meat on special occasions, although milk-curds called *amasi* were a staple – but they provided hides for shields and cloaks, tails as a component of festive dress, and horns as containers. They were an important element in the spiritual life of these people; the Zulu-speaking groups believed that the spirit world, inhabited by generations of long-dead ancestors, co-existed alongside the daily world of ordinary life, and that any misfortune was the result of a disequilibrium between the two. Sacrifice of cattle to the ancestors was a common ingredient of the ceremonies necessary to ensure harmony with the afterlife. Most important, however, was the fact that an exchange of cattle, known as *ilobolo*, was a crucial part of the marriage contract. It was offered by a young man to the family of his bride, as a guarantee of her future well-being and compensation for the loss of her productive capacity. In a polygamous society, cattle therefore assume the role of a physical mani-festation of wealth and status; the more cattle a man had, the more wives and retainers he could support, and the larger his following became.

And the south-eastern coastal strip of Africa was superb cattle country. Cut off from the interior by a jagged wall of the Kahlamba mountains, the coastal strip dropped down in a series of rocky terraces across a hundred miles to the sub-tropical coastal flats. Rain-bearing winds blowing off the Indian Ocean deposited their load as they moved inland, particularly during the wet summer months, and a series of majestic river systems had cut deep gorges through the green rolling hills, taking the water back out to the sea. Before the hand of man had too much affected the landscape, the ridge-tops of the middle and lower reaches were covered with dense primordial forests, and the area teemed with game – elephant, lion, leopard, rhino, giraffe, buffalo and a myriad species of buck. Crucially, the carpet of grassland included a rich range of sweet and sour grasses, which matured throughout the year, and made it possible for pastoral peoples to raise their stock without migrating any great distance; and the relative absence of tsetse fly and other parasitic pests kept bovine mortality levels to a minimum.

In such an environment cattle thrived, and the human community which tended them prospered likewise. In a patriarchal society which practised a rigid division of labour along sexual lines, the hard physical work of planting and raising crops fell to the women, while the task of tending cattle was the exclusive preserve of the men. Zulu stockmen took an astonishing degree of interest in their beasts; the Zulu language included dozens of words to describe the patterns on their hide alone, and it was common for a herdsman to be able to describe the individual characteristics of each and every beast in a herd numbering hundreds.

This pre-eminence was reflected in the physical layout of the homestead, which was arranged in a circle around a central cattle pen. Each homestead (*umuzi*; pl. *imizi*) consisted of a married man and his immediate family and dependants. It was effectively a microcosm of the community at large, for it mirrored the hierarchic relationships of the social group as a whole. At the top of the *umuzi*, opposite the main gate, was the hut of the principal wife, with the huts of other wives arranged according to status on either side. Further round towards the opening at the bottom were the huts of unmarried dependants and retainers. In an ordinary homestead the home-stead-head, the *umnumzana*, had no hut of his own – he slept by rote in the huts of his wives, although the hut of the chief wife was considered his principal residence – but wealthier men had a private hut, screened off at the top end of the *umuzi*, to which they might occasionally retire for a little peace and quiet. The image of the circle, with its implied concepts of wholeness, unity and belonging, pervaded Zulu thought-patterns, and manifested itself in many aspects of the inter-personal relationships of a people for whom the community as a whole, rather than the individual, was pre-eminent.

The huts themselves were also physically circular. They were made by attaching thatch to a rounded framework of supple saplings; a narrow trench was dug to mark out the hut's perimeter, and the saplings stuck in at one end. They were then bent over and fastened on the opposite side, and tied together where they crossed. Poles were used to support the interior of larger huts. When the frame was thatched, the resulting dwelling was dome-shaped, cool in summer and warm in winter. The floor area was cleared and cemented with a mixture of ground ant-heap and clay, and smeared with wet cow-dung which was then polished with stones to produce a deep, dark bottle-green glaze. A raised lip in the centre served as a hearth, but there was no chimney. The smoke had to find a way out of the thatch as best it could; this at least had the advantage of reducing noxious insects in the thatch to a minimum. There were no windows, and the sole opening was a low arched door, which could only be approached at the crouch.

Each man might have as many wives as the practicalities of the *ilobolo* system permitted him to afford. In practice, until European economic systems irrevocably changed the pattern of Zulu family life in the late nineteenth century, this meant that most commoners – 90 per cent of the population – could only support two or, at the most, three wives, and the average *umuzi* probably consisted of no more than four or five huts. Wealthier men, regional chiefs and later the Zulu kings, often had considerably more: King Mpande kaSenzangakhona, who ruled from 1840 to 1872, maintained a household of twenty wives, as well as several hundred female attendants. Marriage was a crucial rite of passage for both men and women in Zulu society, for it marked the onset of full adult status. Whilst unmarried, a young man was considered part of his father's household, and owed a duty to give service to him as a superior. He was considered in a general sense as belonging to his father; any individual rights he may have had were subordinated to his father's will. He was expected to fulfil these duties as a contribution towards the general good, and expected no payment other than his keep. By extension, this duty also extended to his father's immediate superior, the homestead-head writ large, the chief (*inkosi*; pl. *amakhosi*). When a man married, however, he left his father's household, and set up his own homestead. This freed him from any direct obligation to serve his father or the chief, and he assumed all the full rights and responsibilities of adult status. Whatever his age, he remained a youth, an *insizwa*, until he married; only then was he recognised as an *indoda*, a man.

This responsibility of the unmarried man to fulfil duties placed upon him by his superiors was to form a crucial basis for the development of the Zulu military system as it functioned between about 1816 and 1879, and it was this aspect which was so misunderstood by Victorian commentators like Frere. Although marriage signified the onset of full sexual relations, the unmarried state did not imply celibacy; Zulu moral codes accepted that limited external sexual intercourse, known as *ukuhlobonga* or *ukusoma*, was a healthy part of the interaction between young adults, provided full penetration did not take place. Restraint was encouraged by rigorous social taboos against pre-marital pregnancy.

So important was marital condition and the shift in status thus implied that it was marked by an alteration to the physical appearance. Both men and women wore top-knots on their heads to indicate the married state. For men, this took the form of the famous headring, or *isococo*, which was assumed immediately before the first marriage; it was made by binding a fibre in a circle around the crown of the head, then smearing it with black gum. When this was hard and dry, it was polished with beeswax until it had a deep black shine. The hair was often shaved around the back of the head and on the crown, to emphasise the ring itself. The ring could not be removed unless the hair in which it was entwined was cut away, although it did often fall off with the onset of baldness in extreme old age. Some more fashion-conscious men teased out the hair below the ring and allowed it to grow upwards, so that the ring sat on a pad of hair some inches above the crown. Men who had assumed the ring were known as *amakehla* (sing. *ikehla*); and such was the status attached to the ring that it was not unknown for men of rank to don it even though they had not married.

Perhaps the most famous example of this was King Shaka himself who, although he maintained a large household of female attendants, never married; however, both the trader Henry Francis Fynn – one of the first British adventurers to reach Shaka's court in 1824 – and numerous Zulus[9] mention that he wore the ring. Another was Mbilini waMswati,[10] the renegade Swazi prince who proved one of the most daring Zulu commanders in the guerrilla warfare on the northern marches of the kingdom in 1879. Such a practice was, however, unusual, and apparently confined to men whose high rank guaranteed the *ikehla* status without the formality of marriage. For women, the top-knot was known as *isicholo*; until late in the nineteenth century it was the practice of married women to shave their heads, apart from a small patch of hair on the crown which was teased out and dyed with red ochre. By 1879 photographs of Zulu women show that more elaborate hairstyles were becoming fashionable, notably long cones of hair stiffened with clay, pointing out from the back of the head. These were the forerunners of the more extravagant flared headdresses still seen in parts of rural Zululand today.

Politically, each homestead-head and his family recognised themselves as part of an extended social unit – often called, for convenience sake, a clan – who traced themselves back to a common ancestor. Such ancestors might have been real or they might have been mythical, an unconscious means of explaining the foundation of a group, the true circumstances of which had been lost in the mists of time. Thus the Zulu clan explains its relationship with its senior branch, the Qwabe clan, in terms of the rivalry between two sons of a chief named Malandela who, if he really existed, lived sometime in the seventeenth century. The sons were named Qwabe and Zulu – Zulu means 'the heavens' or 'the sky above' – and each struck off on his own to establish his own following, who duly became known after their founding father. Zulu's people called themselves *amaZulu* – 'Zulu's people' – or *abakwaZulu* – 'they of Zulu's place'. Each clan had its dominant lineage, its royal family, and it was from the male line of this family that the hereditary chiefs were drawn. Where several clans were linked by ties of kinship to form a chiefdom, the dominant lineage of the most powerful clan in the group assumed the status of a royal house.

The power of a chief rested on his ability to exact tribute from his followers and to redistribute it as a mark of his favour. In theory, the Zulu philosophy recognised little personal ownership in the case of either land or cattle, though in practice individuals enjoyed almost unlimited rights to use both commodities. Nevertheless, the chief, advised by his council of important men from the chiefdom, had the theoretical right to drive off wrong-doers from their lands, or to confiscate their cattle. These cattle, together with any taken as booty in warfare, were considered the property of the chiefdom as a whole, and the right to dispose of them was vested in the chief. He might present them as a reward to outstanding warriors, to personal favourites, or to anyone else who had served him in some exceptional manner; or he might farm them out to impoverished members of the community, who tended them for him in return for use of their milk products. In addition, the chief was able to call upon the services of the unmarried men of the clan, who might be called together to build him a new homestead, to take part in a hunt or an important spiritual ceremony, and, in extreme cases, serve as the chiefdom's defence unit and internal police force, punishing criminals. Since an alliance through kinship with a chief's family was obviously a highly desirable circumstance, unmarried female members of his household were much in demand, and he was able to fix higher levels of *ilobolo* than those enjoyed by commoners. This process helped to maintain the political status quo and also tended to concentrate wealth – and therefore power – in the narrow circle of the ruling élite.

The clan unit was largely economically self-sufficient; indeed, in theory at least, each homestead produced enough crops and raised enough cattle to support its own inhabitants. Utensils, such as wooden spoons, trays and head-rests, baskets and gourds, were made within each *umuzi*, and the only essential product not made at home was iron, which was necessary for the production of hoe and spear blades. Even this seems to have been readily available, since particular clans were renowned as metal workers – the Cube in the dark Nkhandla forest, above the middle Thukela, for example, or the uMbonambi on the northern coast. The coincidence of appropriate raw materials seems to have been a decisive factor in the apportioning of the smith's art to these clans; most of them lived in areas where there was a good supply of wood to make charcoal, and readily accessible surface deposits of iron ore. The Zulu smiths used a clay furnace to heat the ore, building up the temperature by means of goat-skin bellows. When white hot, the ore was extracted and beaten into rough ingots, using suitable stones; these ingots could then be worked into the required implements. Although the process was technologically simple, it was no less effective for that, and surviving examples display a fine standard of practical workmanship. Like many African cultures, the Zulus regarded the forging of iron with superstitious unease, and the smith, keen to maintain the mystique of his trade, often worked in isolation, accompanied only by his assistants, and away from ordinary dwellings. Ritual was an essential ingredient in the process, and it was widely believed that the best spear-blades were tempered with magical medicine, including human fat, which assured their excellence in combat or the hunt.

The rise of the Zulu kingdom

Given the self-sufficiency of the chiefdoms and clans in the time before the emergence of the Zulu kingdom, historians have yet to explain convincingly why the social order became so stressed at the end of the eighteenth century that it collapsed into violence, and recast itself in a new form. One theory[11] suggests that clan society reached some sort of ecological limit; that human and cattle populations expanded to such a degree that, when further stressed by natural disaster, they outstripped the capacity of the landscape to support them. Certainly the dangers of overcrowding and overgrazing are all too evident in parts of the cramped areas of the former KwaZulu homeland today. Uncontrolled grazing has irretrievably damaged the fragile grass cover, and the heavy summer downpours have stripped away the topsoil, leaving the hillsides scarred by deep run-off gullies – dongas. This is apparently a process natural to Zululand's geological and climatic conditions, and it was under way long before the emergence of the Zulu kingdom, though overgrazing has undoubtedly exaggerated it. It is probably no coincidence that the first inter-clan violence took place in the 1790s, during a period of prolonged drought, remembered as the *Madlantule,* which rather picturesquely translates as 'let him eat when he can and say nought'. With less viable grazing land available to each clan, there would have been clear advantages to maximising the territory each group controlled, either through alliance with neighbours in a similar position, or through direct military conquest.

The stressed resources argument does not, however, explain the radical nature of the change. Another theory – not entirely incompatible with the first – suggests that the conflict was the result of one of the periodic trading drives initiated by the small Portuguese enclave in Mozambique.[12] The Portuguese supplied luxury goods to the Africans in return for hides and ivory, and these goods consisted largely of glass beads and brass ingots, which were worked up by local smiths to produce arm- and neckbands of one form or another. Because of their rarity, these items had a tremendous prestige value, and this was translated into political power through the monopoly of trade exercised by the chiefs. The chiefs granted the right to trade in them to themselves alone, and the articles were distributed among their followers as rewards, in much the same way as cattle. Although the Portuguese trade routes extended throughout Zululand and even as far south as Natal, the Portuguese seldom travelled extensively themselves, but preferred to use African intermediaries. Control of such trade routes was potentially very lucrative and therefore politically important, and it may be that the Portuguese initiative, coming on top of a scarcity of local resources, offered chiefs the chance to expand – or at least retain – their power-base at a time when it was otherwise under threat. Certainly there is a good deal of evidence to suggest that isolated examples of European trade goods were to be found in the heart of Zululand in the 1790s, at a time when Europeans themselves were known only largely by repute as *abelungu* – legendary pallid creatures who apparently lived beneath the sea, and were found now and then washed up on the beaches.

Whatever the reason, the violence which began in the late 1790s rose to a crescendo in the 1820s, and its implications continue to have a profound effect on South African politics to this day. Initially, several larger political groupings emerged, vying with one another to control the area between the Thukela and Black Mfolozi rivers. The Zulus, whose traditional territory lay in the centre of this region, along the middle reaches of the White Mfolozi, were initially no more than subordinate allies to one of these groups, but their rise commenced sometime between 1816 and 1818, when a minor son of the ruling chief, Senzangakhona kaJama, was raised up to assume control of the clan. This man, Shaka kaSenzangakhona, is one of the most extraordinary and controversial characters in southern African history; even today his personality and achievements are the subject of intense scholarly debate. Whatever his true character, however, it was Shaka who ensured that it was the Zulu, rather than any of their rivals, who came to dominate the northern coastal sector.

King Shaka as a military commander

According to tradition, warfare in the age before Shaka was a comparatively bloodless affair. When a dispute arose, armies would meet at an appointed time and place, and contest the issue with light throwing spears and oval oxhide shields. There was a strong element of personal challenge in these exchanges, and at the end of the day casualties would be light, whereupon one side or the other would simply acknowledge defeat and secure peace with the promise of tribute. This interpretation of events, current as early as the 1820s,[13] when they were still within living memory, may be affected by a twinge of nostalgia for a more civilised vanished age, but since the throwing spear is not a particularly effective weapon it is unlikely that such exchanges could have been very destructive. Although the idea that Shaka invented a broad-bladed stabbing spear designed to withstand the stresses of close-quarter combat has been discredited – such a weapon pre-dated him, although it was the preserve of a few 'heroes' – both Zulu sources and nineteenth-century white travellers confirm that it was Shaka who introduced it throughout his army and changed the nature of fighting as a result.[14] His military innovations made an impact on Zulu folklore, if nothing else, for Shaka certainly developed fighting techniques to an unprecedented degree, and there is a wealth of stories concerning his prowess as a warrior: he may, indeed, have been one of the great military geniuses of his age. In place of the loose skirmishing tactics with light throwing spears, Shaka trained his warriors to advance rapidly in tight formations and engage hand-to-hand, battering the enemy with larger war-shields, then skewering their foes with the new spear as they were thrown off balance.

If the results are anything to judge by, Shaka's capacity for conquest must have been dramatic. By 1824 the Zulus had eclipsed all their rivals, and had extended their influence over an area many times larger than their original homeland. Modern research has challenged the view of a generation of imperial historians that Shaka's kingdom was a monolithic and highly centralised autocracy, but nevertheless it was a remarkable exercise in state creation. The old clan system remained intact, but with the new structure of the Zulu kingdom welded over the top. Some of the clans were forced into submission by outright conquest, while in others Shaka intervened in the legitimate royal line to raise up a junior member of the lineage, who thus owed his position directly to the monarchy. Certain clans, such as the Cube, were never conquered by the Zulu kings, but joined the kingdom as allies and considered themselves on an equal footing with the ruling élite. Shaka reigned for perhaps twelve years, and in that time he established a political infrastructure which dominated almost all the territory from the Thukela north to the Black Mfolozi, and from the sea inland to the Drakensberg foothills. On the fringes of this core his control was less well defined, for whereas some groups paid him tribute, others resisted outright. In Natal, parts of the country, extending almost as far as the Mzimvubu river in the south, were abandoned by the inhabitants for fear of Zulu raids, while other groups held fast around local strongholds. Indeed, towards the end of his reign Shaka moved his favourite homestead south of the Thukela. Although it is unlikely that he ever entirely succeeded during his lifetime in instilling his subjects with a sense of common Zulu identity, he left a framework for his successors to consolidate and secure, and his achievement is nonetheless remarkable.

The nature of the Zulu army: the *amabutho* system

It was during Shaka's reign that the Zulu army emerged in a form that endured, with some modification, until the British defeated it in 1879. Without some application of military force, of course, it is unlikely that Shaka's career would ever have proceeded as it did. An army was necessary to secure control of many of the chiefdoms that made up the kingdom, yet if the monarchy's power-base was to grow, the manpower of the newly incorporated groups would also have to be harnessed. There were obvious dangers in forming military units from conquered peoples – they would be an effective focus for dissent – but Shaka side-stepped this problem by organising his warriors not on a regional basis, but on an age basis. This was not a new concept: the custom of banding youths together shortly after puberty was common among the Zulu-speaking peoples long before Shaka's time. These guilds, known as *amabutho* (sing. *ibutho*), probably owed something to the practice of initiating youths into manhood by a communal ceremony of circumcision, although circumcision had died out in Natal and Zululand a generation or two previously. These *amabutho* were the principal means by which the chiefs exercised control over their young men; whenever a chief required them to perform a particular duty, he would summon an *ibutho* to do so. There is considerable evidence to suggest that these guilds were already being used as battlefield tactical units during the wars which preceded Shaka's rise, and that Shaka simply went one step further, turning them into the basis of a fully-fledged national army.

Every few years, Shaka would summon together from across his territory all young men who had attained the age of eighteen or nineteen since the last call-up, regardless of their origins or local allegiance. These were then formed into an *ibutho*, and given a name, and a distinctive group uniform, consisting in the main of a unique shield-colour and a particular combination of ceremonial feathers and furs. They would then be instructed to build a regimental barracks, or *ikhanda* (pl. *amakhanda*) – the word literally means 'head', *ie* of the kingdom – where they would remain in residence for a while, undergoing a rudimentary military training. These *amakhanda* were also a crucial part of the new Zulu administration, being carefully sited around the kingdom, in areas of strategic or political vulnerability, and serving as a focus of royal authority. The *amakhanda* were considered the personal homesteads of the king, and he frequently travelled between them taking up residence in turn; during his absence they were administered by a trusted nominee, often a female member of the household. This system not only provided the king with a large and well-organised pool of labour, but effectively weakened the control of the local chiefs by taking the same resource out of their hands and vesting it directly in the monarchy instead. The common age of the young men in the *amabutho*, and their shared experiences, tended to foster close ties between them, to the extent that many came to refer to themselves by their regimental, rather than their clan, names. The *amabutho* system was therefore an extremely effective means both of centralising power and instilling a sense of national, rather than local, community.

Custom insisted, of course, that when the young men in the regiments married, they should disperse, return to their local areas and establish their own homesteads. This effectively placed them back under the control of their local chiefs, although by that time they were of limited use to him. Shaka countered this by refusing to grant them permission to marry until the men were nearly forty, thereby artificially prolonging the time they were available to serve him directly. Even once they had married, the men remained within the *amabutho* system: they were considered to have passed from the active list on to the reserve, and could be called out again, in their original formations, as circumstances demanded. Although Shaka is popularly held to have maintained his army in a permanent state of readiness throughout his reign, this is unlikely; for one thing it would have been difficult to provision such large concentrations of men for any length of time in the *amakhanda*. Since Shaka ruled for about twelve years, and is known to have allowed at least some of his *amabutho* to marry, it appears that his practice differed from that of his successors only in degree. After they had passed their first period – usually a few months – in the *amakhanda*, the regiments were probably allowed to disperse and spend some months living with their families. There seems little doubt, however, that Shaka frequently called them up again, as his military enterprises, his need to police the kingdom, and the frequent important ceremonies held at his homesteads required a constant level of readily available manpower. Henry Fynn conjured up an image of a landscape teeming with human activity, in which the regiments played a conspicuous part:

> The King came up to us and told us not to be afraid of his people, who were now coming up to us in small divisions, each division driving cattle before it. The men were singing and dancing and whilst doing so advancing and receding even as one sees the surf do on a seashore. The whole country, as far as our sight could reach, was covered with numbers of people and droves of cattle. The cattle had been assorted according to their colour.... After exhibiting their cattle for two hours, they drew together in a circle, and sang and danced to their war song.[15]

One side effect of this system was that it gave the Zulu king some control over the demographic growth of his kingdom. Women were also organised into age-grades, although they were not required to live in *amakhanda* or give military service. Female *amabutho* did, however, provide an administrative framework to facilitate the mass marriages which accompanied the permits for the male regiments to don the headring.[16] Male *amabutho* were simply told to select their brides from a particular female *amabutho*. Although the women were often younger than their husbands, the constraints on marriage imposed limits on their productive cycle according to the king's needs. The longer marriages were postponed, the less children they produced. In some cases, particularly powerful royal homesteads served as the focus for a new self-generating community. In the sparsely populated northern reaches of the country, for example, along the headwaters of the White Mfolozi, Shaka established an *ikhanda* called *ebaQulusini*, presided over by his aunt, Mnkabayi. Many of those attached to this *ikhanda* came from chiefdoms disrupted by conquest, and when they were given permission to marry, they settled in the same location. By the time of the Anglo-Zulu War, they had given rise to a distinct community, the aba-Qulusi, who considered themselves not a regional chiefdom, but an extension of the royal household, directly responsible to the Zulu king.

It is difficult now to gain an accurate impression of the size of Shaka's army. Henry Fynn claimed to have seen forces numbering up to 50,000,[17] but Fynn appears to have been both a poor judge of numbers, and to have had a vested interest in dramatising his story. Alan Gardiner, an ex-Royal Navy captain turned missionary who visited Shaka's successor, King Dingane, in 1835, estimated that the regiment in residence in Dingane's principal homestead, eMgungundlovu, numbered in the region of 900 men.[18] Given that most sources compiled in the nineteenth century suggest that Shaka enrolled about fifteen *amabutho*, this would give a more realistic figure of about 14,000 men. This figure was confirmed by another navy man, the leader of Fynn's party, Lieutenant Francis Farewell.[19] From this figure one historian has estimated that the total number of subjects in Shaka's kingdom totalled between 75,000 and 96,000.[20] Population levels fluctuated widely over the sixty years of the Zulu kingdom's independent existence, but even by 1879, when its internal position was stabilised, the total number of souls who acknowledged the authority of the Zulu king probably amounted only to about 300,000.[21] The British estimated King Cetshwayo's army at a maximum strength of thirty-four *amabutho*, of which seven were effectively beyond active service; some 41,900[22] men were thought to be capable of bearing arms, a figure which still proved something of an over-estimate. Almost certainly the force gathered at oNdini at the start of the Anglo-Zulu War, which probably numbered about 25,000 men, was the largest concentration of troops in Zulu history, considerably outnumbering any army put into the field by Shaka or in the years between.

The effects of colonialism

The arrival of the first whites in 1824 foreshadowed dramatic changes for the Zulu kingdom. These whites, Farewell, Fynn and their colleagues, established a good trading relationship with Shaka, allowing him a new monopoly of prestige trade goods which they exchanged for ivory. They also hired themselves out as mercenaries, adding a small but novel element to the military force at Shaka's disposal – the firepower of European muskets. As a result, Shaka granted them permission to settle around Port Natal, and they soon established themselves as a client kingdom, accumulating wives and followers in the local manner, and being virtually autonomous so long as they enjoyed the king's patronage. The suggestion that access to European trade goods was a useful part of the state-building process might be supported by the fact that Shaka built a new homestead, kwaDukuza, south of the Thukela, in Natal proper, which quickly became his favourite. In 1828, however, Shaka was assassinated in a palace coup led by his half-brother, Prince Dingane kaSenzangakhona. Initially, the new King Dingane was even more sympathetic towards the white enclave, shifting the focus of the kingdom north of the Thukela once more, and building his capital, eMgungundlovu, in the old Zulu heartland, just south of the White Mfolozi. The southern border had never been clearly defined in Shaka's time, but Dingane allowed the small white community almost exclusive use of that land south of the Thukela over which he held sway. Almost immediately, however, a problem arose which was to have profound consequences for the Zulu kingdom. There had always been a tendency for Zulu criminals to attempt to flee the kingdom, but in Shaka's time sanctuary was difficult to find. In the political uncertainty that followed Dingane's accession, however, this exodus was swollen by a large number of refugees who promptly fled across the Thukela to *konza* – give allegiance to and claim the protection of – the whites in Natal.[23] Dingane protested and some refugees were returned, but it proved impossible to contain this traffic without an open rupture with the whites, and in due course a community emerged south of the Thukela which effectively provided a political and economic alternative to the Zulu kingdom. It soon became impossible for the later Zulu kings to maintain the monopoly of power that Shaka had enjoyed.

War with the Voortrekkers

This situation was further exaggerated by the first serious conflict with the whites. Throughout the 1830s, the Afrikaners at the Cape had become increasingly disenchanted with British rule, and they began to drift away in search of new lands where they could live independently of foreign interference. This movement, known as the Great Trek, reached its peak between 1836 and 1838, and one strong trekker thrust was made into Natal from across the Drakensberg. The trekker leader Piet Retief attempted to persuade Dingane to grant the immigrants land in Natal, but Retief's heavy-handed manner unsettled the already suspicious Zulu leadership, and Dingane reacted by ordering the murder of Retief and his unarmed colleagues. The Zulu army was then sent against the trekker encampments in the Drakensberg foothills, catching several family groups by surprise and massacring them. The result was a bitter war in which both the Afrikaner and British settler communities suffered heavily, but ultimately it was the Zulus who were defeated. On the banks of the Ncome river on 16 December 1838, the Zulus repeatedly charged a Boer wagon-circle, and in an action which set the pattern for future conflict, were unable to penetrate the Boer defences and were mown down in reply. So many Zulu were killed that the river was said to run red with their blood, and the Boers ever after knew the battle as Blood River.

The war against the Voortrekkers had involved the most concerted national resistance in the kingdom's history and defeat almost led to a collapse of the Zulu state. It was narrowly avoided when Dingane moved his principal homestead yet further north, out of the Boers' reach, but in 1840 his brother, Prince Mpande kaSenzangakhona, defected to the enemy. Such was Mpande's support in Zululand that this incident is still known as 'the breaking of the rope that held the nation together'. With limited Boer support, Mpande defeated Dingane and drove him out, but the price of Boer support was the alienation of huge tracts of Zulu territory. The territorial integrity of the kingdom was only saved by the timely arrival of the British. The British government had watched the progress of the Boers with some concern, and finally decided to act in support of Lieutenant Farewell's claim to the bay of Port Natal. Troops were marched up overland, and a sharp fight took place among the sand-dunes, but despite an initial British reverse, the Boers were forced in the end to give way. Most of the Afrikaners – who had come to Natal to escape British influence – abandoned it in disgust, and in 1843 Natal was officially recognised as a British colony. Negotiations with King Mpande agreed that the border between it and independent Zululand should run along the line of the Mzinyathi and Thukela rivers. This boundary was not challenged until the crisis of 1879. No formal boundary, however, was agreed between Zululand and its north-western neighbour, the Transvaal, and it was this wild, sparsely populated area that was to become the cause of so much conflict thirty years later.

Rebuilding the kingdom, 1840–78

The struggles of those two years between 1838 and 1840 deeply affected the nature of the internal mechanics of the Zulu kingdom. The mystique of the monarchy, which Shaka had striven to build up, had inevitably been damaged by the civil war, and the Zulu army was weakened and demor-alised, both by defeat and by divisions within the ranks. The natural tendency for power to slip away from the centre and into the hands of the regional chiefs, which Shaka had tried so hard to resist, was once more unleashed. By giving the chiefs the chance to choose between two rival kings, Dingane and Mpande had acknowledged their *de facto* power in a way that would prove impossible to reverse. Mpande, whose carefully cultivated air of indolent stupidity masked the subtle mind of a shrewd political survivor, spent most of his reign trying to rebuild the authority of the state.[24]

Powerful factors, however, were working against him. White authority in Natal was apparently secure, with the entire might of the British empire to back it up, and the king had little sanction against those who chose to abandon him and 'cross over'. In the thirty years that Mpande ruled, several entire chiefdoms moved out of the Zulu orbit and into Natal, while the number of individual Zulus who slipped across the border numbered thousands. In 1852 one white observer estimated that the outflow numbered about 4000 people a year. Not all of them were accused criminals or political refugees; many simply sought an easier life, away from the restrictions that service to the Zulu king entailed. Although African custom accounted for the administration of the vast majority of blacks in Natal, there was no highly developed *amabutho* system there, and the price of *ilobolo* was generally lower. It was much easier for a young man to marry and set up his own homestead in Natal than it was in Zululand. Also in the 1850s, two separate estimates suggest that the number of men actively serving in the king's army was not more than 10,000, and perhaps as few as 6000 – far less than in Shaka's day, despite a general increase in the region's population, and more than ten years of peace. Not all these refugees found life under colonial rule quite as they had expected, and the efforts of first Mpande and then Cetshwayo gradually stemmed the haemorrhage; but it was still necessary for the king to relax some of the more vigorous prohibitions that accompanied life in the *amabutho*. The age at which regiments were allowed to marry was lowered, and Mpande created a number of *amabandla mhlope*, 'white assemblies'; these were regiments who had been allowed to marry, but who were still required to muster regularly at the *amakhanda*. They were, however, permitted to take their wives and families with them.

The increase in trade following the gradual expansion of white settlement in Natal from 1843 also undermined the king's power. With few enough whites to deal with, both Shaka and Dingane had been able to monopolise European trade goods, and use them to accrue further power and prestige. With the proliferation of traders eager to make a quick profit, it became increasingly difficult for the king to control the commerce. Many of the subordinate chiefs began to trade on their own account, expanding their personal power and influence at the expense of the crown. The goods most in demand in Zululand were mainly European tools, particularly hoes, beads, metal wire for decorating the handles of spears and clubs, cloth and blankets. So many beads entered the country that they almost lost their value as a reward from the king, whilst the indigenous metal industry is generally accepted to have declined after European metal became freely available. Hitherto the Zulu kings had enjoyed a monopoly on ivory, a commodity which Europeans always desired, and which the *amabutho* could be sent out to hunt. But hunters, as well as traders, were now regularly working in Zululand, and this monopoly, too, was in danger. The hunter William Baldwin, in 1853, describes the king's reaction when one of his parties decided not to await the royal permission to hunt:

We had not gone more than two miles, when one of Panda's captains came up to us in a great fury, swearing awfully by the bones of Dingaan, Chaka, the much-dreaded and cruel, and other renowned warriors of the nation, that if we did not immediately turn back, an *impi* (regiment 500 strong) would be down upon us and kill us instanter. He was in a great state of excitement, and would not hear of our outspanning or delaying our return a moment, said the signal for attack was crossing that watercourse (pointing to a running stream not twenty yards ahead); and as we were entirely in their power, we thought discretion was the better part of valour, and we did as we were ordered, looking very foolish in both our own and our followers' eyes. Panda had always opposed our wish to go that way, and it was bearding the lion in his den, and most foolish and misjudged on the part of White [Baldwin's companion] to go in direct opposition to his orders. On passing his kraal gates we went through two lines, at least 200 yards long, of magnificent men, armed with assegais, shields, knobkerries, and knives, in close file, waiting only the slightest intimation from his majesty to annihilate us instantly. It was a nervous moment; I did not half admire it, and all our Kaffirs were in the utmost alarm: a dead silence was maintained by everyone . . .

Eventually all was settled amicably; but our long-meditated route was peremptorily forbidden, and we were obliged to rest satisfied with the shooting Panda thought fit to give us in the Slatakula bush, where the old fellow knew well there were rarely any elephants worth shooting. . . .[25]

Typical though this may have been of King Mpande's efforts to control European commercial activity, such sanctions were increasingly ineffective. One commodity which he did attempt to control rigorously was the firearm, since the king was all too aware that widespread possession of guns had an important bearing on the internal balance of power. In these, however, he faced a further complication, in that many traders, nervous about their long-term safety, were unwilling to become involved in the gun trade, which was, in any case, illegal in Natal. The king attempted to overcome this inhibition by demanding guns as the price of his permission to hunt or trade in Zululand.

If Mpande's programme to rebuild royal authority was in general terms successful, it nonetheless received a serious setback in 1856. Unlike his brothers who preceded him, Shaka and Dingane, Mpande had a number of wives and produced many children, including boys. Although Zulu tradition provided some guideline for the nomination of his heir – the senior son of his appointed Great Wife – in practice such distinctions disappeared as Mpande's sons grew to manhood and became aware of their potential. The king himself, mindful that by publicly nominating an heir he was undermining his own security, refused to state his preferences. Moreover, he sought to play one son off against another in an attempt to keep them guessing. By 1856 two principal contenders had emerged, the Princes Cetshwayo and Mbuyazi, each of whom had enthusiastically courted the support of chiefs in their own districts. The issue was resolved in December 1856 when Mbuyazi tried to emulate his father's roads to success, and fled to the Natal border. Unfortunately the Thukela was in flood, and his followers could not cross. Cetshwayo's faction caught them there, and in one of the bloodiest battles in Zulu history Mbuyazi's faction was annihilated. Some estimates put the number of dead as high as 20,000, and their bodies, carried out to sea by the river, were washed up on nearby beaches for days afterwards. Although this effectively secured Cetshwayo's rights to the succession, Mpande continued to procrastinate, and remained in rather more than nominal charge until his death from natural causes in 1872.

Zululand under King Cetshwayo, 1873–9

The kingdom that Cetshwayo inherited was rather stronger than it had been when his father had become king thirty-nine years earlier.[26] The exodus to Natal had slowed to a trickle, and the position of the king seemed secure. Nonetheless, the principal chiefs of the kingdom – known as *izikhulu* (sing. *isikhulu*), literally 'great ones' – had grown used to exercising a degree of local autonomy that they had not enjoyed since Shaka's day, and their position on Mpande's royal council gave them an authority that Cetshwayo could not readily subvert. This council, known as the *ibandla*, met with the king to discuss all important issues, and it was so powerful that the king rarely rejected its advice. Indeed, Cetshwayo had himself made matters worse, since his victory over Mbuyazi had only been achieved with the support of two *izikhulu* in particular, both of whom lived in the northern reaches of the country, a long way from royal authority. They typified the powerful regional nobles whose allegiance Cetshwayo would have to ensure if he was to continue the process of reviving monarchical power. One of them, Zibhebhu kaMapitha, was chief of the Mandlakazi, a section of the Zulu royal house that was descended through a brother of Shaka's father, Senzangakhona, and whose status was therefore a reflection of the king's own. The other was Hamu kaNzibe, who was actually a son of Mpande and therefore a brother of Cetshwayo; but, because of a quirk of the complicated Zulu laws of genealogy, he was technically an heir, not to Mpande, but to his brother. Hamu's section, the Ngenetsheni, was also powerful, and

Hamu's power within his own region was as great as the king's. It was typical of the subtle interplay of Zulu politics that it was because these men had been so influential in supporting his own cause that Cetshwayo was most concerned how they might now be contained.

His solution was to appeal to the Natal government to send an embassy to the ceremonies which marked his accession as king, as a token of British support for his claim. Accepting the offer quite unofficially, Theophilus Shepstone duly rode with a small escort into Zululand, and proclaimed Cetshwayo king by placing a stage-prop crown on his head. Rather more significantly, Shepstone proclaimed a series of conditions upon which British support for Cetshwayo would in future depend; they stipulated that only the king should be allowed to pass the death sentence on those found guilty of criminal activity, and that anyone found guilty by a chief of a crime should have the right to appeal to the king. Almost certainly,[27] Cetshwayo believed that these 'laws' were aimed not at limiting his personal power, but at his chiefs, since they confirmed that the ultimate judicial sanction lay with the king. Like Shepstone's presence at the 'coronation', the 'laws' were part of the new king's policy of reclaiming administrative power. They set the bench-mark for Cetshwayo's reign, which was characterised by a vigorous attempt to revive the authority of the royal house; but, in one of the many ironies that bedevil the history of the Zulu kingdom, it was this policy which so provoked the British. King Cetshwayo's attempts to restore something of the structures that had supported the monarchy in Shaka's day ultimately brought about their total destruction.

The crisis of 1879

The 'coronation laws' provided the basis of one of the British complaints addressed in Frere's ultimatum. Cetshwayo had broken the laws, it claimed, and the Zulus were oppressed. It was an accusation that took the Zulu envoys who gathered to hear the ultimatum by surprise. 'Have the Zulus complained?' one is said to have asked.[28] Indeed not, and the Zulu nation, although as riven with internal political differences as any nation-state the world over, would vigorously defy British intervention. Fifty years later, on the eve of the 1929 anniversary, two journalists from a local newspaper, the *Natal Mercury*, travelled up from Durban to a Swedish mission station in the Ngoye mountains, deep in old Zululand. The local missionary, the Reverend Mr Aadnesgaard, had arranged for them to interview a handful of the surviving Zulu veterans of the Anglo-Zulu War. Sitting 'under the spreading branches of a large tree outside [a] cattle kraal which afforded welcome shade,[29] these elderly men recalled how they had been called together to fight in defence of their country. Most of them, inevitably, had been in the youngest regiments in the army in 1879, and by 1929 were in their seventies; at least one was 'just on his ninetieth year'. They recalled the last great musters of the Zulu army with a nostalgia born of pride, and of a knowledge of what came after. A man named uNsuzi, who had been in the uVe regiment, summed up the causes of the war as they appeared to the ordinary Zulu when he remembered how King Cetshwayo had addressed them, saying:

'I have not gone over the seas to look for the white men, yet they have come into my country and I would not be surprised if they took away our wives and cattle and crops and land. What shall I do? I have nothing against the white men and I cannot tell why they come to me. They want to take me. What shall I do?'

'Give the matter to us,' we replied, 'we will go and eat up the white men and finish them off; they are not going to take you while we are here. They must take us first.'

'The matter is in your hands,' he answered...

And so it was, for better or worse. When the great army marched off that afternoon, it was 25,000 strong, and it seemed to Gumpega Kwabe that the 'regiments there had so many men in them that they seemed to stretch right from there to the sea'.[30] It was probably the largest army mustered during the history of the Zulu kingdom, and it included representatives from every part of the land. Within a few days, the main section of this army had fallen on the British camp below Mount Isandlwana, leaving 1300 British soldiers and their African allies lying dead in the green grass at its foot. Yet if Isandlwana offered the prospect of a Zulu military victory over the invaders, it would soon prove an illusion, for rather than persuading the British to reconsider their policies, it provoked a bitter backlash. British reinforcements poured into Zululand. Isandlwana had been a costly victory, a type of fighting which the Zulu army had not before experienced, and the terrible consequences of the horrific casualties they suffered became more apparent with each new battle. The Zulus had no answer to the concentrated might of British firepower, and the staggering body-blow in the latter part of the campaign of three successive defeats, at Khambula, Gingindlovu and finally oNdini (Ulundi), broke the army physically and emotionally.

The end of the old Zulu order

For the British, the end of the war brought about that romanticisation of the enemy which comes with military victory and political disentanglement. Now that the spectre of the ghastly field at Isandlwana had been safely exorcised, the British came to see a tragic grandeur in the wild and hopeless Zulu charges, and Frere's bogeyman, the African demon with blood-dripping spear, was steadily recast in the image of the noble savage – an image which has, incidentally, persisted to this day. The great Liberal politician Gladstone, campaigning in the Midlothian by-election in late 1879, seized upon the suffering of the Zulus, and thundered: 'In Africa you have before you the memory of bloodshed, of military disaster, the record of 10,000 Zulus ... slain for no other offence than their attempt to defend against your artillery, with their naked bodies, their hearths and homes, their wives and families.'[31]

It was an emotional appeal which contributed to the downfall of the expansionist Disraeli administration, and thereby put an end to the Confederation policy. It had, in any case, been ailing since Isandlwana, for Frere had gambled on a swift and successful outcome to the Zulu war, which he intended merely as the precursor to proper exploitation of the region. The human and financial cost of the war had, however, called into question the whole expansionist view of southern Africa, and it was abandoned – Frere himself recalled – under Gladstone's severe programme of retrenchment. Yet in practical terms, the reversal of British policy offered no hope of Zulu recovery; it merely resulted in a vacillating and parsimonious approach to the internecine struggles, half-hearted rebellions, and white filibustering which characterised the decade following the war. Having broken the Zulu monarchy, Britain refused to annex Zululand outright, and instead opted for indirect rule through appointed chiefs. It was a system that fostered conflict, but little attempt was made to restore order. With no great military adventures to focus the attention of the wider empire, the popular romantic image of the Zulu flourished amongst their former enemies even as their country went to the dogs. When King Cetshwayo was brought to London in 1882, curious crowds cheered him through the streets. When, however, it was suggested that he might be restored to his throne in an attempt to reduce the violence, the response of the Lieutenant-Governor of Natal, Sir Henry Bulwer – who had been, incidentally, no admirer of Frere's policies – summed up the extent to which British attitudes were still shaped by a lingering fear of Zulu prowess.

> Unfortunately, the [Zulu] military system is not a system that has to be created. It is not something that has to be laboriously, and with difficulty, thought out and brought into existence. The system exists already. It exists – a dormant, inactive power, it may be, at the present moment, but it exists – a perfect organisation, such as it has been from the time of Tshaka. The system which was then established has, during a period of half a century, taken deep root in the Zulu nation. It is part and parcel of the Zulu life.... And, as a time-piece which has been suffered to run down and lie in disuse is silent, but no sooner is the action of the mainspring restored than, complete in all parts

of its mechanisms, it begins again to tell the hours and moments of time, so is the wonderful mechanism of the Zulu military system. . . .[32]

Bulwer need not have worried: King Cetshwayo was restored, to part of his kingdom at least, but the fissures within the nation which had been unleashed by defeat in 1879 were too great, and civil war broke out. The king was defeated; no united Zulu army sprung up to challenge the inexorable progress of colonialism. It was left to the old men sitting in the shade to recall the glory days of old.

NOTES

1. This story is quoted by J.Y. Gibson, who served as a magistrate in Zululand towards the end of the nineteenth century, in his *The Story of the Zulus*, London, 1911. Prince Mgidlana kaMpande told James Stuart the same story in 1903; see C. De B. Webb and J.B. Wright (eds), *The James Stuart Archive* (hereafter *JSA*), Volume 3, Durban and Pietermaritzburg, 1983. The author was told the same story by Mr Lucas Mncube at Rorke's Drift in 1991.

2. For a history of the Anglo-Zulu War, see Ian Knight, *Brave Men's Blood*, London, 1990. On the Isandlwana campaign, see the same author's *Zulu; The Battles of Isandlwana and Rorke's Drift*, London, 1992.

3. For a discussion of the various factors leading to Anglo-Zulu confrontation in 1879, see Norman Etherington's *Anglo-Zulu Relations 1856–78* and Bill Guest's *The War, Natal and Confederation* in A. Duminy and C. Ballard, *The Anglo-Zulu War; New Perspectives*, Pietermaritzburg, 1981. Graham Dominy's *'Frere's War'? A Reconstruction of the Geopolitics of the Anglo-Zulu War of 1879*, published in the *Natal Museum Journal of Humanities*, October 1993, outlines the debate concerning Frere's role, and seeks to place his policies within the specific context of contemporary southern African politics.

4. For Frere's correspondence with Hicks Beach, see *British Parliamentary Papers* (hereafter *BPP*) C 2220 and C 2222.

5. Quoted in Bill Guest, *The War, Natal and Confederation*, in Duminy and Ballard, *The Anglo-Zulu War; New Perspectives*, Pietermaritzburg, 1981.

6. *BPP* C 2222: the terms of the ultimatum are also quoted in the official *Narrative of Operations Connected with the Zulu War of 1879*, published by the Intelligence Department of the War Office, London, 1881.

7. For an analysis of the economic basis of the socio-political structure of the Zulu kingdom, see Jeff Guy's *The Destruction of the Zulu Kingdom*, London, 1979.

8. *The Diary of Henry Francis Fynn*, compiled and edited by James Stuart and D. McK. Malcolm, Pietermaritzburg, 1950. Fynn is a rather controversial and unreliable source, since the published form of the diary was written up years after the events he witnessed, and was clearly distorted to reflect Fynn's own agenda. Nevertheless, the present author sees no reason to mistrust such details of observation.

9. See, for example, the testimony of Jantshi kaNongila in Webb and Wright, *JSA* 1, Shaka 'put on the headring . . . among the Zulu', and Mbovu kaMtshumayeli, *JSA* 3, 'Tsaka had put on the headring.'

10. 'Mbilini . . . was still unmarried, but was already wearing the headring, because it was said that he was to be appointed as head of an *umuzi*, and as such should appear as

having entered a man's estate.' *Paulina Dlamini, Servant of Two Kings*, compiled by H. Filter, translated and edited by S. Bourquin, Pietermaritzburg and Durban, 1986.

11. See, for example, Jeff Guy, *Ecological Factors in the Rise of Shaka and the Zulu Kingdom* in S. Marks and A. Atmore (eds), *Economy and Society in Pre-Industrial South Africa*, London, 1980.

12. Summarised by Charles Ballard in *Trade, Tribute and Migrant Labour; Zulu and Colonial Exploitation of the Delagoa Bay Hinterland 1818–79*, in J.B. Pieres (ed.) *Before and After Shaka*, Grahamstown, 1981.

13. 'Shaka . . . disapproved of the old custom of carrying many assegais and throwing them at the enemy.' Fynn, *Diary*.

14. J.B. Pieres comments that the Xhosa on the Eastern Cape Frontier were using stabbing spears in the early nineteenth century, quite independently of Zulu influence; *The House of Phalo*, Johannesburg, 1981.

15. Fynn, *Diary*.

16. On the role of female *amabutho* see *Control of Women's Labour in the Zulu Kingdom*, by John Wright, in Pieres (ed.) *Before and After Shaka*.

17. Of the Ndolowane campaign Fynn estimated of Shaka's forces, 'The whole body of men, boys and women amounted, as nearly as we could reckon, to 50,000.' Fynn, *Diary*.

18. Alan Gardiner, *Narrative of a Journey to the Zoolu Country*, London, 1836.

19. Quoted in A.T. Bryant, *Olden Times in Zululand and Natal*, London, 1929.

20. Ibid.

21. Guy, *Destruction of the Zulu Kingdom*.

22. *Precis of Information concerning Zululand with a map prepared by the Intelligence Division, War Office*, London, 1895.

23. On the exodus to Natal see Philip Kennedy, *Mpande and the Zulu Kingship*, in the *Journal of Natal and Zulu History*, Vol. IV, 1981. For a first-hand account of King Dingane's attempts to have such refugees returned, see Gardiner, *Narrative*.

24. See Kennedy, ibid.

25. *African Hunting and Adventure from Natal to the Zambezi*, by William Charles Baldwin, London, 1894.

26. See *The Zulu Political Economy on the Eve of War*, by P.J. Colenbrander, in *The Anglo-Zulu War; New Perspectives*, edited by Andrew Duminy and Charles Ballard, Pietermaritzburg, 1981.

27. See R.L. Cope, *Political Power Within the Zulu Kingdom and the Coronation Laws of 1873*, in the *Journal of Natal and Zulu History*, Vol. VIII, 1985.

28. Quoted in J.Y. Gibson, *The Story of the Zulus*, London, 1911.

29. *Natal Mercury*, Tuesday, 22 January 1929.

30. Ibid.

31. Quoted in D.M. Schreuder, Gladstone and Kruger; *Liberal Government and Colonial 'Home Rule', 1880–1885*, London and Toronto, 1969.

32. *BBP*, C. 3466:79, enc. Report by Bulwer, *Settlement of Zulu Country*, August 1882.

CHAPTER 2

Drinking the King's Milk

For much of the nineteenth century, Africa was the dark continent, a well of the unknown on the reflective surface of whose murky waters the expanding European colonial powers could project their own attitudes and preconceptions. Even before Darwin muddied the waters still further, Africa was fertile ground for those imbued with the myth of white racial and cultural superiority. It was both the fabled home of King Solomon's Mines, to be plundered for adventure and profit, and the haunt of the unspeakable and unnameable terrors of the human soul, the Heart of Darkness. The accounts of the first whites who encountered the Zulu kingdom are fraught with ambivalence. 'We were astonished at the order and discipline maintained in the country through which we travelled,' wrote Henry Francis Fynn of his 1824 journey. 'It was a most exciting scene,' he said, witnessing a grand review of the army staged by King Shaka for their benefit, 'surprising to us, who could not have imagined that a nation termed "savages" could be so disciplined and kept in order.'[1]

Here it is again: 'savages' and 'discipline', that disconcerting equation which so alarmed Bartle Frere sixty years later. In an age when public hangings were still common in Britain, where children could be transported to the other side of the world for stealing a loaf of bread, and where miscreants in the Royal Navy could be flogged round every ship in the fleet, white travellers could nonetheless he shocked by the sudden death, and the more subtle and disturbing manifestations of sexuality and the spirit, which they encountered in Africa. To such an outlook the Zulu kingdom was the perfect conundrum; Europeans could see much in it to admire – honesty, courage, discipline – yet still thrill with the horror of its 'savagery', and justify the nation's overthrow.

Often the expression of this dichotomy was superficially trivial. The hunter William Baldwin was not alone when he admitted he was particularly impressed with Zulu honesty. Having been caught up in the panic which surrounded the civil war between Cetshwayo and Mbuyazi in 1856, he had fled the country in a hurry, leaving the contents of his wagon with a chief who promised to guard it. 'I have never yet,' he wrote in 1862, 'returned to reclaim my property, but, should I ever do so, I shall no doubt get what the rats have left, as Zulus are scrupulously honest.'[2] The traveller Bertram Mitford, writing in 1882 with just a touch of a guilty conscience, found that three years after their defeat, the Zulus still had a proper degree of respect for an Englishman and his property:

> More than once I have returned to the wagon, after leaving it alone and unprotected for some hours, to find several natives squatting round awaiting my return, pointing out to each other such of its contents as were visible, which contents they knew to consist of the very articles most prized by themselves, yet not a thing was touched.... I believe that, save in actual war time, any Englishman may go all over Zululand alone and unarmed, with perfect safety, provided he is friendly and courteous towards the natives....[3]

An ordered society

Even at such a mundane level, there was clearly a sufficiently evident degree of order and discipline within the Zulu kingdom to impress outsiders. Zulu society was intensely hierarchic; it revered all forms of authority, and regarded the king with an awe that went far beyond respect for the physical manifestations of his power. The king represented the authority of the nation entire, and of all its most potent ancestral spirits personified, and commoners dared not look upon the face of his anger. Even the *izikhulu*, who held the power of life and death over their subjects in their own regions, and who were confident enough to cross the king on occasion within the *ibandla* council, quailed when he lost his temper: they 'would look shamefaced, and cast down their eyes,' commented one Zulu, 'their penis-covers would fall off.'[4] This dread pervaded all levels of the state administration, since to offer disrespect to one of the king's functionaries implied offence to the king himself. Lunguza kaMpukane, whose father was a messenger of King Dingane, recalled: 'My father was feared; people did not come up to him face to face, but turned aside.... "Would you meet him face to face?" he would be asked.'[5] The *induna* Zulu kaNogandaya was a famous warrior, and so awe inspiring that 'fear would overcome [one] even though no words had passed; the very sight of him was enough'.[6]

It is true that the power vested in the Zulu state was considerable. Laws were few enough, but commonly understood; transgressors would be tried before their chiefs, the local *izikhulu*, or ultimately the king himself. Minor infractions were usually punished by confiscation of livestock, but in a culture that was horrified by the slow torture of imprisonment, all major crimes were punished by death. The most heinous crime of all, and one which tainted not only the accused but his immediate family and homestead as well, was of witchcraft. The Zulu believed that the spirit world, inhabited by generations of long-dead ancestors, lived cheek by jowl with the world of the living, and that almost all misfortune was the result of a disequilibrium between the two. Any wilful interference in the spirit world to bring about such misfortune to others was regarded as an appalling crime. Those guilty of witchcraft or possessed of evil spirits – *abathagathi* – could only be identified by *izangoma*, diviners whose mystic powers allowed them to commune with the spirit world and 'smell out' practitioners of evil. Those found guilty of such a crime were liable to a particularly gruesome death; they were impaled with a short wooden stake, thrust into the rectum, and left to die in the bush. Their families and attendants were thought to be contaminated, and were also killed off. The only chance of escape was to flee the country, for the Zulu kingdom was 'like a pit, or a snuffbox, for you did not know where to run to; that is, if a man had to be killed it was inevitable that he would be killed, for there was nowhere to run to.'[7]

Yet although it was such obvious and external constraints that forcefully impressed outsiders, the true discipline within Zulu society came from a culture in which laws of custom dictated behaviour at every stage of personal development. These attitudes, too, provided the psychological framework that made the Zulu military system viable.

From conception, every aspect of the Zulu child's development was hedged around with cycles of ritual to ensure that it grew up free of misfortune. Strict observances had to be kept during pregnancy and labour, and the new-born babe was subject to a number of important ceremonies before it could be exposed to the dangers of daily life. Furthermore, as the child grew, each stage of its development was recognised by further ritual and ceremony. At the age of about six, children of both sexes would have their ears slit to enable them to wear the large plugs in the ear-lobe which were a feature of Zulu body decoration. This ceremony marked the assumption of a certain level of maturity, and children who had been through the process were allowed some authority over those who had not; as a small part of the homestead community, for example, they were required to take a share in the daily chores. As they grew older, so the amount of work apportioned to them increased. The onset of puberty was an event of considerable importance – although of course it did not signify adult status – and marked by ceremonies that extended over several days for both sexes. By the time young men had reached the stage of giving service to the Zulu king, they had already absorbed a view of society that was highly structured, in which each individual had a clearly defined developing role. They had been trained, too, both in the ideals of service and in some of the necessary physical skills they would need as adults.

The sort of life a man would lead in the king's service differed only in degree and detail from the upbringing he received as a child. Zulu culture stressed the community rather than the individual, and individual identity and achievement was always framed by the need to belong to society at large. This manifested itself most obviously in the concept of the age-grade, or *intanga*. Every child belonged to an age-grade simply by virtue of being born within the same four- or five-year span as other children. In even the smallest homestead, there were usually two or three children who fitted into the same span, and were considered of the same group, and these played freely with each other, developing a sense of common identity and belonging. Children of the same age in neighbouring homesteads, and indeed in homesteads throughout the clan and kingdom, were all considered to belong to the same *intanga*, even though the physical formation of such a group did not take place until later life. This eventual grouping was applicable in the main to boys. Although girls were nominally formed into *amabutho*, they did not serve the king directly, and were called together as a group only on very rare occasions – it was quite normal for a girl to belong to such an *ibutho* without ever meeting other members who lived beyond her locality. For boys, however, the system worked to gradually bring them together, and ultimately expressed itself in the military system.

Zulu boyhood

Until the age of about four or five, life for the Zulu boy was fun-filled and carefree. He slept in his mother's hut, and passed the day playing with boys of his own age, or watching curiously the activities of his elder brothers, who formed the *intanga* above him. At about that age, however, boys were required to give assistance with the principal male pursuit, care of the livestock. At first, they were only permitted to look after the smaller stock, goats, sheep and calves, but sometime after the ear-slitting ceremony, they graduated to herding fully grown cattle. Given the role of cattle in Zulu society, this was a position of immense importance, and it taught boys to assume responsibility and become self-reliant; if they lost a beast, or allowed cattle to wander into fields and damage the mealie crop, they were likely to be severely punished. At the same time, it taught them how to function as part of a group and how to survive in an outdoor environment. As Ndukwana kaMbegwana, who grew up during King Mpande's reign, recalled:

> Little boys would go out with the boys who herded calves, and so learn. Even a very small boy carries his stick – grows up with it. It would be cut for him by his elder brother or (he would be) given a switch. Herding was the main occupation of boys – cattle, calves, goats and sheep. They had dogs and hunted too. . . .[8]

Hunting and games instructed Zulu boys in the rudimentary skills of military life. They were not allowed to use spears until they were older – and then only a small and fairly harmless type – but, as Ndukwana says, they were seldom without sticks. These were a means of self-defence, and a way of testing skill and courage among themselves, since stick-fighting was an art learned at an early age. With no tradition of wrestling or fist-fighting, Zulu boys learned instead to spar with their sticks. One stick was held in the left hand, and used to ward off blows; the other held in the right and used to strike. Fights were fast and furious, although any combatant losing his temper was likely to be at a severe disadvantage. The object was to hit the opponent's head; this could produce some spectacular but essentially superficial injuries, and among bigger boys drawing blood was considered the proof of victor. The combatants were then expected to disengage and tend each other's wounds to prove that there was no ill-feeling. Hunting of small game, rabbits and birds, was achieved by means of the throwing-stick, while a popular game among older boys involved rolling an *insema*, a vegetable tuber, down a slope, and trying to impale it by throwing sharpened sticks at it. The *insema* bounced past two lines of boys, careening off obstacles and spinning away, and it required speedy reflexes, a good eye and accurate throwing skill to transfix it.

By the time a boy had reached eleven or twelve, he had moved out of his mother's hut and shared a special 'boy's hut' with lads of his own age within the same homestead. He was now ready to assume a new duty, acting as a servant to his father or elder brothers when they travelled on long journeys. Homestead-heads were often called up to attend the king, or simply visited him to *konza*, to pay allegiance, in the hope of winning royal favour or persuading him to intervene in some local dispute. Youths who were already formally enrolled in the *amabutho* were, of course, called up for several months each year to attend the king in his *amakhanda*. These twelve- to fifteen-year-old boys were known as *izindibi* (sing. *udibi*).

The first duty of an *udibi* boy on such occasions was to carry all the possessions his father thought necessary for the journey – his carved wooden headrest, a skin cloak or blanket, a gourd for water, a pot, a spoon, and perhaps some maize, all rolled up in a sleeping mat made of rushes and usually carried on the head. Journeys of several days' duration were commonplace, and in a country with no roads, this often meant travelling across difficult terrain which teemed with dangerous wildlife – everything from lions to poisonous snakes. Zulu men grew up hardy, tough and self-reliant, and much of their first experience of their wider environment beyond the confines of their homestead came as an *udibi*. As Ndukwana put it, 'Boys became tough and wily in this constant carrying.'[9] Lunguza kaMpukane, whose father was a noted official and messenger of King Dingane, recalled how he and his father would set off on a long journey to the outlying chiefdoms:

On these occasions I had to carry my father's skin blankets (i.e. his sleeping cover), mat and headrest. There was also a calabash. My father would carry a couple of assegais and a shield (white, or with markings). My father wore his black sheepskin loin cover, with the front part made of genet skin. He might stick in his ring a little bunch of feathers, possibly of dove feathers. He was otherwise naked.... [It] took us four or five days to [reach] the capital.... We used to put up at people's kraals.... We returned the same way we had gone.... I never ceased carrying my burden.[10]

The *amakhanda*

It was probably during such trips that most Zulu men became acquainted with the wider world of the Zulu state, represented by the *amakhanda*. Since the king travelled frequently between the various *amakhanda*, almost all contact with him took place in them. They were, moreover, scattered throughout the kingdom, and were a deliberately visible expression of royal presence of power. The missionary Alan Gardiner wrote that when he visited Dingane's kingdom in 1835, he was told that 'there were fourteen to sixteen *ekandas*, and several smaller ones',[11] whilst by 1879 it was estimated that Cetshwayo controlled no less than twenty-seven *amakhanda*,[12] thirteen of them concentrated at Mahlabathini, north of the White Mfolozi, in the very heart of the kingdom. Not all of these were barracks – the 'smaller ones' noted by Gardiner served as regional outposts controlled by members of the king's household – and in any case they varied considerably in size. Although each one was royal property, and therefore potentially a seat of government, each king inevitably had his favourite – known as the *komkhulu*, or 'great place' – where he spent most of his time, and which served effectively as the nation's capital.

Such establishments were very large indeed. Henry Fynn estimated that King Shaka's kwaBulawayo homestead, overlooking the Mhlatuze valley, was surrounded by an outer palisade fully two miles in circumference,[13] while his colleague Nathaniel Isaacs believed it contained 1400 huts.[14] King Dingane's favourite residence, eMgungundlovu in the Mkhumbane valley, included over a thousand huts, and from a distance Gardiner likened it to a giant racecourse.[15] David Leslie, a trader who flourished in the 1860s, thought King Mpande's resident, kwaNodwengu, contained about five hundred huts, but admitted he had not counted them all himself.[16] The hunter Baldwin judged it rather 'fully two and a half miles round, and contains nearly two thousand huts'.[17] Archaeological evidence has confirmed that King Cetshwayo's residence, known variously as oNdini or Ulundi (from the common root *uNdi*, meaning 'the heights'), had significantly more than a thousand huts. Bertram Mitford, visiting the site of oNdini a few years after it had been razed by the British, observed that

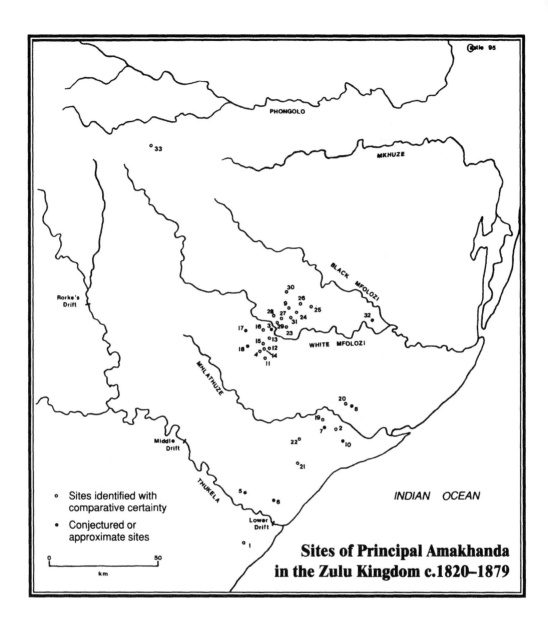

PHONGOLO

MKHUZE

° 33

BLACK MFOLOZI

Rorke's
Drift

30
°
28 9 26
° ° ° 25
27 °
° 31 24
17 • 16 ° 29 °
° 3 ° 23
15 °13
18 • ° °12
4 ° 14
°
11 WHITE MFOLOZI

32
•

MHLATHUZE

20
• • 8
19 °
7 • ° 2
22 ° • 10

° 21

Middle
Drift

THUKELA

5 •

• 6

INDIAN   OCEAN

Lower
Drift

° 1

○   Sites identified with
    comparative certainty

•   Conjectured or
    approximate sites

0 _____ 50
       km

**Sites of Principal Amakhanda
in the Zulu Kingdom c.1820–1879**

'some ideas as to the dimensions of the kraal may be gleaned when I say that it takes fully five minutes of tolerably quick walking to cross it'.[18]

Although perhaps two or three favoured *amakhanda* might have reached similar proportions during each of the kings' reigns, the majority were rather smaller, usually sufficient to house one *ibutho*. At the 'Escapene' *ikhanda* (uSixepi, at Mahlabathini) David Leslie counted 338 huts catering for the uNokhenke *ibutho*,[19] whilst when the British burnt King Cetshwayo's kwaGingindlovu *ikhanda* on 21 January 1879, they found it consisted of about sixty huts surrounded by a stout palisade eight feet high.[20] KwaHlalangubo and emaNgweni, two important *amakhanda* in the northern coastal strip, destroyed by the British in the closing stages of the 1879 war, consisted of 'about 600 huts' and 'three or four hundred huts' respectively.[21] KwaHlalangubo had been established in the 1850s by Mpande for his son Cetshwayo, and had remained the focus of Cetshwayo's household until the death of his father in 1872. At that time it had been called uNdi or oNdini, and was still sometimes referred to as 'old oNdini' even after Cetshwayo had removed his household to the new oNdini at Mahlabathini in 1873. Indeed, it was common for homesteads of the same name to exist in different forms in different places at different times, since

Key to Map 1, opposite: principal *amakhanda*, c.1820–1879

NB It has not been possible to include the sites of several of the smaller royal homesteads, and only those which served as barracks for the *amabutho* have therefore been included. Furthermore, *amakhanda* were sometimes moved from one site to another, and the location of several sites, particularly from the early period, remains obscure. *Amakhanda* known to have existed at the time of the Anglo-Zulu War, 1879, are marked with an asterisk.

 (1) KwaDukuza (late 1820s)
 (2) KwaBulawayo [KwaGibixegu] (mid-1820s)
 (3) emBelebeleni (1820s)
 (4) eMgungundlovu (1830s)
 (5) Illomendlini mhlope (1830s)
 (6) Hlomendlini mnyama (1830s)
 (7) KwaKhangela (1830s)
 (8) KwaDlangezwa (1820s/30s)
 (9) KwaNodwengu (1840s–1872)
(10) ezinGulubeni (1840s–)
(11) KwaKhangela (1840s–)
(12) emaKheni*
(13) esiKlebheni*
(14) KwaDukuza (1840s–)*
(15) ezinGwegweni*
(16) KwaNobamba*
(17) oDlambedlweni*

(18) uSixepi*
(19) Old oNdini (Hlalangubo)*
(20) emaNgweni*
(21) KwaGingindlovu*
(22) eSiqwakeni*
(23) eSangqwini*
(24) emLambongwenya*
(25) KwaMbonambi*
(26) KwaGqikazi*
(27) KwaNodwengu (1873–1879)*
(28) KwaKhandempemvu*
(29) KwaBulawayo (?; 1870s)*
(30) KwaNdabakawombe*
(31) oNdini (Ulundi)*
(32) oLandandlovu*
(33) ebaQulusini*

the royal households occasionally moved from one spot to another according to the king's needs, but retaining the same name. Hence King Shaka originally constructed a small homestead known as kwaBulawayo near the White Mfolozi river at the beginning of his reign, and later built a much larger establishment with the same name further south, also known as kwaGibixhegu, 'Take Out The Old Man', celebrating his defeat of a rival chieftain, Zwide kaLanga of the Ndwandwe. The homestead was kept alive after Shaka's death and moved to Mahlabathini, where an *ikhanda* of the same name still existed in 1879. In any case, the natural materials of which each hut was built only lasted for four or five years before they began to succumb to the ravages of the weather and parasitic insects; at the very least, huts had to be refurbished regularly, and occasionally it was decided to move the site of the homestead altogether. Gardiner saw some rebuilding in progress at eMgungundlovu:

> The town, which had been rebuilt, appeared in the distance like an immense assemblage of hay-stacks, the rays of the mid-day sun shining brightly upon the newly arranged thatch. The whole was not yet completed – numbers of women, bearing bundles of grass upon their heads, were approaching from all sides, while ... we observed several hundreds of the young amabooto (young soldiers) hastening forward in compact lines, bearing mimosa boughs for the fences.[22]

Physically, each *ikhanda* was laid out on the same basic principles as an ordinary *umuzi* homestead. Catherine Barter, who wrote an account of a journey through the Zulu country in 1855 under the blunt pseudonym 'A Plain Woman', described the *ikhanda* of the iSangqu *ibutho* (probably eSangqweni, near oNdini):

> An immense circumference like a large field is fenced in, and constitutes the kraal. Inside this fence is a row of huts for the accommodation of soldiers and other persons attached to the place or visiting there. At the upper end, opposite the entrance, is a very high fence, carefully constructed with wattles, and behind this are the huts of the great ladies – either old wives or mothers of the king....[23]

Like the ordinary *umuzi*, the *ikhanda* consisted of huts arranged in a circle, surrounded by a palisade, and enclosing a large open area which constituted both the pen of the royal cattle attached to the homestead and the place of assembly and parade ground of the warriors. The huts were set in rows up to four deep, while at the top of the homestead was a fenced-off area known as the *isigodlo*, which served the king in much the same way as the private quarters of the *umnumzana* in an ordinary homestead. Here a hut was set aside for the king's personal use, when he was in residence, and here, too, were the huts of the *isigodlo* girls.

The *isigodlo* was a means of abstracting tribute from the population through female service in much the same way as the *amabutho* did for the men. The various great men and chiefdoms of the nation offered teenage girls to go into the king's service. This was part of the usual web of patronage and obligation, and it was generally looked upon as an honour to be nominated for the *isigodlo*; if some girls did not themselves regard it so – and some did not – it was most unwise to object. The girls were housed in the *isigodlo* sections of *amakhanda* about the country, and for the most part were required to perform the chores of the king himself or his family. The king had the right to dispose of them in marriage, and they were an effective means both of cementing internal alliances, and enriching the royal herds, as they naturally commanded a much higher *ilobolo* rate than commoners. A select few, known as the *umdlunkulu*, were picked out by the king, and with them he enjoyed the pleasures of *ukusoma*. They were housed in an inner sanctum known as the 'black *isigodlo*', and it was strictly prohibited on pain of death for any male except the king to enter their quarters. Even access to the remainder of the *isigodlo*, the 'white *isigodlo*', was restricted to the senior councillors or those invited by the king, and when an *ibutho* was in residence at the *ikhanda*, guards were posted outside the entrances to the royal quarters to keep the young men at bay. This was not only to prevent sexual transgression, but also to prevent evil-doers from gaining access to the king to work some supernatural evil over him.

To control the *isigodlo*, the Zulu kings appointed senior female members of their household as guardians. Because of the system of polygamy, each king 'inherited' a large number of his father's widows, all of whom were considered of equal rank to his mother, and, indeed, referred to as his 'mothers'. Because of their relationship with the late king, their prestige was enormous, and they were generally considered above the marital intrigues of the new king and his own wives. By placing them in charge of the *amakhanda*, the king was able both to secure trusted administrators of his own extended household and also provide a means of support for the widowed queens themselves. As a logical extension of this system, the raising of royal offspring was also entrusted to these women when they became old enough to leave their mothers' huts, thus preventing friction between rival heirs by separating them geographically. Their authority was, however, largely confined to household matters, for when an *ikhanda* was fully occupied by warriors, these had their own officers in charge of them. Catherine Barter describes meeting the royal ladies at the iSangqu *ikhanda*:

The driver escorted me to the gate of the tall fence of the Isigohlo or preserve of the women; after he had announced me I went on by myself. The old creatures were highly flattered by my visit. They were immensely fat, and tolerably well decorated with beads and brass buttons. They asked me all manner of questions, were beyond measure surprised that I could understand and answer them, and we had a long chat....

The ladies insisted on my waiting till they had prepared some food for me. After a long while a young girl brought in a bowl of stuff not unlike thin water gruel without salt or sugar.... I did not like it at all. They were not sorry, for they consumed all that I left....[24]

The duties of the *udibi* at the *amakhanda*

For the young *udibi* boy, attending his father on his first visit to an *ikhanda*, it must have seemed an exciting but terrifying place. Ndukwana remembered how, 'as boys, we used to run to the huts near the gate of the kraal when we heard the king was coming, and peep out of the doors to have a look at him as he passed by'.[25] When fully occupied, the *amakhanda* teemed with life, and the boy found himself with new duties to be performed. Important men, at least, seem to have lived in the same huts whenever they were called up, and the first job given to the *udibi* was to clean up any rubbish which had accumulated since the hut was last occupied. As Lunguza kaMpukane recalled of his visit to eMgungundlovu:

If (a man) went off and stayed at home it would be well if he left someone to look after his hut, for if he merely shut it up and went away, others in the royal kraal would open it and use it as a closet and throw their ashes and refuse there, on the grounds that the owner was away enjoying himself and drinking beer at home. And coming back to such a hut he could not occupy it the first day because of refuse; it must first be cleaned out by a mat-bearer and then smeared with cow-dung allowed to dry. My father always stayed until relieved by Manzezulu kaJobe....[26]

But for an over-awed newcomer it must have been difficult to tell which was which. Lunguza again:

The mat-bearers used to go and collect firewood for the huts to which they belonged. It was very difficult to know what hut one belonged to. I accordingly stuck a stick on our hut so that I could see which it was, for if one went to the wrong hut they would smack you in the face or throw a bone at you, and want to know why you made the mistake and why you did not take care.[27]

Other indiscretions might, moreover, have more serious consequences

The Ultimate Ikhanda:
King Dingane's eMgungundlovu 'Great Palace' c.1836

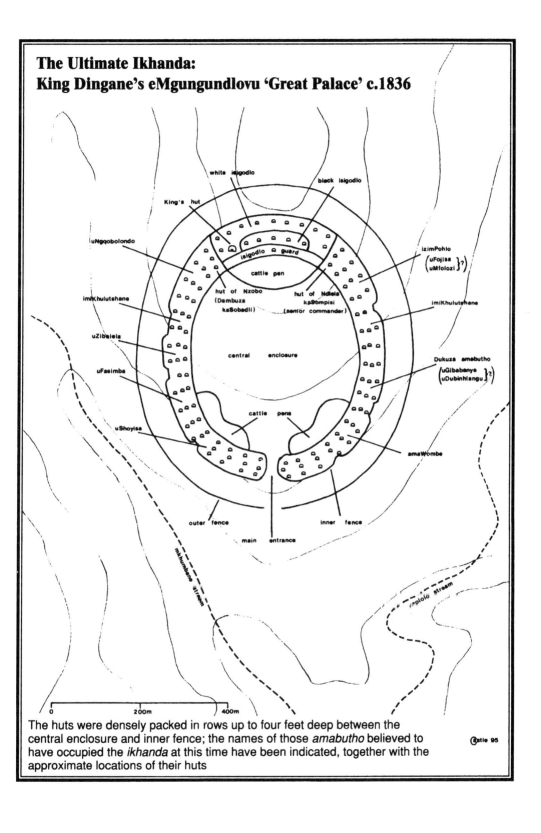

The huts were densely packed in rows up to four feet deep between the central enclosure and inner fence; the names of those *amabutho* believed to have occupied the *ikhanda* at this time have been indicated, together with the approximate locations of their huts

than a clip round the ear. Living in daily proximity of the *umdlunkulu* could prove fatal for the unwary.

> The umdhlunkulu were stark naked, only a strip of beads around the waist.... When they went out to the river to wash they were escorted and guarded by men armed with shields and assegais, and if you came in sight you must fall right down into the grass and face downwards in order not in any way whatever to look. The umdhlunkulu were very fat.... They perspired though they did nothing.... When called to the white isigodhlo I never dared to look up at any of the umdhlumkulu. I never had a feeling of affection for them, for it was death to do so.[28]

Indeed, Lunguza remembered eMgungundlovu with little affection: 'They used ... to aim a bone at one as one passed by a hut, merely for passing there, and nothing else. It was a place of death. One always lived in a state of trembling and dread at Mgungundlovu, and was only relieved when one went off home.'[29]

Life at the *amakhanda* was clearly not easy for the *udibi*, as Ndukwana confirmed, but it was not without its compensations:

> When work is over boys play about – but he has plenty of work. He has also to roll up the sleeping mats, for these will be left by the young men on the floor. He also has to spread out the mats at night-time.... Udibi boys had boiled mealies (izinkobe) poured out for them on the ground, they did not get ... porridge. Potsherds – these became boys' dishes at the cooking place outside. They will not wait for a boy to bring his potsherd; if he is not ready with it – the mealies will be thrown on the ground.[30]

If boys were in attendance at an *ikhanda* on the occasion of the annual *umKhosi* ceremony – the great festival of national rejuvenation which ushered in the new harvest each year – they might be required to fulfil a rather more uncomfortable duty. Mpatshana kaSodondo, a member of the uVe *ibutho* who fought at Isandlwana in 1879, remembered that before the war, during such a ceremony, 'boys serving the regiments (udibi), who have not yet reached puberty [were] searched out'. A black bull had been killed in an important ritual by one of the *amabutho*, and the boys were told to

> come and eat the bull; but when they go (being commandeered) they may not urinate the whole night, nor may they leave the place in the kraal where the bull is being eaten until the following morning.... Boys used to hide when they saw they were wanted to eat the bull, just because they knew they could not make water until the following day. Boys eat as much as they can,

and what cannot be finished is burnt. I was warned not to go, as a dibi, because those warning me saw they would have no one to cook for them.[31]

Drinking the king's milk

Of course, *udibi* boys only lived at the *amakhanda* while the man they were serving attended the king; even then, if they were serving elder brothers, their fathers might recall them to resume their duties at home, sending their sisters to fetch them. Despite the poor treatment they received – lack of food, hard work, constant teasing from the warriors, and occasional punishment – they do not generally seem to have been put off military life, since the next stage in their development required them to report to a local *ikhanda* to be enrolled as a cadet. The timing of this decision seems to have been left to the individual boy, since, according to Ndukwana:

> Boys used to go of their own accord to the amakhanda and [enlist as cadets] there, even though their father refused and said they must still herd cattle. They would not be called; they would go seeing that their elder brothers, whom they had seen [as cadets] had been ... turned into a regiment.[32]

By this time the boys were perhaps sixteen or seventeen years old. They simply reported to the nearest *ikhanda* in their locality, where they were taken in and given huts with other boys of their *intanga* who had done the same thing. Other youths of the same age would also be gathering at the other *amakhanda* throughout the country. This process was known as *ukukleza*, from a verb *kleza*, meaning to drink milk straight from a cow's udders. It was meant quite literally, since this was the main source of sustenance for the cadets, but it had a deeper significance, too, since it implied they were giving themselves up to the physical protection of the king, accepting his bounty, and offering service in return.

During this period the cadets were known as *inkwebane*, a term referring simply to those who were old enough to *kleza*, but had not yet been formed into an *ibutho*. While they were still living at the various *amakhanda*, and before they had been summoned by the king, the latter might give their cadet unit an identifying name. Mtshapi kaNoradu of the uKhandempemvu regiment recalled that as cadets they were known as the uNgangezwe,[33] while Ndukwana remembered that 'the Dhlambedlu, when still *kleza*ing, in Dingane's time, were called Insewane',[34] and according to Baleni kaSilwana of the uDloko *ibutho*, 'we cadets ... were known as the Inyati'.[35] In addition, it was during this period of cadetship that the foundations were laid for the internal formation of the future *ibutho*, since the groups which gathered at each *ikhanda* formed the basis of the various sections of the regiment proper.

Whilst at the *amakhanda*, the cadets were formed into companies, known as *amaviyo* (sing. *iviyo*). For reasons that remain obscure, these companies varied widely in size, with some as small as fifty cadets apiece, and some as large as two hundred. This may have been due in part to the king tinkering with their demographic structure; if some *amaviyo* were reported to be particularly small, it was not unknown for them to be merged with *amaviyo* at other *amakhanda*, to keep the numbers up. *Amaviyo* who *kleza*'d at the same *ikhanda* constituted an *isigaba* (pl. *izigaba*), or division, within their regiment when it was formerly enrolled. These *izigaba* also varied considerably in extent, both because of the fluctuating numbers of youths who gathered at a particular *ikhanda* and because of the unpredictable size of the *amaviyo*. As a result, it is often difficult to assess accurately the strength of a Zulu army on any given occasion as a result, since the Zulu themselves merely counted the number of companies. Because of their common experience at a formative age, however, ties between members of the *amaviyo*, and their sense of belonging to a particular *isigaba*, were intense. Almost forty years after the Anglo-Zulu War, Mtshapi kaNoradu could remember that there were forty-nine companies forming twelve *izigaba* in the uKhandempemvu *ibutho*, and list the names of the *izigaba* commanders.[36]

The duties of cadetship

Whilst *kleza*'ing, the cadets were supervised by the senior officer in charge of the regiment at whose *ikhanda* they were based. No officers were appointed from their own ranks, although it was common for natural leaders to emerge among the *amaviyo*, who would be acknowledged by the others as leaders of their particular group. Often the part played by these youths would be formally recognised when they were enrolled as a regiment. Life as a cadet was not particularly hard – most Zulus who remembered it seem to have spoken of it with more affection than of their time as an *udibi* – and, in addition to the usual menial chores, they underwent a rudimentary form of military training. Baleni kaSilwana described the lifestyle:

We used to sleep in huts nga kwesikulu, i.e. on the right side going in, and near the gate of the cattle enclosure. There were very many of us indeed.... We drank from the cows at midday and sunset, for there were two milkings. What happened was this. The cattle would all be driven into the great cattle kraal. Those for the king's or isigodhlo's use were driven to their accustomed spot, a little way up the enclosure, whilst the main lot stood below. After a time, the king's milk pail would emerge from the isigodhlo, carried by [a royal attendant] who would whistle loudly. This whistle would be heard and responded to by several in different parts, who would shout 'Zi jubekile!'

['They have been set apart!'] Upon this, whilst the king's or royal cattle were being milked, we cadets would make for the main herd and proceed to drink from the cows . . . two or three boys to drink from one cow, for they stood all about in the cattle enclosure. There would be no rushing at the cattle, for the cows had all been appropriated.

According to Baleni, work duties were light: 'The cadets used to collect firewood and thornbush for the isigodhlo. The thorns were very painful. The thornbush would surmount the isigodhlo fence. Cadets also hoed the fields, carried the amabele [millet] when it was being reaped, and threshed it. That was about all.'[37]

The cadets were not allowed to carry spears, and training was informal. When out in the bush, cadets would stab at tubers with their sticks, just as they had as herdboys, or engage in stick-fighting. There are suggestions that they were occasionally taken on cross-country runs, to keep them fit. They were encouraged to perform war-dances, either together, or engage in the solitary display of physical and weapon skill known as *giya*. A man *giya*ing would jump out from among his comrades and leap about, enthusiastically shadow-fighting with his sticks, showing off his athleticism and prowess, fighting a mock fight in which he triumphed over his enemies. This was an important aspect of the life of an adult warrior, and the art was learnt in cadetship. As a man danced, his companions would shout out his praises, calling out the nicknames he had earned as a warrior and obscure phrases that recalled his heroic deeds. Of course, the cadets had no actual military experience to boast of, but it was quite acceptable for their friends to make up praises to encourage them. This process also helped to build the esprit de corps of the future *ibutho*, and it was common for established *amabutho* to vie with each other, trying to outshine one another with their praises and *giya*. It was not unusual for such contests to end in a stick-fight.

Enrolling the *amabutho*

Cadets *kleza*'d for two, three or four years, until the king decided that there were enough of them in the regional *amakhanda* to form into a regiment. It is not entirely clear whether the cadets lived in the barracks for the whole of that time, although Baleni's comment that he 'was a number of years at Ndabakawombe [*ikhanda*]. I grew up there'[38] suggests that they did. It may be, however, that they were allowed periodic leave to visit their families and to take part in important functions at home. Eventually, though, the time would come when the king called them together at his principal residence to *buta* them, to form them into a proper regiment.

Given the ritual which controlled almost every aspect of Zulu life, the ceremony to *buta* a new regiment seems curiously matter-of-fact. The cadets were simply called together by the king, given a new name, and told to go and build themselves a new *ikhanda* at a place specially appointed to them. Thus Mtshapi recalled, rather proudly, 'We Kandempemvu built our own ikhanda, called the uKandempemvu. It was built between the Mabedhlana hills. It was built by us alone.'[39] Occasionally, a newly *buta*'d regiment might be ordered to join an existing *ikhanda*, perhaps because the original occupants had married and seldom used it, or even be incorporated into an existing regiment. Thus the uVe regiment, which *buta*'d shortly before the Anglo-Zulu War, was incorporated into the iNgobamakhosi, the regiment which had been *buta*'d immediately previously. This was almost certainly due to King Cetshwayo's attempts to revitalise the *amabutho* system, and to increase the number of young men at his disposal; it was more common, however, for a new regiment to be incorporated into an existing one, simply to keep the numbers up. The uThulwana, who had been raised by King Mpande and whose ranks had included a number of the *abantwana*, or royal princes, including Cetshwayo himself, enjoyed the status of an *ibandla mhlope* when Cetshwayo himself was king; its members mustered with their wives and were based at the oNdini homestead itself. It enjoyed a particularly high prestige, and because of that the younger iNdlondlo and iNdluyengwe regiments were allowed to marry early in order to be drafted into it, to keep it strong – a decision which, in due course, would have unfortunate repercussions for the kingdom.

Once safely established in an *ikhanda*, the new *ibutho* was usually allowed to disperse. Thus, for most of the time, the average *ikhanda* was occupied only by female members of the king's household, cadets and a handful of warriors who kept it in good repair and maintained its security. The new *ibutho* could expect to be summoned for several months of the year, whenever the king had a particular need for it, or to take part in important national ceremonies. When it did so, the *ikhanda* remained its headquarters, although regiments who were based in outlying districts might be called to the king's principal residence, where they would have to erect temporary grass shelters in the nearby veld to house themselves. Now that they had been properly enrolled, the young warriors were entirely at the king's disposal. Waging war, of course, was a primary duty, and serving as an internal police force, but in peacetime they were required to perform a variety of other tasks – as King Cetshwayo himself described when interviewed during his captivity – 'building military kraals, planting, reaping, and making gardens for the king. These are the men who look after the king'.[40] 'The king's fields were cultivated by us,' confirmed Mtshapi, '. . . [we] went to pick torches for the king. . . . The order was continually being given, "Go out and do such and such".'[41] Lunguza, who served with the Isiziba section of King Dingane's uKhokothi *ibutho*, summed up his experience in the king's service:

The Isiziba did not live at Mgungundlovu but only came when specially summoned. We were called together for the special purpose of cutting wattles of the umnqandane bush. After finishing this work we were given cattle to eat and then told to disperse to our homes. That is an illustration of what occurred.[42]

Mundane as this work seems, it was necessary to keep the king's royal homesteads in working order. It did not appear much to David Leslie, the trader, who was a great advocate of the civilising power of physical labour – especially when practised by Africans for the benefit of white settlers:

It is amusing to see the natives doing what they call *work*. The other day the king wanted some wattles for a hut; and immediately, instructions were sent all round all the kraals in the Mahlabate, to the Amakanda (heads) as they are called. The whole of the young men turned out to the bush, each cut a wattle (or branch), leaving the leafy head upon it, and returned marching up the hill, looking as if 'Burnham wood had come to Dunsinane'. When they came into the kraal each man threw down his wattle with the air of one who had done some great deed; then they had a dance, and each 'went his way', entirely satisfied with the great day's *work* which he had done.[43]

Occasionally, European visitors were treated to spectacular examples of the sort of dedication the Zulu kings required of their regiments. Although most tales of the whimsical cruelties practised by the various kings – such as the missionary story that Cetshwayo once ordered an *ibutho* to stamp out a burning bonfire, to prove his contempt for hell-fire – were grotesquely exaggerated, there can be no doubt that the kings occasionally expected their followers to demonstrate their loyalty. Alan Gardiner witnessed such an incident at King Dingane's court:

Several men from a distant part of the country, and who had never yet seen a horse, were standing near, when Dingarn, in one of his frolicsome moods, suddenly turned round, and, pointing to my horse quietly grazing at a distance, cried out, 'There's a lion – go and bring it alive.' Instantly the whole party were in pursuit. I did not witness the circumstance, but my interpreter informed me, that as they approached they extended themselves to surround him, one standing out in advance as though to tempt the attack, while those behind were prepared to seize and master the animal after he had, as they expected, sprung upon his victim. But they soon discovered their mistake, and on their return were ironically rebuked by their sovereign for not bringing in the lion. Had it been a lion, as Dingarn himself asserted, it would have been brought, and from this specimen I have little doubt of the fact, notwithstanding the great loss of life that must have attended so unusual an enterprise.[44]

Rare as these demonstrations were, they served to remind both the king and his subjects of the extent of the obligations placed upon them. It was a common boast of the king – and some of his more presumptuous *izikhulu* – that the lives of the ordinary people belonged to him. So powerful were the bonds of service that it was not without an element of truth.

Appointing *izinduna*

When a new regiment was *buta*'d, the king appointed two officers, or *izinduna* (sing. *induna*) to command it. The term *induna* perhaps requires some amplification; the *izinduna* were state officials, specifically chosen by the king to fulfil particular roles within the administrative system. Be they military commanders, messengers or functionaries within the royal homestead, they owed their position directly to the king himself. This was another apparatus intended to centralise power, since the *izinduna* were not necessarily men of rank in themselves. It was not unknown for the Zulu kings to raise up individuals who were commoners and appoint them to positions of authority in a field where they had known some distinction; indeed, this was particularly true of the army, where outstanding warriors were often raised up and rewarded.

Inevitably, however, hereditary rank and state recognition often overlapped at the highest level, and it was unusual for the king to appoint the most senior functionaries from among any but his most trusted advisers. These advisers, who constituted the *ibandla* – the inner council composed of the great nobles of the pre-Shakan chiefdoms – met to discuss all decisions of national importance with the king himself, and the king could ill afford to ignore their counsel. As Cetshwayo explained: 'The king has not the power of electing an officer as chief without the approval of the other chiefs. They are the most important men. But the smaller chiefs he can elect at his discretion.'[45] Even a quick glance at the individuals who held the highest commands within the Zulu army suggests the extent to which such appointments were made from within this circle of powerful men. King Shaka's most senior military commander, trusted with handling those campaigns which the king himself did not accompany, was Mdlaka ka-Ncindi, a lineage-head of the eMgazini people, who had been among the first incorporated into the kingdom. Mdlaka was assassinated in the coup which followed Shaka's death, and his role under Dingane was taken by Ndlela kaSompisi. Ndlela had been an officer under Mdlaka, and had been made head of the Ntuli people, who had suffered heavily during Shaka's wars, and whom Shaka had relocated along the middle reaches of the

The raw material; a Zulu man, photographed sometime during the nineteenth century, carrying his weapons –
a large-bladed stabbing spear, throwing spear and, in his right hand, a knobkerrie. This man does not wear the headring,
and so is an *insizwa* – an unmarried youth. (Bryan Maggs Collection)

Left: Marriage was an important rite of passage for Zulu men and women; among the men it was recognised by the adoption of a ring, the *isicoco*, which was bound into the hair on the crown of the head.

Right: A famous study by G. F. Angas of warriors in King Mpande's army in the 1850s, suggesting the splendour of the full ceremonial costumes worn at the umKhosi ceremonies. The regiments are the iSangqu (left) and iNdabakawombe (right).

Right: A Zulu *induna* in festive dress, sketched by Angas; his status is suggested by the large beads around his neck, and by the bunches of lourie feathers on either side of his headring. (British Library)

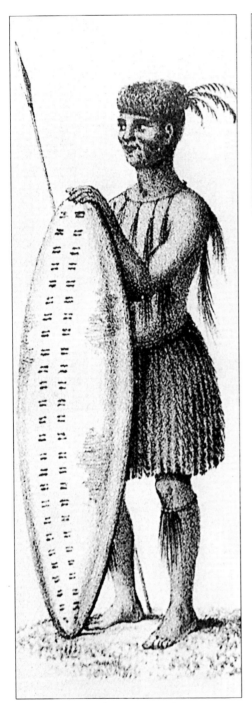

Two sketches by the missionary Gardiner of warriors in 'war dress' – the simplified version of ceremonial regalia worn into action – in the 1830s; they are wearing the full kilt around their waists, but a reduced necklace of cow-tails, and a solitary bunch of feathers in their headbands.

Right: A Zulu 'chief' and his wife, photographed in England in June 1853. This picture suggests something of the magnificence of Zulu ceremonial costume in the middle of the nineteenth century. (Royal Archives)

Above: A Zulu 'chief' in dancing costume, with his attendants, photographed in a British studio in 1853. Note that his attendant is holding a shield over him to protect him from the sun. (Royal Archives)

Right: A remarkable study of a Zulu warrior, one of a party brought to England as curiosities in 1853: these are some of the earliest known photographs of traditional Zulu costume. This man is wearing cow-tails suspended from a necklace, and carrying a full-sized *isihlangu* war-shield. (Royal Archives)

Three photographs from the 1860s of the *inkosi* Ngoza kaLudaba, whose followers broke away from the Zulu kingdom and settled in Natal. They depict the full range of male costume.
Left: Ngoza in his everyday dress.
Right: With his unmarried warriors, wearing the *amaphovela* head-dresses characteristic of the younger *amabutho*.
Lower right: With his senior men, wearing typical otter-skin and crane-feather head-dresses. Note both the full *izihlangu* war-shields, and the smaller variants, similar to the *umbumbuluzo*. (Africana Museum)

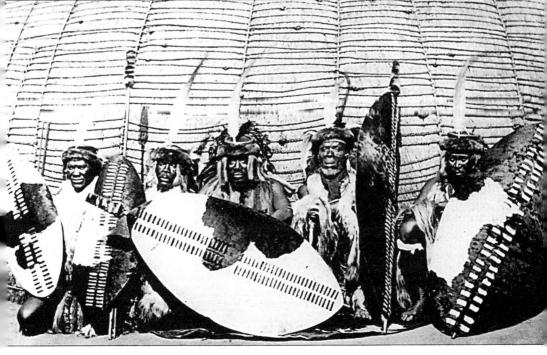

The *amabutho* in all their splendour; although these photographs probably show men from one of the Natal chiefdoms, rather than the Zulu king's warriors, they date from the 1860s, and give a striking impression of the appearance of large bodies of men in full ceremonial regalia. (Africana Museum)

A striking study of an unknown man, carrying his stabbing spear and knobkerrie and wearing a necklace of charms to ward off evil. (Natal Museum)

Rank and status were indicated within the Zulu army by prestige items, such as the lourie-feather head-dress and necklace worn by this *induna*; the necklace is made of red beads and pieces of bone, carved to resemble leopards' claws. (Natal Museum)

Right: The *umqele;* a headband of animal-skin which formed the basis of the Zulu warriors' head-dress. (Africana Museum)

Below: Despite the poor quality of this photograph, it none the less gives a good impression of the magnificence of the *amabutho* on ceremonial occasions. (Natal Archives)

A warrior in full regalia, apparently photographed at King Cetshwayo's 'coronation'. These pictures amply demonstrate the lavishness of the full ceremonial regalia. His body is almost hidden by a profusion of cow-tails, and his head-dress consists of leopard skin headband and earflaps, ostrich feathers, and (at the back of the head) lourie feathers.
(S. B. Bourquin)

Two of the most authentic studies of Zulu military costume, taken before the war of 1879.
Above left: A warrior in the typical ceremonial costume of the younger *amabutho* in the Zulu king's army; cow-hide *amaphovela,* and a tall plume of *isakabuli* feathers. Note that the shield is predominantly dark in colour.
Above right: A warrior in the costume of the senior *amabutho* in the Zulu king's army; he is headringed, wears a crane-feather in the front of his headband, and carries a predominantly white shield. (Royal Archives)

Thukela. Although King Cetshwayo appointed Ntshingwayo kaMahole, chief of the Khoza, one of Mpande's *izinduna*, and one of Cetshwayo's closest personal friends, as senior commander in the 1879 campaign, Ntshingwayo's second-in-command was Mavumengwana, a son of Ndlcla. Furthermore, Mavumcngwana's elder brother, Godide kaNdlela, who was now the principal chief of the Ntuli, was given command of the forces in the coastal sector, opposing the advance of Colonel Pearson. During the Khambula campaign of March 1879, the army was accompanied by none other than Mnyamana kaNgqengelele, chief of the powerful Buthelezi people, and effectively Cetshwayo's most senior adviser; although Mnyamana was not strictly a military commander, he attended the *impi* as the king's personal representative — an indication of the importance of the coming fight.

The senior officer of a newly formed *ibutho*, and his second-in-command, were chosen by the king from outside the regiment, usually from an experienced *ibutho* whose members had already married and assumed the headring. Thus they were given the necessary authority to control the exuberant young men in the ranks, who could on occasion be quite unruly. This was a particular problem when an *ibutho* contained a number of *abantwana*, the king's sons. The uThulwana, for example, formed by King Mpande about 1851, was Cetshwayo's own *ibutho*, and contained a number of other royal princes. It was notoriously arrogant, and Mnyamana had been made its senior *induna* on the grounds that only he was held in sufficient awe to control it. Mtshapi recalled the disputes that arose when Qethuka kaManqondo was also made one of its senior officers:

> Qetuka was of the Umdhlenevu regiment (the Ingwegwe). He was taken from that and made an induna of the Thulwana when the princes Cetshwayo, Mbuyazi, Mantantashiya, Thsonkweni, Dabulesinye, Ziwedu, Siteku, Dabulamanzi, and Hamu were in it. He was the chief son of Manqondo. He was directed to take up the position of his father Manqondo. The princes complained, saying that Quetuka should not go to the old men. Tshonkweni said, 'Why is it that the king places him over old men when we are here?"[46]

Nevertheless, the king had his way and Quethuka retained his command. He was known to be a strong personality, which perhaps accounts for the choice; indeed, at Isandlwana he led part of the regiment out to attack the British camp against the wishes of the senior generals. As this incident demonstrates, civilian rank, even royal blood, was not necessarily enough to overturn the authority of the *izinduna*, since they spoke on behalf of the king himself. Nevertheless, the *abantwana*, whose status as members of the royal house was unassailable, enjoyed authority within the army even when they held no official command. Prince Dabulamanzi kaMpande, for example, had been given no military appointment in 1879, but still led the uNdi *amabutho* across the Mzinyathi river to attack Rorke's Drift in Natal. This was despite the king's prohibition to cross the border, and, indeed, against the urgings of the king's *izinduna* on the day.

Each *iviyo* within an *ibutho* had its own officer, and those *amaviyo* who had *kleza*'d at a particular *ikhanda*, and therefore constituted a section within a regiment, also had their own commander. Baleni kaSilwana of the uDloko regiment recalled how these officers were appointed:

> Some time after we had been butwa'd, it was proclaimed, when we were drawn up in a circle formation at Nodwengu [King Mpande's favourite residence] who were to be izinduna. I was made one of these. The induna called out the names on behalf of the king. The induna (smaller one) was Mfinyeli ka Nguzalele of the Xulu people and was the one who called out. The 'bigger' induna was Ndungundunu ka Nokokela of the Zulu. All of those who were made izinduna afterwards gave the king an ox as thanks for having been so appointed.
> I do not know how I came to be appointed an induna....[47]

Sometimes, as this account suggests, such appointments might have been made at random, the king appointing as junior officers those who had caught his eye when the regiment was brought before him. More often, however, the king relied on the advice of the officers at the *amakhanda* where the sections had *kleza*'d, on reports from the senior officers of an *ibutho*, who were already in charge, and even on reports from district chiefs and *abanumzana*. The king had 'eyes and ears' throughout all levels of society in Zululand, retainers whose duty it was to pass on local gossip, and such spies were not generally regarded with suspicion by the population at large; it was considered the king's right to know exactly what was going on across the length and breadth of his kingdom. White travellers were often struck by the king's knowledge of events that occurred, and individuals who lived, in districts remote from the centres of royal authority, and this system of intelligence no doubt served to influence important decisions such as the selection of army officers. When a man was appointed an *induna*, he was expected to inform both his own *umnumzana* and his district chief of the choice, so that they should respect the duties which the king had imposed upon him.

Nevertheless, the king did have his personal favourites, and this gave rise to another layer in the class structure of Zulu society, the *izilomo*. *Izilomo* were simply friends of the king, those who had caught his eye, his ear and his confidence. Often, they were warriors who had particularly distinguished themselves in battle, and were therefore rewarded, appointed *izinduna*, and sometimes consulted on important military matters within the royal council. Some were junior chiefs whom the king liked and trusted, and who therefore had an influence far in excess of their social position. Indeed, the king often cultivated men of limited hereditary rank, since it gave him access to a fresh range of opinions which were not coloured by the concerns of the *izikhulu* – the representatives of the great pre-Shakan clans who made up the kingdom. This seems to have been particularly true of King Cetshwayo, the early part of whose reign was overshadowed by the existence of the immensely powerful *ibandla*, assembled by his father, Mpande. One of Cetshwayo's favourites was Sihayo kaXongo, the chief of the Qungebe people who lived on the kingdom's western border, opposite the crossing at Rorke's Drift. Sihayo had a number of contacts in colonial Natal which made him useful to the king, and Sihayo's son Mehlokazulu was one of Cetshwayo's personal attendants. Indeed, so much did Cetshwayo enjoy the company of younger men like Mehlokazulu, who was an *induna* in his favourite iNgobamakhosi *ibutho*, that a new class of young royal favourites emerged, called the *zembekwela*, [48] much to the disgust of the older *izikhulu*, who strongly resented their influence over the king. These tensions were summed up by Ndukwana in a anecdote about an argument over the right to occupy a particular hut at oNdini: 'Sirayo was an isilomo but he even disputed about a hut with Ntshingwayo ka Marole, the isikulu. Sirayo was ordered to be removed from the hut.' Ndukwana was quite clear that 'the precedence ran: *izikulu*; *izinduna* … *izilomo*', but because of their influence with the king, '*izikulu* must treat *izilomo* with respect.'[49] Interestingly enough, it was Mehlokazulu kaSihayo's sortie across the border in July 1878 which finally provoked the British ultimatum; the *izikhulu* on the *ibandla* urged the king to surrender Sihayo's sons, but the king could not do so without abandoning both a friend and some of his own prestige.

Life in the king's service
There appears to have been no very great routine to the duties undertaken in the *amakhanda*. The warriors lived four or five in a hut, with *udibi* boys to serve them if they were lucky. When the king wanted them to fall in, his attendants would shout out, 'Let the men of the regiments muster! In the order heard?' According to Lunguza:

> They replied 'It is heard'. Then they would come hurrying out of the huts and start singing, both sides of the kraal. This is the way the whole kraal was called into the cattle kraal. The king at the time would be looking over the fence of the isigodhlo at the troops. In going into the cattle kraal thus, the men would not bring their arms.[50]

The singing and dancing mentioned by Lunguza was a feature of *ama-*

khanda life. Kings Shaka and Dingane both enjoyed composing songs and dances for their regiments to perform, and white travellers were struck by the extreme order with which large numbers of men and women went through complex movements. For men, the dancing usually consisted of advancing and retreating in ranks, stamping with each foot in turn; often they were required to attend armed with shields and sticks, and the rhythmic beating of shields was part of the performance. And herein lies the true significance of these manoeuvres; they were not merely social entertainment, they were perceived as a part of the army's military training. Gardiner recognised this when he described such a dance:

> ... the feet regulate the time, and impart that locomotive effect in which they so much delight; sometimes the feet are merely lifted, to descend with a stamp; sometimes, a leaping stride is taken on either side; at others, a combination of both; but they have yet a more violent gesture; forming four deep, in open order, they make short runs to and fro, leaping, prancing, and crossing each other's paths, brandishing their sticks, and raising such a cloud of dust by the vehemence and rapidity of the exercise, that to a bystander it has all the effect of the wildest battle scene of savage life, and which it is doubtless intended to imitate.[51]

Dancing taught the warriors to move in formation with their regiments, to keep pace, to change front without confusion, and to perform particular tasks on a given command. Indeed, such displays constituted almost the entire book of Zulu drill. Occasionally, regiments were detailed to take up facing positions in ranks, and to charge down on each other, practising the use of the shield and stabbing spear at close quarters; but there was nothing to compare with the European concept of repetitive 'square bashing'.

When the *amabutho* had been called into the *amakhanda* by the king, he was expected to repay their service by providing the food with which they sustained themselves. This, however, extended only to meat and beer, and as Ndukwana observed:

> The true food of Zululand regiments was boiled grain (izikobe). They also ate amabele porridge (inyambazi). At the king's kraals girls had to bring food, for there was none to be got there. Girls were repeatedly carrying food to their brothers, who might be serving at different stations, and do so until the hair wore off the crowns of their heads.[52]

In other words, warriors attending the king were entirely dependent on their families for the same foodstuffs that had sustained them in ordinary life. This was acceptable if a warrior's family *umuzi* was located near the *ikhanda* at which he served, but for men whose families lived a long way off, and therefore could not bring fresh food regularly, it resulted in considerable hardship. According to Ndukwana, most men accepted this philosophically: 'When one went to konza . . . he would get no food, but that did not matter. He got used to being without food and did not feel the pangs of hunger';[53] but there is evidence to suggest that lack of food *was* resented within the *amabutho*. The king was expected to slaughter cattle from the royal herds, and the warriors appreciated any obvious signs of generosity. Lunguza remembered that at eMgungundlovu, 'sometimes the warriors were called up and had cattle doled out to them on the ground that they were hungry. Dingana was fairly liberal with cattle. He gave five, three, two, one, sometimes ten or even more as presents. He killed many cattle, and freely, for the men if hungry.'[54]

Alan Gardiner was a witness to this apparent generosity, and was fascinated by the spectacle of meat being distributed and cooked:

The carcasses of several oxen, recently killed, were at this time lying in several heaps not far from the gate of his fence, the quarters divided and piled one upon another, and in order, no doubt, to exhibit at once his wealth and his munificence; he again appeared slowly emerging from the arched gateway, and advancing with a measured step to the nearest animal mound. Instantly he was surrounded by fourteen or fifteen men who ran up from a distance and crouched before him; a word and a nod were then given, and as quickly they arose and carried off the meat at full speed, holding it up the whole way with extended arms, and singing as they went. Another heap was then approached, and as systematically distributed, and so on until the whole had been conveyed away with a similar pantomime manner. . . .

The evening meal is most characteristic, and which, from the situation of my hut near one of their feeding places, I had the most frequent opportunities of witnessing. Every regiment is divided up into sections, and over each of them an officer is appointed, whose particular charge are the shields and distribution of the meat, of which he is the carver. The beer is always drunk in the area included within the inner fence, and often in the presence of the King; but, for the supper, every section is separately collected in some convenient spot in that quarter, within the fences. The meat is generally stewed in a large black earthen bowl, with a smaller one inverted, and cemented round the top to prevent the steam from escaping; but with all this, and notwithstanding it may have been cooking during the greater part of the day, it is generally so tough, that my teeth could make but little impression upon the pieces which I now and then attempted by way of experiment. It is usually dark before their repasts are ready, when the meat is brought upon a mat about two feet square, and placed upon the ground, round which the whole party thickly crowd in a dense circles, often two or three deep. The carver then, with an assegai head upon a short stick, which constitutes his knife, apportions rations to every second or third man, who, in his turn, divides it with his collateral neighbours, by the joint effort of their teeth; the recipient being always privileged with the first bite. So positive is the labour which is necessary before they can venture to swallow these tough morsels, that the operation is distinctly audible at a considerable distance. . . .[55]

The later kings do not appear to have been as forthcoming as Dingane. No doubt the economic decline of the nation from the 1840s contributed to this, exaggerated by a series of cattle diseases which decimated the royal herds. By the 1870s it seems that a prolonged period in the *amakhanda* resulted in severe want, bordering on starvation.[56] At least part of this was due to the temperament of the king, Cetshwayo, himself, as a remarkable account by one of his *isigodlo* girls, Nomguqo (Paulina) Dlamini, reveals:

Cetshwayo was very stingy. He had inherited this trait from his mother, Ngqumbazi Zungu, who had a reputation of never offering anyone a drink of beer. . . . Cetshwayo did not distribute food readily; only after it had been reported to him that the people were hungry was food released. On the other hand we girls never went hungry. We shared his food and surreptitiously kept some. He received supplies of amadumbe [an edible tuber] sweet potatoes, potatoes, bananas and pineapples. Much of it rotted away because he alone could not eat it all; but he would not allow it to be distributed, until it was reported to him that the foodstuffs were perishing. Only then did he order that the people should receive some. Excess supplies were then dished out to various huts. Then the people ate and became satisfied. Then they approached his quarters and proclaimed their gratitude.[57]

Rivalry between the regiments

Inevitably, when large numbers of young men are gathered together in a martial atmosphere, it is possible for over-exuberance to lead to aggression and violence. The Zulu army had no code of military lore like its Western counterparts, simply because the king's law prevailed throughout all levels of Zulu society. Catherine Barter was not the only outsider to comment on the truculence of the *amabutho*: 'These young soldiers are very insolent at times, and it was rather a questionable proceeding for a [white] woman to go alone to a military kraal'.[58] Senior *izinduna* were usually nearby, however, to keep them strictly in hand. Trouble most often occurred when more than one regiment was quartered in the same *ikhanda*. *Amabutho* used to vie with each other to attract the king's praises or to boast of their past glories, and this often led to fighting between them. Indeed, even if only one regiment was present in an *ikhanda*, the warriors were so competitive that the different sections would contest with one another in dancing displays or at the tasks set by the king, and this might lead to scuffles and blows. Ndukwana described how the uKhandempemvu and uMbonambi regiments clashed once, as they were dancing outside oNdini:

> At that point the uKhandempemvu regiment approached, passing below us, as the Mbonambi regiment was about to go in at the gate. The Ingobamakosi had not yet performed the isiqubulo dance, and was still waiting. At that point a fight broke out at the gate. It was drizzling, and the shields made little noise. Then Mahlapahlapa [an *induna*] came up to me and said, 'There is trouble here. Go and see what is happening, so that we do not take fright if they come on top of us.' I then ran towards the gate, until I could see what was going on there. Matters were serious. There was no reason for this fight, as so often was the case among Zulu regiments – even though no quarrel of any kind.
> Nothing was done, no fine etc. . . .[59]

Such friction was connived at by the senior officers and the king himself, who felt it enhanced the warriors' esprit de corps and fighting ardour. It was, however, strictly prohibited for spears to be used in such fights, which were waged instead with sticks. David Leslie witnessed a number of such fracas, and commented on the usual means of restoring order:

> A wry word or a crooked look sets the whole in a blaze like a spark among powder; and then the captains immediately commence to hammer away with sticks or 'knob-kerries' till they cry 'hold, enough!' The stick is the great disciplinarian and 'argumentarian' in the Zulu. The young men have a saying, 'We never can hear, unless we first feel the stick!'[60]

For some faint-hearted, the incidence of such fights and the prolonged privation made for a reluctance to join the *amabutho*. In theory, the system was one of universal conscription, but compliance was customary rather than obligatory. It was possible for young men to opt out and refuse to join the *amabutho*, although of course this exposed them to the derision of their more conventional age-mates,[61] and considerably damaged their chances in the courting stakes. Nevertheless, there were alternatives available to those who did not wish to serve the king; many simply crossed over into Natal, where the chiefs maintained only nominal *amabutho* and levels of *ilobolo* were in any case lower. Others sought some legitimate excuse for not joining, as Mpatshana kaSodondo of the uVe explained in 1912:

> About 42 years ago there were very many izangoma [diviners]; a regular craze set in, so that in every valley one found six to ten of these men. The reason for

the abnormal increase was because they wanted to get out of military service, for this meant something akin to starvation and being beaten by one another; for at headquarters men were always, as individuals, picking quarrels with one another and fighting with sticks, or a section (isigaba) might fight another section, thereby causing many heads to be injured (open wounds). It was owing to the abnormal amount of this sort of thing going on that led to many turning into *izangoma* and so escaping military service.[62]

To combat this tendency, the Zulu kings had both to make service in the *amabutho* more attractive, and at the same time more rigorously enforce adherence to the system. In this particular instance, Mpande, under some pressure from his indignant heir Cetshwayo, apparently rounded up most of the new *izangoma* and drafted them into a new *ibutho*, the uKhandempemvu, which was just about to *buta*.[63] Cetshwayo himself pursued a deliberate policy of revitalising the *amabutho* after his accession in 1873; although he only formed two *amabutho* before the 1879 campaign, the iNgobamakhosi and uVe, both were unusually large. There was some resistance to this among the district chiefs, many of whom had adopted the habit of keeping back their young men during King Mpande's reign; indeed, Cetshwayo was to complain after the war that 'the many disorders that have existed in Zululand lately are the outcome of so many men pretending royalty, keeping assemblies, and not allowing my people to come and serve me as in the days of old.'[54] Furthermore, his efforts to ensure that the customary observances regarding the marriage of *amabutho* were obeyed resulted in an incident which played into the hands of his enemies in Natal who wished to cast him in the mould of a bloodthirsty despot.

Marriage

The *amabutho* were usually given permission to marry when an age-group reached the mid to late thirties, after perhaps fifteen years of service. Thus the uThulwana *ibutho* was formed by Mpande in 1851, and given permission to marry in 1866. British observers were convinced that this permission was only given after a regiment had distinguished itself in war, the so-called 'washing of the spears' in blood, and were haunted by the image of hordes of frustrated black warriors bent upon slaughter on a promise of sexual gratification. In fact, the *amabutho* system had nothing to do with sexual abstinence, and the phrase 'washing of the spears' was only truly relevant in the context of the *ihlambo*, a ceremonial hunt in which the nation cleansed itself after some momentous event such as a royal death. King Cetshwayo denied emphatically that a recent military success was a prerequisite of permission to marry; asked exactly that during an interview in captivity after the war, he replied, 'No, that has nothing to do with the matter.'[65]

A number of factors affected the final decision. As a regiment matured, the men themselves began to press for the right to marry, and the king could not afford to deny them too long for fear of desertions to Natal. *Izikhulu* whose sons were serving in that *ibutho* might also lobby the king on its behalf, whilst the girls who formed the corresponding female *ibutho* also begged to be allowed to choose husbands. The king usually delayed the process as long as possible, both to maximise the time the regiment was at his disposal, and also to demonstrate his authority over them. Sometimes he would require one last task from them, and this might indeed include a military expedition. Finally, advised by his *ibandla*,[66] the king would grant permission for the *ibutho* to *tunga*, to sew on the headring, and to choose wives from a female age-grade which he had specified.

The marriages did not take place all at once, in one grand ceremony. The individuals of the permitted *ibutho*, wearing their newly fastened headrings, dispersed around the country, searching out suitable mates from among the ordinary civilian homesteads where unmarried girls still lived. According to Lunguza:

> A man who belonged to a regiment allowed to marry would take his shield and assegais and, with a boy to carry his mats, proceed to a kraal he had in mind where there were some of the girls he had been allowed to marry. On getting there he would salute the umnumzana, saying, 'Son of——, I request a comfortable place to sleep.' A girl would be ordered by the kraal head to go and sweep out a particular hut for the use of the new arrival. The girls (eligible) would then be collected and told to go into this hut. When there, the man would look at them and then fix on a particular one and invite her to come and sit by him, side by side. She would then do so, thereby causing the others to laugh at her. He would then proceed to court her, and during the night his mats would be spread out and each of the other girls would occupy the same hut during the night. The mat bearer would sleep alongside the other girls. The man might *hlobonga* with her. There was no sense of shame in this, even though the others heard what was going on. None of the girls were afraid for this was the general custom, hence the girls saw nothing extra ordinary or alarming about it.[67]

After a night spent with the girls, the warrior would share food with the *umnumzana*, and when he left the next morning, 'the girls carry his shield for him and his assegais, for they were very pleased at having been visited by one of the king's warriors.'[68] This appears to have been part of a selection process, since it did not imply that the warrior and his chosen partner were betrothed, although if both were happy with the match, they often became so. In practice, naturally, both warriors and girls alike had often already formed attachments within the appointed regiments, and merely took the opportunity to seek out their lovers and marry. Girls were, of course, particularly keen to form alliances with young men who had already earned some mark of royal favour, since it offered them the prospect of a more comfortable life in the future. Although *ilobolo* rates were low – only one or two cows – and a man might marry several girls from the same *ibutho* if they all wished it, only those who enjoyed the king's favour were realistically in a position to do so, since unmarried men had little opportunity to obtain cattle of their own except by the king's reward. Indeed, there are suggestions that whereas girls in the appointed female *ibutho* were prohibited from marrying among men younger than their authorised partners, they might nevertheless marry, as a second or third wife, older men who had already been through the process. As Lunguza put it, with just a touch of cynicism: 'They liked to marry men of importance, men, that is, who were well off – had plenty of food. Food was the great attraction. Girls liked being the wives of wealthy men.'[69] The marriage ceremonies took place in the ordinary homesteads of the country, and were carried out according to the usual customs, although the number of marriages taking place around the same time may have led to them being more rushed than was usual.

The 'Marriage of the iNgcugce'

In 1876 King Cetshwayo ordered the iNdlondlo *ibutho* to marry, and to select their wives among a younger female age-grade, the iNgcugce. The iNgcugce were disappointed, for they had apparently expected Cetshwayo to allow all of King Mpande's surviving *amabutho* to *tunga*, as King Dingane had allowed Shaka's on his accession; in particular, the iNgcugce girls were of the same age as the uDloko *ibutho*, and many already had lovers in that regiment. They refused to marry the iNdlondlo men, saying derisively that 'the string of beads does not meet around the neck',[70] meaning that there were too few men in the iNdlondlo to go around. The king, determined to assert his authority, insisted, and numbers of iNgcugce girls slipped across the border into Natal. Cetshwayo determined to make an example of the remainder, and set a date by which he expected them to comply with his orders. When the time was up, he called up members of the uKhandempemvu, iNgobamakhosi and iSangqu *amabutho* and told them to kill any girls of the iNgcugce who remained unmarried. This caused an uproar in Natal, where stories of indiscriminate slaughter were spread by the Zululand missionary community, who were implacably opposed to Cetshwayo's regime. These stories were later used to justify British intervention in 1879, although there seem, in fact, to have been few enough killings. Bishop Colenso, a champion of the Zulu royal house, quoted the evidence of one white observer who thought that ten were killed 'at the outside', and claimed that his own informants put the figure as low as five or six.[71]

Nevertheless, the evidence of Mtshayankomo kaMagolwana, who was in the killing party, suggests that the king's reaction was deliberately severe:

> We Ngobamakosi were sent to the Cube country ... and to the Magwaza country ... and to the Ntuli country. ... We killed the girls; we killed many of them; we killed them in their father's homes. We Ngobamakosi were twelve companies (amaviyo) strong. We killed thirty-one girls. We found them hiding among the people of their fathers; others were with their men in the forests. ...
>
> The king had ordered, 'If you come across a girl travelling with a young man, put her to death right there in the path. Lay the body across the place where paths join. Do the same with the young man with whom she is travelling. Kill them both. When you have killed them, place the bodies together, face to face, so that other girls and youths will see.' Indeed that is what we did. There were three who were killed in this way. ...[72]

When news of this incident reached Natal, it provoked a sharp rebuke from the Lieutenant-Governor, Sir Henry Bulwer. Cetshwayo was furious, and responded curtly, 'Why does the Governor of Natal speak to me about my laws? Do I go to him and dictate to him about his laws? ... The Governor of Natal and I are in like positions; he is Governor of Natal, and I am Governor here.'[73] In Zululand, the lesson was learned; the iNdlondlo and the iNgcugce were married off, and the king's decree was not ignored so lightly again.

In more normal circumstances, once a warrior had married, his status had immeasurably improved. He was no longer merely an *insizwa*, a youth, he was an *indoda*, a man with a very clearly defined role in society. Furthermore, since he owed this elevation to the king's permission, he carried with him some reflection of the king's authority, symbolised by the *isicoco*, which was often referred to as 'the king's ring'. In the strict hierarchy of Zulu society, the married man could now impose duties of service on those younger than him. According to Ndukwana:

> Going along a path – meeting one another – it was recognised that an unmarried youth (insizwa) must make way for a mature man (indoda). If he failed to do so, the latter would go to the men of the place of the mnumzana, who would fine the boy, asking how he came to regard himself as the equal of a man, and why he did not reserve his spirit of disputation for those his own size.
>
> A headringed man was always shown respect by a youth (hlonitshwa'd) and never touched by a youth. A man smoking the smoking-horn would say, 'Go, boy, and fetch me a light.' Men hlonipa'd {respected} one another, i.e. according to age and regiments. A younger always hlonipa'd an older man

even though both had headrings. Youths hlonipa'd one another, i.e. the younger and older ones.[74]

This change of status marked a shift in the responsibility of the men concerned. No longer did they owe their first duty to the king, but instead they owed it to their own homesteads and, by extension, to their local chiefs; it was, in effect, the end of their period of national service. As Cetshwayo put it, 'The old men of the country are called the white part of the nation, that is to say they are not soldiers; the young men are the soldiers.'[75] Although they remained linked to particular *amakhanda*, married men were not required to attend the king except under very special circumstances, such as serious military threat, when they would be expected to muster to fight as before. Married regiments were generally signified by carrying white shields. In an attempt to manage the resource crisis which affected the kingdom from the 1840s, both Mpande and Cetshwayo maintained *amabandla mhlope*, 'white assemblies', married regiments who continued to serve in the *amakhanda*. In Cetshwayo's time, this was the uThulwana and the regiments incorporated with it, who remained based at oNdini. However, attending the king seems to have been a purely voluntary affair, and men stayed at the *ikhanda* or returned home at will, often taking their wives with them.

The clash between the uThulwana and iNgobamakhosi

The strict laws and observances regarding social stratification, set within the context of a system in which every individual in turn had the opportunity to enjoy the privileges of his particular stage of development, reduced the potential for inter-generational conflict. Nevertheless, it did occur; older men were jealous of their privileges, as we have seen, and younger men naturally resented their exclusion from the world of wives, cattle and social standing. Younger men, moreover, in the manner of soldiers the world over, considered themselves fitter, stronger and braver, and belittled the stories of military glory told by the older generations. Under ordinary circumstances, these tensions were scarcely significant, but they were dangerous when a younger regiment was thrown into too close proximity with an older one. This happened when the iNgobamakhosi *ibutho* clashed spectacularly with the older uThulwana at the annual *umKhosi* (harvest) festival in December 1877 – the last such festival held before the British invasion. It is worth considering the incident in some detail, since it reflected many of the broader divisions within the kingdom in its last days.

As a 'white assembly', the uThulwana were quartered at oNdini itself. This *ibutho* enjoyed a particularly high degree of prestige, since it had been a favourite of King Mpande, and included in its ranks many of the *abantwana*, or royal princes. It had been kept up to strength over the years by the incorporation of a number of *amabutho* drawn from younger *izintanga*, notably the iNdlondlo and, recently, the iNdluyengwe. It was, moreover, commanded by Prince Hamu kaNzibe, an immensely powerful *isikhulu* from northern Zululand, who was a biological son of Mpande, and who quite clearly resented Cetshwayo's position as king. By contrast, the iNgobamakhosi were young men in their mid-twenties, who, as the first *ibutho* formed by King Cetshwayo,[76] enjoyed his particular indulgence; they were a particularly large *ibutho*, representing the success of the king's attempts to shore up royal authority over the nation's young men. They were commanded by Sigcwelegcwele kaMhlekeleke, who, although a chief of the Thembu, did not rank as an *isikhulu*, but was apparently an *isilomo*, one of the king's favourites. Incorporated into the iNgobamakhosi were the younger uVe. It is also possible that some of the iNgcugce girls, married off to the iNdlondlo, had been forced to abandon sweethearts in the iNgo-bamakhosi.[77] Between them, therefore, the uThulwana and iNgobama-khosi represented in microcosm the full range of the nation's generational and political rivalries.

Because the king liked the iNgobamakhosi, he had not established a new *ikhanda* for them, but rather ordered them to find what room they could among the uThulwana already based at oNdini. During the *umKhosi* ceremony, when both were fully in attendance, conditions became somewhat cramped. According to Magema Fuze, one of Bishop Colenso's informants:

> ... when a wife visited her husband of the Thulwana, a junior of the iNgobamakhosi would have to sit outside and wait whilst the [uThulwana] discussed private matters with his wife, and eventually there developed a rift between the [uThulwana] and the uNgobamakhosi. For these youths of the iNgobamakhosi would call out to the men of the Thulwana when it was dark and now time to sleep, 'Hurry up, old chap, we want to come in and sleep.' Matters remained as such for some time, until these men complained that they were being treated with disrespect by the youths.[78]

In the excitable atmosphere of the ceremonies, passions overflowed. Sigcwelegcwele himself had already apparently argued with some of the most senior *izikhulu*, including Chief Mnyamana kaNgqengelele of the Buthelezi, Cetshwayo's most senior adviser and a commander of the uThulwana, during a meeting in the *isigodlo*. Mnyamana had dismissed the fighting qualities of the iNgobamakhosi, and Sigcwelegcwele had been bold enough to reply, 'You shall see when the regiments go out.'[79] Shortly after this, both regiments were summoned by the king, who had already left oNdini for kwaNodwengu nearby, where the *umKhosi* ceremonies were due

to be held. Sigcwelegcwele refused to hurry his men, saying they were still
eating.[80] Instead, the uThulwana began to emerge from their huts and
formed up in *izigaba* in the central enclosure. They duly began to march off.
By the time their principal sections were leaving by the gate, however, the
iNgobamakhosi had now mustered, and as the iNdluyengwe (incorporated
into the uThulwana) were leaving, congestion arose with the uVe, who
served as the vanguard of the iNgobamakhosi. Outside the gate, in front of
the *ikhanda*, a stick fight broke out, which soon spread throughout both
regiments.

Prince Hamu was in a homestead nearby when the news of the clash
was brought to him. He was outraged that the iNgobamakhosi had been
insolent enough to attack their seniors, and when he heard that his men
were in danger of losing the fight, he cried out: 'Here are the youths
climbing over us and covering the king's things (dancing dresses) with
blood. Arm with assegais and stab them. This has been caused by the
king, who has shoved them in with us, whereas it is we who live with
the king.'[81]

According to Ndabazezwe kaMfuleni, who was present with the iNgobamakhosi: 'They then armed and stabbed us, chasing us away and killing
very many. We ran away, for it was impossible to arm with assegais, seeing
that the Tulwana was in possession of the Undi kraal where our assegais
were.'[82]

The iNgobamakhosi rallied on a nearby hillside, and the uThulwana,
chanting an impressive war-song, poured out of oNdini. The iNgobamakhosi, who did not appreciate that the uThulwana were now fully armed,
advanced to meet them. As soon as they realised their mistake, the iNgobamakhosi broke and scattered, with the uThulwana chasing and spearing
them. The fight raged across the plain before oNdini and on to the surrounding hills. The first clashes had taken place in the early afternoon, and
the uThulwana did not retire until sunset. Ndabazezwe again: 'We turned
on them when they retired to Undi and caught them at Ntukwini. Many of
us succeeded in snatching their assegais and stabbing them with those so
obtained. The pursuit was continued until they reached the kraal and
entered their huts. They shut the doors.'

That night, the iNgobamakhosi slept out in the veld, or tried in vain to
secure entrance to other *amakhanda* nearby, which were already full of men
attending the *umKhosi*. Cetshwayo had watched the fight from Nodwengu
with astonishment turning to fury; when he sent messengers to try to stop
the fighting they were unable to get close enough to restore order without
being attacked themselves. The white trader John Dunn had been attending
the king; when he returned to his camp that night he found that the fight
had raged through it:

On lighting up in my tent I found that one poor fellow must have run for refuge there and been stabbed in the tent, and there was a squirt of blood right round the canvas, over the table, and covering a Worcester Sauce bottle and salt cellar all over. On going to my sleeping tent I also found the front of it covered with blood, and my servants told me that one man had been killed there, whom they had dragged outside, and there he lay about three yards from my wagon. Another was lying against the fence where my cook had his kitchen. This poor fellow was not dead, but unconscious, and moaning frightfully. I tried to get him to drink some water, and then tried to make him swallow some spirits, but he was too far gone and died during the course of the night. All round the cattle kraal the dead and wounded were lying, and everything was covered in blood, the hottest of the fight having taken place there.[83]

Dunn estimated that about seventy men had been killed, mostly from the iNgobamakhosi, although some Zulu accounts put the figure in the hundreds.

Order was restored the next morning. The king was furious with Hamu for ordering the uThulwana to arm with spears, but dared not act overtly against him. Hamu retired to his own district in the north of the country, and instead the king vented his anger on the iNgobamakhosi who had started the fight; each warrior was fined a beast – the seized cattle were 'as numerous as trees in the forest,' recalled Ndabazezwe regretfully. Sigcwelegcwele was also fined, and for a few days it seemed his life was in danger; he had made powerful enemies among the *izikhulu*, and only a timely warning by John Dunn allowed him to slip away safely to his homestead near the coast. The king decided that the iNgobamakhosi should no longer be 'shoved in' at oNdini, and they were sent off instead to Hlalangubo, the old oNdini, not far from Sigcwelegcwele's residence. According to Ndukwana, 'the whole country sided with uHamu',[84] blaming the king instead, for having pushed the two regiments together; the incident undoubtedly soured the already distant relationship between the two men, with significant repercussions during the Anglo-Zulu War a year later. Hamu kaNzibe was the only member of the royal house to abandon Cetshwayo and go over to the British before the king had been defeated in the field.

NOTES

1. Fynn, *Diary*.
2. Baldwin, *African Hunting and Adventure*.
3. Bertram Mitford, *Through the Zulu Country; Its Battlefields and Its People*, London, 1883.
4. Account of Mtshayankomo kaMagolwana, Webb and Wright, *JSA* 4.
5. Account of Lunguza kaMpukane, Webb and Wright, *JSA* 1.

6. Account of Mkehlengana kaZulu, Webb and Wright, *JSA* 3.

7. Account of Lunguza kaMpukane, Webb and Wright, *JSA* 1.

8. Account of Ndukwana kaMbengwana, Webb and Wright, *JSA* 4.

9. Account of Ndukwana kaMbengwana, Webb and Wright, *JSA* 4.

10. Account of Lunguza kaMpukane, Webb and Wright, *JSA* 1.

11. Gardiner, *Narrative*.

12. Cornelius Vijn, (Translated and edited by Rt Rev. J.W. Colenso), *Cetshwayo's Dutchman; Being the Private Journal of a White Trader in Zululand during the British Invasion*, London, 1880. See also John Laband, *Kingdom in Crisis; The Zulu Response to the British Invasion of 1879*, Manchester, 1992.

13. Fynn, *Diary*.

14. Nathaniel Isaacs, *Travels and Adventure in Eastern Africa*, 2 vols, London, 1836.

15. Gardiner, *Narrative*.

16. David Leslie, *Among the Zulus and Amatongas*, Edinburgh, 1875.

17. Baldwin, *African Hunting*.

18. Mitford, *Through the Zulu Country*.

19. Leslie, *Zulus and Amatongas*.

20. Report in *Natal Mercury*, 24 January 1879. An anonymous correspondent with the Durban Mounted Rifles claimed there were precisely forty-seven 'commodious' huts; *Natal Mercury*, 3 February 1879.

21. Correspondent of *The Illustrated London News*, in edition of 23 August 1879.

22. Gardiner, *Narrative*.

23. *Alone Among the Zulus* by A Plain Woman (Catherine Barter), *c.* 1879.

24. Ibid.

25. Account of Ndukwana kaMbengwana, Webb and Wright, *JSA* 4.

26. Account of Lunguza kaMpukane, Webb and Wright, *JSA* 1.

27. Ibid.

28. Ibid.

29. Ibid.

30. Account of Ndukwana kaMbengwana, Webb and Wright, *JSA* 4.

31. Account of Mpatshana kaSodondo, Webb and Wright, *JSA* 3.

32. Account of Ndukwana kaMbengwana, Webb and Wright, *JSA* 4.

33. Account of Mtshapi kaNoradu, Webb and Wright, *JSA* 4.

34. Account of Ndukwana kaMbengwana, Webb and Wright, *JSA* 4.

35. Account of Baleni kaSilwana, Webb and Wright, *JSA* 1.

36. Account of Mtshapi kaNoradu, Webb and Wright, *JSA* 4.

37. Account of Baleni kaSilwana, Webb and Wright, *JSA* 1.

38. Ibid.

39. Account of Mtshapi kaNoradu, Webb and Wright, *JSA* 1.

40. Cetshwayo's evidence to the Cape Commission on Native Laws and Customs, 1883, reproduced in C. de B. Webb and J.B. Wright (eds), *A Zulu King Speaks*, Pietermaritzburg, 1978.

41. Account of Mtshapi kaNoradu, Webb and Wright, *JSA* 4.

42. Account of Lunguza kaMpukane, Webb and Wright, *JSA* 1.

43. Leslie, *Among the Zulus and Amatongas*.

44. Gardiner, Narrative.

45. Cetshwayo's evidence in Webb and Wright, *A Zulu King Speaks*.

46. Account of Mtshapi kaNoradu, Webb and Wright, *JSA* 4.

47. Account of Baleni kaSilwana, Webb and Wright, *JSA* 1.

48. 'Cetshwayo was, I think, about to make the Zembekwela *izikulu*. This is not the name of a man but of the class of his *izinceku* [personal attendants]. The *izinduna* objected to the king always speaking to young men. . . .' Ndukwana kaMbengwana, Webb and Wright, *JSA* 4.

49. Ndukwana, ibid.

50. Account of Lunguza kaMpukane, Webb and Wright, *JSA*, 1.

51. Gardiner, *Narrative*.

52. Account of Ndukwana kaMbengwana, Webb and Wright, *JSA* 4.

53. Ibid.

54. Account of Lunguza kaMpukane, Webb and Wright, *JSA* 1.

55. Gardiner, *Narrative*.

56. On the shortage of resources needed to feed the *amabutho*, see Kennedy, *Zulu Political Economy*, in Duminy and Ballard, *The Anglo-Zulu War; New Perspectives*. A number of reports of men actually dying of starvation in the *amakhanda* reached the Natal authorities on the eve of the 1879 war; see John Laband, *Kingdom in Crisis; The Zulu Response to the British Invasion of 1879*, Manchester, 1992.

57. Filter and Bourquin, *Paulina Dlamini*.

58. A Plain Woman, *Alone Among the Zulus*.

59. Account of Ndukwana kaMbengwana, Webb and Wright, *JSA* 4.

60. Leslie, *Among the Zulus and Amatongas*.

61. According to King Cetshwayo, 'If anyone stops at home, the others laugh at him, and say he is a *Ungogo* = button quail.' Cetshwayo's evidence, Webb and Wright, *A Zulu King Speaks*.

62. Account of Mpatshana kaSodondo, Webb and Wright, *JSA* 3.

63. Ibid, and account of Ndukwana kaMbengwana, Webb and Wright, *JSA* 4.

64. Cetshwayo's Letter to the Governor of the Cape, 1881, reproduced in Webb and Wright, *A Zulu King Speaks*.

65. Cetshwayo's evidence, ibid.

66. 'The King . . . consults with the chief men in the country and agrees with them that a certain regiment or regiments are to put on the headrings.' Ibid.

67. Account of Lunguza kaMpukane, Webb and Wright, *JSA* 1.

68. Ibid.

69. Ibid.

70. Account of Mtshapi kaNoradu, Webb and Wright, *JSA* 4.

71. Bishop Colenso's notes, in Vijn, *Cetshwayo's Dutchman*.

72. Account of Mtshanyankomo kaMagolwana, Webb and Wright, *JSA* 4.

73. *BBP* C1748, November 1876.

74. Account of Ndukwana kaMbengwana, Webb and Wright, *JSA* 4.

75. Cetshwayo's evidence, Webb and Wright, *A Zulu King Speaks*.

76. The iNgobamakhosi were formed from men born in the early 1850s (Bryant, *Olden Times*), and *buta*'d in the early 1870s. Since Mtshayankomo kaMagolwana (Webb and Wright, *JSA* 4) was a member of the iNgobamakhosi and took part in the last umKhosi ceremony of Mpande's reign, they were obviously formed before Cetshwayo's accession. Most contemporary sources agree, however, that Cetshwayo had assumed much of his father's real – if not ceremonial – power by the last years of his reign, hence his involvement with the raising of the iNgobamakhosi.

77. Gibson is of this opinion; *Story of the Zulus*.

78. Magema Fuze, *The Black People and Whence They Came: a Zulu View* (translated by H.C. Lugg and edited by A.T. Cope), Pietermaritzburg and Durban, 1979.

79. Account of Ndabazezwe kaMfuleni, Webb and Wright, *JSA* 4. Ndabazezwe was present during the incident as a member of the iNgobamakhosi.

80. Account of Ndukwana kaMbengwana, ibid.

81. Account of Ndabazezwe kaMfuleni, ibid.

82. Ibid.

83. John Dunn, *Cetywayo and the Three Generals*, edited by D.C.F. Moodie, Pietermaritzburg, 1886.

84. Account of Ndukwana kaMbengwana, Webb and Wright, *JSA* 4.

CHAPTER 3

The Love Charm of the Nation

On 22 January 1879, the Zulu army lay concealed in a valley some five miles from the mountain of Isandlwana, where the Centre Column of the invading British forces was camped. The Zulus were not expecting to launch an attack that day, since the omens were inauspicious, but at about noon they were detected by British patrols. Without waiting for final instructions from their commanders, most of the *amabutho* rose up and streamed off to attack the camp. The senior *izinduna* were able to restrain only the regiments associated with the oNdini royal homestead – the uThulwana, with its incorporated *amabutho*, the iNdlondlo and the iNdluyengwe, and the uDloko – who had arrived late at the bivouac, and were therefore furthest from the point of encounter. Ntshingwayo kaMahole, the great commander, formed with oNdini regiments into an *umkhumbi*, the circle traditionally formed on the eve of combat, in order to perform the last-minute rituals, and to hear the *izinduna*'s commands. After calling out the praises of Shaka and his father, Senzangakhona, Ntshingwayo apparently held up his warshield, and said: 'This is the love charm of our people. You are always asking why this person is loved so much. It is caused by the love charm of our people. There is no going back home.'[1]

It was, of course, just the sort of speech any commander might give when sending his men into battle: a reminder of past glories, an evocation of the honour of their military tradition; 'victory or death, boys, there's no going back home'. Yet the symbolism of the shield could hardly have been more appropriate, since it was not only a military icon, but a reminder that the *amabutho* were bound to the king's service, and that their hopes of future well-being, of cattle and marriage, depended upon it. The love charm of the people, indeed. In the subsequent fight, of course, it was the oNdini *amabutho* who swept behind the British camp at Isandlwana and went on to attack the border post at Rorke's Drift. Curiously enough, the valley where the great army lay hidden that day is remembered locally for the spectacle of the thousands of shields that were gathered in it; in the first light of dawn, they flitted like ghosts in the mist, the dark patterning on the hide standing out alone, and seeming to dance of their own volition.[2] It is called *Mahaweni*, the place of the shields.

Perhaps no single artefact symbolises the old Zulu army than the great war-shield. True, shields were made and carried for a variety of purposes among the Zulu-speaking peoples long before the advent of Shaka, and they are still a feature of life in parts of rural Zululand today. Nevertheless, the use of a uniformed size and pattern of shield was very much a part of the military system of the independent Zulu kingdom, and has come in many ways to epitomise it. The Zulu shield carried with it particular associations of security. As the great kings had attendants who held shields above them by long shield-sticks, to serve as umbrellas on hot days, so the shield in general symbolised the protection afforded by benevolent authority. To live 'under the shield' of a powerful patron was to enjoy the benefits of a life free from danger and insecurity. Shields were used in almost every aspect of Zulu life; there was a small shield, about nine inches by nine inches (*umgabe-lomunye*) for dancing, a slightly larger shield, about twelve inches by eight inches (*igqoka*), carried by youths when courting, and a sturdier shield, *ihawu*, about twenty-four inches by twelve inches, used for everyday pur-poses of protection, including fighting.[3] All these shields were made for an individual from the hides of his own cattle, and were his personal property. The true war-shield, however, belonged to no one but the king himself. It was kept with the *amakhanda*, and only issued to the *amabutho* when they were in the king's service. The king's shield, therefore, was not carried lightly, and any man bearing it carried with him a portion of the king's majesty. Indeed, a man who bore the king's shield – as most of the male population of Zululand did at one time or another – was entitled to respect as someone who accepted his place under the king's protection, and the obligations that were placed in him in return.[4]

The war-shield

All Zulu shields were oval in shape; the regimental war-shield was known as *isihlangu* (pl. *izihlangu*), from a verb meaning 'to brush aside'. Most examples which survive date from the 1879 war, when the victorious British looted them from the battlefields or *amakhanda* as souvenirs. The largest of them measure fifty-four inches tall by thirty inches across, although a smaller variant, about forty-eight inches by twenty-seven inches, is com-mon. No examples appear to have survived from the reigns of the early kings, but the accounts of early white travellers suggest that the larger type was more popular in Shaka's time. Fynn, for example, commented that 'they are supposed to reach from the feet to the chin in length and nearly twice the body's breadth'.[5] The later preference for a smaller variant probably had much to do with the changes in fighting techniques over the kingdom's history. In King Shaka's time, fighting was conducted hand-to-hand, usually against a foe armed with similar stabbing weapons, and a tall, wide shield offered the very real prospect of protection. From 1838, how-ever, the Zulu army increasingly faced Europeans armed with firearms, against which a shield was of more limited use. A small reduction in size was probably more than compensated by increased manoeuvrability and a lighter weight in the field.

Indeed, during the civil war of the 1850s, Prince Cetshwayo introduced a variant among his faction, the uSuthu, which was smaller still. Called the *umbumbuluzo*, it measured forty inches by twenty inches, and was to prove the most popular type carried in 1879.[6] The *umbumbuluzo* was more rounded at either end, noticeably lighter, easier to carry, and much easier to wield in combat, although the choice of type seems to have been a matter of personal preference, and both types were carried, even within the same *ibutho*.

War-shields were cut from cowhide that had been scraped, cleaned and prepared by being buried in the soil for several days. Although the hide was by no means soft, it was at least pliable, enabling the shield-maker to cut it, and the shield itself to be rolled up for storage. The hair was left on the outside of the shield, which served as part of the *amabutho*'s distinctive uniform. Slits, known as *amagabelo*, were cut in parallel rows down the centre of the shield, and strips of hide about two inches wide were threaded through. These strips not only strengthened the centre of the shield, but, since they folded over on the back and were threaded down the opposite row, also provided a means of fastening the hide to the shield-stick. The shield-stick served to stiffen and strengthen the whole shield; it projected beyond the hide at either end, for as much as a foot at the top and a few inches at the bottom. The top was carefully trimmed so that a strip of genet skin could be fastened to it and wound round. This may have been purely decorative, although in a close-quarter fight the projecting end must have quivered with every movement of the shield, and may have served to distract the enemy. The bottom end of the stick was cut to a point, and could be used to jab at an enemy's feet and ankles during a fight. The threaded strips of hide also had hair left on the face, and this was arranged so as to contrast with the pattern on the front of the shield.

The shield in combat

Certainly, there is evidence that Shaka used the shield as an integral part of his fighting techniques. According to Mayinga, whose father Mbekuzana had been one of Shaka's favourite warriors, Shaka 'told the men to carry their shields under their arms and only to bring them out when they got in among the enemy. In the attack they would run in a stooping position, at a great rate'.[7]

This would have been an easy way to carry the shield when advancing rapidly through long grass or bush, and the sudden displaying of the shield just before contact must have had an unnerving effect on the enemy. Shaka, indeed, seems to have had an instinctive understanding of the psychological advantages of display under such circumstances, and it was common for Zulu forces to perform an action known as *ingomane* whilst advancing to the attack – to strike the shield rhythmically with the butt of the spear. This heightened the Zulus' own morale and at the same time gave the enemy a warning of what lay in store for them.

The well-worn idea that Shaka taught his warriors to hook their shields over that of their opponent in combat and to wrench them to the left, exposing the enemy's body to an under-armed spear thrust, is little more than a myth encouraged by early biographers of Shaka who were keen to draw unwarranted parallels with ancient Roman fighting techniques. Nonetheless, it is clear that the shield was used offensively as well as defensively – that a warrior would strike forwards and upwards with it, hoping to batter his opponent in the face or torso, knocking him off balance, pushing his enemy's own shield and weapons back into him, blocking his movements, and exposing his torso to the Zulu's under-arm stab.

Making shields

Making war-shields was a skilled job; one bad cut in the shape or in the *amagabelo* slits, and a hide could be ruined. Nevertheless, the ability to cut shields correctly seems to have been common enough, and large numbers of people were employed in the art at the royal centres. With constant practice, shields could be cut remarkably quickly; the author has seen a modern specialist, working with today's knives, produce a small shield from the hide in a matter of minutes. It is interesting to note that surviving authenticated shields, recovered from a variety of battlefields or looted *amakhanda,* follow the basic patterns and measurements to within an inch or two of each other, despite the fact that the craftsmen would have had access to no sophisticated measuring or marking equipment. Alan Gardiner was fascinated by the extent of shield production he witnessed at eMgungundlovu in 1835:

> ... all the cattle folded in the military towns belong to the King, and but few are killed there in proportion to the numbers which are daily slaughtered at the capital, that is, in consequence, the great deposit of shields, the manufacture of which is the constant and almost only occupation of the men; two being formed from each hide.[8]

As this passage suggests, the shields were made from the hides of the king's cattle, the national herd: the hides of any of these beasts, including those slaughtered to feed the *amabutho,* were apparently used in this way. The standard method of slaughter was to stab the animal in the side, a method that was efficient, if not always quick. It sometimes took several minutes for the animal to die, and to the disgust of European observers, the Zulu took a particular interest in its death-cries. A beast which bellowed long and loud was thought to be calling to the spirits, who would be impressed by its strength and vitality, since robust bellowing was believed to bridge the gap between the living and the dead. Shields were cut from both sides of the flayed hide, and that from the side that bore the death-wound was considered especially favourable. When King Mpande ordered shields to be made for the rival Princes Cetshwayo and Mbuyazi, he gave Mbuyazi the one from the side with the wound, which Cetshwayo took as an indication that he preferred him as an heir — an act that many saw as the start of the civil war between the two.[9] Henry Harford, a young lieutenant of the 99th Regiment who served with the Natal Native Contingent during the war of 1879, saw shields produced under circumstances that filled him with horror, and revealed the very different European and Zulu attitude towards animal suffering:

> For some reason (I forget now what), some short time after the Column had marched I had to return to the camping-ground, and as I rode in I saw clumps of Kaffirs sitting round the oxen that we had been unable to take on. I went up to see what they were about, thinking that they had despatched them and were going to have a feast, but to my horror found that they were calmly carving out a large shield out of the back of each ox and skinning it off while the poor beasts were still alive, some extraordinary superstition being attached to this particular method of obtaining a shield![10]

By cutting a shield whilst the beast was still alive, Harford's men pre-sumably hoped to secure the blessings of the ancestral spirits, to make the shield particularly effective. All such preferences, however, were only applicable when shields were cut for particular individuals, usually men of rank and status. When producing shields in large quantities, to equip entire *amabutho,* it would have been impractical to observe such niceties.

The colour of the hide

Early travellers in Zululand were struck by the fact that the shields carried by each *ibutho* were all cut from hides of the same colour. A description by Henry Fynn of a dancing display at Shaka's court suggests how this was achieved:

> A grand cattle show was now being arranged. Each regiment drove towards us thousands of cattle that had been allotted to their respective barracks, the colour of reach regiment's cattle corresponding with that of the shield the men carried, which, in turn, served to distinguish one regiment from

another. No cattle of a differing colour from those allotted to a given regiment were allowed to intermix.[11]

In order to provide large numbers of uniformly coloured shields, clearly thousands of cattle had to be accumulated, and during the formation of the Zulu state under Shaka, this was apparently accomplished through warfare. When cattle were looted from neighbouring peoples in the course of a successful military expedition, a number were distributed as individual rewards, but the rest were apparently sorted by colour and given into the care of the appropriate *amabutho*. A comment by Mtshapi kaNoradu, a veteran of the uKhandempemvu *ibutho*, although referring to a specific ceremony in which cattle were sacrificed to the nation's ancestral spirits, suggests how this was done:

> A large herd of various-coloured cattle would be picked out and driven to Emakosini, i.e. to the kings' graves, where the departed kings would be praised at length, and chants (amarubo) sung. After this the herd would be driven back then divided up into tens and twenties and then sent out in these small lots to the various amakhanda, where . . . [they would] be actually sacrificed and slaughtered.[12]

According to Henry Fynn's colleague, Nathaniel Isaacs, such sorting took place regularly after a major campaign: 'Several months have been occupied in killing bullocks – the spoils of [Shaka's] successful and inhuman carnage – for the purpose of fattening and diverting his people, as well as for occupying their minds in manufacturing shields from the hides of the slaughtered animals.'[13]

It is interesting to note that this passage seems to confirm Gardiner's comment that the manufacture of war-shields was carried out principally at the king's residence, rather than at the district *amakhanda* themselves, but is at odds with Mtshapi. Presumably the ordinary slaughter of cattle continued at the various *amakhanda* on a daily basis, but any significant or wholesale issue of shields took place centrally. A revealing passage by Lunguza also makes it clear that the Zulu kings extracted tribute from the regional chiefdoms in the form of cattle to be used as shields. Lunguza's father, Mpukane, was a royal messenger of King Dingane, and was frequently sent to Chief Jobe of the Sithole people, to 'say that war shields were needed for the Dhlambedhlu [*ibutho*]. Black oxen, with markings of the side (amawaba) would then be picked out, say 60 of them. The cattle requested of Jobe would be taken from his (Jobe's) own stock, not Dingana's. . . .'[14]

Interestingly enough, another Zulu informant, Madikane kaMlomowetole, observed the 'the best cattle, the handsomest, with the best hides, came from Jobe's country in the Nkandla district near the Mzinyati, and that was where Tshaka's shield used to come from'.[15]

In the early days of the kingdom, when there appear to have been ample cattle available from one source or another, the colour-coding of the regimental shields was quite precise. Nathaniel Isaacs outlined the basic principles: 'The great warriors have white shields with one or two black spots; the young warriors have all black shields; the middle warriors, or those that have wives, form distinct regiments, and are called Umfaudas [possibly *umfokazana* – inferior],' have red shields.'[16]

The broad distinction between black and white is significant; black carried associates of youth and vigour, while white, perhaps because of its association with grey hair and therefore wisdom, conveyed seniority. This distinction prevailed, with some modification, throughout the kingdom's history. As the changing political and economic climate from the 1840s forced the Zulu kings to modify aspects of their control over the military system, so permission to marry was given earlier, and the reserve force of married men increased. White shields, as well as red, therefore came increasingly to be associated with married regiments; as King Cetshwayo himself put it, 'soldiers that are married and have rings are called Amabandhla amhlope, *ie* 'white assemblies' . . . they have white shields.'[17] It was some of these men, like the uThulwana *ibutho*, who still attended the king's principal *ikhanda*, but came and went as they pleased, often taking their wives with them.

Judging from the extensive terminology used to describe the patterns on hides used for shields, the distinctions between the different *amabutho* were, in Shaka's day at least, quite specific. Mayinga, describing a particular shield he associated with King Shaka, noted that 'it was speckled in one portion of it, at the lower end, not all over. This was like ubuwanga; if the same colouring had been all over it would have been called nala.'[18] Such precision implies the extent to which different patterns were recognised and kept distinct. Similarly, an *insana* shield was black or dark brown, with speckled markings on the lower part, *amalunga* shields had a base of one colour with several distinct contrasting markings, whereas red hides with white spots were known as *imitshezi* and black ones with white spots *nkone*.[19] According to Lunguza, 'It was a great offence for a man not belonging to a particular regiment to carry a shield of the colour proper or reserved to that regiment. The reason was, "How could such a man be distinguished as to what he was if he carried a shield of a colour used by a particular regiment [*ie* if he was not entitled to it]?" '[20]

By 1879, however, these distinctions were less strictly observed. Although a pamphlet compiled by Lord Chelmsford's agents on the eve of war listed the colour of shield of each of Cetshwayo's *amabutho*,[21] evidence from Zulu sources suggests that it was no longer usual for a regiment to carry shields wholly of one colour. Mpatshana kaSodondo, who fought with the young uVe *ibutho* at Isandlwana, listed three *amabutho* who, he claimed, had 'shields of any colour; no particular ones'.[22] Mtshapi kaNoradu, describing the shields of his own uKhandempemvu regiment, commented:

> Our shields were black, with white markings (amalunga), while others were brown with white markings (marwanqa) ... Cetshwayo mixed our shields with white ones, ncu ones [meaning unclear], hemu ones [i.e. black or red on one side, white on the other], and mtsheko ones, i.e. black top and bottom, with large white patch running across.[23]

One can only speculate as to the reasons for this. Perhaps, after several decades of comparative peace, the Zulus had simply let the system of colour-coding lapse; this seems unlikely, however, given King Cetshwayo's attempts to revive the military system, and even the precise royal directives implied in the passage above. A more plausible explanation is that by the 1870s, the Zulu kingdom no longer had the tremendous cattle resources which had been available to previous generations. The process of impoverishment had begun in 1840, when the Boers extracted thousands of head from King Mpande as part-payment for their help in ousting Dingane. Traders in the 1850s commented that cattle seemed to be in short supply – in 1861 Mpande asked John Dunn to shoot 600 buffalo, to supply his *amakhanda* with meat, because there were insufficient royal cattle available[24] – and, of course, their own activities depleted herds still further. More disastrously, the traders introduced a number of bovine diseases that had hitherto not been known in Zululand, notably bovine pleuropneumonia – lung-sickness – which spread rapidly among herds which had developed no immunity. When Cetshwayo became king in 1873, one of his first acts was to call together the royal herds for a grand review. John Dunn estimated that over 100,000 beasts were paraded before the new king; some among them were infected, and when they were returned to their respective posts, they spread the disease throughout the country.[25] Within two years as many as half of them were dead. Of course, the national herd still numbered thousands of beasts, and the hides from stricken animals could still be used to make shields. There are suggestions, however, that the Zulu economy was by this time heavily involved with the Natal trade, and that many of the hides were exported; a Durban firm of merchants recorded that in one year alone in the early 1870s it exported 90,000 hides from Zululand.[26]

Clearly such a mortality rate must have had some effect on the use of hides for shields. With fewer cattle, it must have become increasingly difficult to assemble a matched herd of the 500 or more animals necessary to equip the average *ibutho*. It is perhaps no coincidence that it was the younger *amabutho* in Cetshwayo's reign, many of whom, like the uKhandempemvu and the iNgobamakhosi, were abnormally large, who included a mix of shield colours. Of course, the markings on a particular beast might not in any case be uniform; with two shields being extracted from the same hide, it is possible that markings on one side of the hide – and therefore one shield – might vary noticeably from the other. Again, a shortage of cattle must have exaggerated this tendency. Nevertheless, it seems clear that despite these problems, the majority of *amabutho* in 1879 still followed the basic black/white distinctions of previous decades.

If the colour of a shield indicated the seniority of a regiment, at which point did a particular *ibutho* graduate from one shield colour to another, if at all? It seems obvious that the transition from black shield to white shield was made when permission was given to *tunga*, but did a given *ibutho* change its shield pattern several times during its career? The evidence is inconclusive; certainly Cetshwayo is described as carrying a black war-shield with a single white spot at the battle of 'Ndondakusuka in 1856, when his *ibutho*, the uThulwana, was still unmarried.[27] By 1879 the uThulwana were listed by the British as carrying white shields with some markings.[28] Examples that survive, and believed to belong to the uThulwana, prove to be white with small red patches.[29] Whether there were any intermediate stages it is impossible to say. Since war-shields were kept in stores made of natural materials, they were inevitably vulnerable to varying degrees of damage from damp or parasites. It seems unlikely that the serviceable life of an individual shield would have been more than five or six years, necessitating at least one change and possibly as many as three, during the period between a regiment's formation and the granting of permission to marry.

Granting shields

The missionary Gardiner witnessed a fascinating ceremony at eMgungundlovu, which suggests that this was indeed the case, and gives some clues regarding the mechanics of the operation. An *induna* named 'Georgo' (possibly Jojo kaSondata, commander of the amaGovu or uDlangubo *ibutho*) arrived at the royal homestead, together with a large detachment of his regiment, with the purpose of 'begging shields' from King Dingane. Summoned to the *isigodlo*, they ran up, 'brandishing their sticks in a most violent manner'. The king first appeared inside the *isigodlo*, standing on a small mound, which allowed him to overlook the fence; he was greeted with a roar of the royal salute, '*Bayethe!*' He then emerged from his enclosure and sat in front of the assembled regiment, with his councillors at a respectful distance. His senior *induna*, Dambuza kaSobadli, stepped out, and began berating 'Georgo' and his regiment for their supposedly poor performance in a recent campaign. The regiment was required to listen to this public humiliation, and

> Georgo's countenance can better be imagined than described at this moment. Impatient to reply, he now rose from the centre of the line, his person decorated with strings of pink beads worn over his shoulders like a cross belt, and large brass rings on his arms and throat. 'Amanka' (it is false) was the first word he uttered. Then various chivalrous deeds of himself and his men were set forth in the most glowing colours, and a scene ensued which I scarcely know how to describe. Independent of his own energetic gesticulations, his violent leaping and sententious running, on the first announcement of any exculpatory fact indicating their prowess in arms, one or more of the principal warriors would rush from the ranks to corroborate the statement by a display of muscular power in leaping, charging, and pantomimic conflict, which quite made the ground to resound under his feet; alternately leaping and galloping (for it is not running); until frenzied by the tortuous motion, their nerves were sufficiently strong for the acmé posture – vaulting several feet into the air, drawing the knees towards the chin, and at the same time passing the hands between the ankles. In this singular manner were the charges advanced and rebutted a considerable time....[30]

Throughout this procedure, King Dingane, 'who [Gardiner] remarked could scarcely refrain from smiling', acted as a referee, interposing between 'Georgo' and his tormentor Dambuza, until at last he asked: 'When have I ever heard anything good of Georgo? What has Georgo done? It is a name that is unknown to us. I shall give you no shields until you have proved yourself worthy of them – go and bring me some cattle from Umselekaz, and then shields shall be given to you.'

This decision was greeted with some applause and the king retired, leaving beer to be distributed to the warriors, who soon marched off to return to their *ikhanda*. The whole ceremony had been largely symbolic, as Gardiner realised: 'I am inclined to think,' he commented, 'that there was much of state policy in the whole of these proceedings, particularly as the order for the attack on Umselekaz was shortly after countermanded, and not more than ten or twelve days elapsed before the same party returned, and received their shields.'

It is obvious from this account that Georgo's *ibutho* had seen previous military experience, so it must presumably already have been in possession of some shields; it is not clear, however, whether it was begging new shields as the result of some specific and recent achievement. Nor was the ceremony apparently related to any imminent permission to marry, so presumably the new grant was merely a display of royal approval. Sadly, Gardiner does not give us any clue as to whether the new shields were of a different colour to the old. Ironically, the uDlangubo regiment was still active five years later, during the struggle between Mpande and Dingane, and it sided with Mpande.

Gardiner was present when the new shields were later claimed. Typically, they had been housed in thatched stores, known as *unyango,* which were raised on stilts seven or eight feet off the ground, to keep them out of the reach of rats. Rats thrived on the refuse inevitably left around the *ama-khanda* – Gardiner was frequently tormented by them running across his body as he slept in Zulu huts at night – and they were capable of consuming entire shields. He recalled:

> At this time I was quietly writing in my hut; one of the shield houses adjoined; and I shall never forget the unceremonious rush [the warriors] made. Not contented with turning them all out, and each selecting one, but, in order to prove them all and shake off the dust, they commenced beating them on the spot with sticks, which, in connexion with this sudden incursion, occasioned such an unusual tumult, that I almost thought a civil war had started.[31]

No doubt part of this selection process included trying out the individual shields to ensure that any minor variations in size fitted a warrior's height and build. Perhaps proven warriors were allowed a greater degree of choice, since there is evidence that well-known heroes were recognised at a distance by the particular markings on their shields. A warrior called Nombango kaNgedhi, for example, was known, rather sinisterly, as 'the white-marked shield that asks no questions',[32] while both Shaka and Cetshwayo are said to have watched out for their *izilomo* in battle by the colour of their shields. A number of important men are also remembered to have carried particular shields, and it seems that men of status may even have stored their shields in their own huts. For the most part, however, as Isaacs noted, the warriors 'retired to put away their shields'[33] in the communal stores at the end of their day's duty.

The spear

Unlike the shield, however, the spear remained an individual's property. The spear *(umkhonto)* was, of course, the inevitable counterpart of the shield, and it remained the Zulu army's principal weapon throughout the kingdom's existence, despite the increasing availability of firearms. Zulu traditions universally attribute Shaka with having introduced the large-bladed stabbing spear. As Mayinga put it, 'Tshaka said the old system of hurling assegais was bad; it caused cowardly behaviour'.[34] The story that Shaka invented the stabbing spear has now been discredited but the weapon had previously been regarded as an exceptional one, the preserve of a few *abaqawe*, champion warriors such as Shaka himself had been as a young man. Its widespread adoption among the Zulu following his accession was undoubtedly a factor in subsequent military successes since Shaka developed both the practise and psychology of the stabbing spear to a certain logical conclusion. Warriors were no longer allowed to carry throwing spears, and so had no excuse to avoid close-combat; those who returned from battle without their stabbing spears were similarly liable to be accused of cowardice, on the grounds that they too had hung back. Although Dingane seems to have revived the practice of carrying one or more throwing spear, this was in addition to the stabbing weapon, which remained the most important part of a warrior's armoury until the early part of the twentieth century.

The stabbing spear of Shaka's day apparently had a tapering blade some eighteen inches long and an inch and a half wide.[35] The crude smelting process employed by local smiths enabled a certain amount of charcoal to mix with the molten ore, so the resulting metal was, in effect, an inferior quality steel. If the technology was limited, however, the craftsmanship was not; a skilled smith could produce a beautifully finished blade which was strong and kept its edge well. By the 1870s, however, the availability of superior European metalwork had led to a decline in the Zulu iron industry, and a number of blades dating from the Anglo-Zulu War show signs of having buckled in use.

Although the smith fashioned and tempered the blade, it fell to the spear-maker – *inyanga yoku pisela* – to fit it to the haft. The wood for the haft *(uti)* was carefully selected from one of three or four varieties, according to whether the spear needed to be light, for throwing, or strong, for stabbing. A hole was bored in the end with a hot awl, and into this the tang on the spear-blade was set. A strong vegetable glue, from the tuber of the *ingcino* plant *(Scilla rigidifolia),* was used to cement it in place. A strip of the bark of a particular bush was bound around the join, and this was then covered over, either with a tube of hide peeled from a cow's tail, or with a binding of split cane. The join was therefore a strong one, well able to withstand the stresses of repeated and powerful thrusting into flesh and bone. Indeed, the weakest part of the whole spear was probably the haft, which sometimes snapped in combat. The best stabbing spears therefore had a haft about thirty inches long, as thick as a man's thumb, and with a swollen butt at the end, to prevent the hand, wet with blood, from slipping right off the haft when trying to withdraw the blade from a deep body thrust. Each of the various types of spear used by the Zulu-speaking peoples had a specific name and purpose; the prototype stabbing spear was usually known as *iklwa,* which is said to be an onomatopoeic word resembling the sucking sound it made on being pulled out of a wound.

Unfortunately, no examples survive which can be dated with any certainty to the Shakan period, nor is it possible to tell how long this pattern remained pre-eminent. Certainly, stabbing spears with impressive blades were common throughout Natal and Zululand until the early twentieth century; the traveller Bertram Mitford in 1882 described meeting a veteran of the uDloko *ibutho,* who had fought at Rorke's Drift with a spear which had a blade 'like a small claymore'.[36] Photographs taken in the region until about 1910 show men proudly posing with similar weapons. Nevertheless, most examples which survive from 1879 suggest that types with shorter and narrower blades, like the *ntlekwane* (blade twelve inches long by one-and-a-quarter inches wide) were by then more popular. It may be that these had a wider range of practical everyday uses than the Shakan prototype, which was specifically designed for combat; or it may simply be that any decline in the quality of craftsmanship was reflected in the size of the blade.

Certain individuals and clans in specific parts of Zululand enjoyed a high reputation as smiths, although, as Ndukwana commented, 'there were not many smiths who made assegais, but there were a considerable number of smiths who made hoes'. Most of these were undoubtedly made for individual use, but there is some evidence that the smiths also supplied spears directly to the Zulu kings, who in turn distributed them to their *amabutho.* According to Ndukwana: 'No order was ever issued ... to smiths to make assegais. They used to arrive periodically at the king's kraal, carrying quantities (bundles) of assegais, and the king, as often as these bundles arrived, would give them to izinduna to distribute to the regiments that required them.' [37]

Beleni kaSilwana, speaking of Mpande's day, added that the smith received 'say three beasts each time he bought a bundle'.[38] Although, no doubt as a result of this, the stabbing spears used in warfare were sometimes called 'the king's spear', it is likely that this distribution of spears was largely symbolic, another demonstration of the king's role as the notional provider of the nation. These spears were in fact probably destined for the *izilomo,* the king's friends and favourites, whose services he wished publicly to recognise. Otherwise, all the evidence suggests that Zulu men acquired their own spears; Ndukwana himself mentions that two spears could be obtained, presumably by anybody, for the cost of a goat. This would be only natural in a country which had a strong military tradition, where a man needed to be able to defend himself against wild animals, and where spears provided the only means of slaughtering domestic livestock. Indeed, although the spears belonging to men of great rank were destroyed after their death, to prevent their spirits wreaking havoc with them in moments of wrath,[39] the spears belonging to ordinary *abanumzana* were regarded as family heirlooms. All such spears would have been stored at private homes; when a man reported to serve the king, he would simply bring the appropriate spear or spears with him. It is interesting to note, however, that it was considered an unforgivable breach of etiquette to take a spear into the presence of the king, and that in the great dancing displays at the *amakhanda*, sticks, not spears, were carried. As late as the 1930s, Denys Bowden, a collector of Zulu traditions, recorded how one of his informants broke off a conversation to put his spear away, 'as it was not polite to talk over a spear'.[40]

Weapon training

Training in the use of the stabbing spear appears to have been largely symbolic. There is a conspicuous absence of accounts describing how the use of the spear in combat was passed on; this appears to have been something a Zulu man absorbed in the course of his upbringing. Some techniques were clearly more highly regarded than others, however, since according to Mandlakazi kaNgini, his grandfather, Zulu kaNogandaya, who was a noted warrior in Shaka's day, and who commanded an *ikhanda* in Dingane's,

> ... used to jeer at a man if he did not hold his stabbing assegai in the imfukule position. He himself used to hold his assegai in this position, pointing upwards, with the blade above his head and the shaft below it [*ie* underarm]. Not ... ukukabukomo [overarm, above the head]. Zulu said that the assegai should be held in the imfukule position. Our fathers learnt this from him.[41]

This was sound practical advice. Used overarm, striking downwards, the length of the blade mitigates a strong, well-directed blow, but hefted underarm, with the weight of the body behind it, and used in co-ordination with the shield, the stabbing spear could inflict ghastly body wounds which soon incapacitated the enemy. There was, perhaps, rather more attention given to the need to fight within a coordinated battle formation, and Isaacs describes how King Shaka once organised a demonstration to prove the effectiveness of the stabbing spear. He armed two parties with reeds; one was given a bundle, to be hurled at the enemy like throwing spears, whilst the other had only one, representing a stabbing spear. 'The latter,' observed Isaacs, 'covering themselves with their immense shields ... soon beat off their adversaries, and thus it was decided that Shaka's new regulation was best.'[42] It is interesting to note that traditional dances are still remembered in Zululand today which include a carefully choreographed use of the shield and stabbing spear, and it is quite probable that such dances formed the basis of weapon training in Shaka's kingdom.

When throwing spears were carried, the usual practice was for the warrior to carry them in the shield hand – usually the left – and to draw them out one at a time and fling them as he closed on his enemy and only the stabbing spear was left. There was no great distinction in the patterns of throwing spears between those used for war and those for hunting, with the exception of a few heavy-bladed types like the *isiphuphu*, used to bring down elephant, buffalo or other large game. The most common type of throwing spear, the *isijula*, had a blade about seven inches long on the end of an exposed shank three or four inches in length, which was set into a shaft up to three feet long. Other patterns had smaller blades and longer shanks. The throwing spear's effectiveness was dictated almost entirely by range. Over short distances it could be hurled with considerable accuracy and 'astonishing force', according to Isaacs, who was on the receiving end of one, and would have had sufficient velocity to transfix a human torso. Beyond a range of thirty yards or so, however, the drag on the shaft caused it to slow down and waver in flight, with a dramatic decrease in accuracy and velocity. In 1879, Lieutenant Colonel Evelyn Wood, commanding a British column, organised a spear-throwing contest for the diversion of his troops and was disappointed to note that 'the first prize [was] won by a Hottentot about 5 feet in height, who propelled an assegai 70 yards, the second man being a Colonial born Englishman, while no Zulu threw an assegai farther than 50 yards'.[43]

In addition to spears, the Zulu armoury included a number of striking weapons. It has already been noted that sticks were carried for dancing and sparring; a variety with a heavy knob on the end – known in English as the 'knobkerrie' and Zulu as *iwisa* – was also used as a club in war. These clubs were cut from a single piece of wood, often of a characteristic light and dark colour, and had a stout, straight handle about eighteen inches long, and a round head which might vary from four inches to six or seven inches across. Such clubs were as a result beautifully finished and highly polished, and occasionally decorated with a twisted binding of metal wire around the handle, a feature introduced into Zululand by traders from Natal in the 1840s.[44] Some surviving examples are mounted with a fearsome array of metal studs, embedded in the head but it is not clear whether these post-date the Anglo-Zulu War. Two or three lighter variants were also known, including the *chopho*, a knobkerrie with the head set to one side of the stick, and scooped out at the top and bottom; this was more often used during ceremonial dancing displays. The knobkerrie was used with considerable skill, but no great subtlety; it was simply a club with which to beat the enemy's brains out. Curiously enough, the knobkerrie is likewise associated with mercy, since it was the weapon employed to put a badly wounded man, who had no hope of recovery, out of his misery.

Lastly, the Zulus also knew of the battle-axe, although it was usually only carried by men of status, and as a ceremonial weapon rather than for fighting. Lacking the technology to pierce metal or work it into a tube, most southern African groups employed an axe blade which fitted into a wooden handle, rather than the other way round. Among the Shona people of Zimbabwe and the Sotho groups of the interior, axes with half-moon blades were common; the curved edge was the cutting edge, whilst a tang emerged from the straight back and pierced the handle horizontally, a few inches below the top. There is some evidence that such axes were traded into Zululand, although the true Zulu axe – known as *isizenze* – seems to have been a heavier weapon, with a steeply angled blade, the top edge projecting noticeably above the handle. When employed in battle, it was wielded with a chopping movement, and the lower portion could be used to hook the edge of an enemy's shield, and pull it aside.

The ceremonial dress of the *amabutho*

The colour-coding of the big regimental war-shields was not the only component of an intricate uniform system which distinguished each *ibutho*. Isaacs was one of the early European travellers to realise this:

> This morning three regiments of boys arrived to be reviewed. There appeared to be nearly 6,000, all having black shields. The respective corps were distinguished by the shape and ornament of their caps. One regiment had them in the shape of Malay hats, with a peak on the crown about six inches high, and a bunch of feathers at the top. Another wore a turban made of otter skin, having a crane's feather or two on each side; and the third wore small bunches of feathers over the whole head, made fast by means of small ties . . . [later] a regiment of men arrived with white shields, having on them one or two black spots in the centre. . . .[45]

These differences were quite specific and military by association, although their fullest importance was ceremonial rather than practical. In fact, the basic dress of Zulu males in the nineteenth century was minimal, to say the least; it consisted of a small box made of dried grass and banana leaves, known as the *umcedo*, which was worn over the end of the penis. For a man to be naked without an *umcedo*, outside the privacy of his own hut, was a shocking breach of etiquette, but conversely a man was considered decently dressed on almost all occasions even if he wore nothing but an *umcedo*. It was far more usual, however, to wear a loin covering over the top of the *umcedo*. This consisted of a thin strip of hide around the waist, with covers of animal skin hanging front and back, and was known as the *umutsha*. The front portion, known as the *isinene*, consisted of a number of strips of animal skin, each wound round a central core of fibre so that the hair stood on end, and the whole strip resembled an animal's tail. Sometimes strips of two different skins were wound together, so that the colours contrasted or blended in each tail to produce an attractive visual effect. The skins most commonly employed were those of the civet cat or the blue monkey, *isimango*, although other skins, including lamb and goat, were sometimes used. Perhaps a dozen or more of such 'tails' would be needed; an ordinary *umutsha* hung perhaps half-way down a man's thigh, but more extravagant examples, worn on special occasions, hung to the knees and beyond. The back part of the loin-covering was known as the *ibeshu*, and consisted of a soft square of bullock-hide, hairy side out, hanging over the buttocks. For everyday wear, the *ibeshu* was small and practical, but a longer variant was often worn on ceremonial occasions, hanging to the back of the knees.

This loin-covering formed the basis of male dress amongst the Zulu-speaking peoples until the widespread adoption of European clothes in the twentieth century. It was worn regardless of age or rank, although a man's status might be suggested by the quality of the skins he wore. When attending a muster of the *amabutho*, however, a man would be expected to wear an extravagant costume over the top of his everyday loin covering. On such occasions further 'tails' made of twisted monkey skin might be added in a bunch over the hips, or a lavish waist kilt, the *insimba*, consisting of beautifully worked skins which hung all the way round the waist like a skirt, might be worn instead. The rest of the costume consisted of a striking headdress, which varied from regiment to regiment, and, about the body, an extraordinary profusion of cows' tails.

The basis of the headdress was the *umqele*, a padded headband of animal skin.[46] This usually consisted of leopard skin for the unmarried *amabutho*, and otter skin for the senior men, and each skin was carefully sewn around a bulrush or a wad of dried cow-dung, so that it formed a roll, which was then tied at the back of the head. Often long tails, made in the same way as those for the *umutsha*, were attached at the back, to hang down over the shoulders. Square or oblong pieces of skin (*amabheqe*), usually of the *isamango* monkey, were sewn to either side of the headband, so as to hang down over the ears and the cheekbones to the jawline. Some regiments displayed additional flaps at the back of the head, hanging down on to the shoulders. This headband formed the basis of the feathers worn above it. Young unmarried regiments boasted large quantities of the tail feathers which the long-tailed widow-bird (*isakabuli*) develops during the mating season; these are up to two feet long, and black in colour. They were either tied to porcupine quills to form a plume which was then inserted into the headdress on either side above the ears, or were fastened to a grass framework which was worn directly on top of the head. Long white ostrich feathers, and their shorter black counterparts, were borne in various combinations according to regiment; some, for example, had bunches of black ostrich feathers at the front of the head, surmounted by a few long white feathers, while others wore both types fixed at different points around the whole headdress. Senior regiments – married men – displayed the tail feathers of the *indwe*, the blue crane, either singly in the front of the headdress, or in ones and twos on either side. Other plumes, such as a clipped ball of feathers worn over the forehead, might, like the eagle feathers granted to the iNdabakawombe *ibutho* by King Mpande, be approved on the whim of the king himself.

Perhaps the most bizarre feature of the headdress was an arrangement common to many of the younger *amabutho*, the *amaphovela*. This consisted of two stiff strips of cowhide, fastened under the front of the headband so that a couple of inches showed below it, over the temples, while the rest stood up above it for eighteen inches or so, like horns. The tops of these strips were split in two, and to the points were attached cow-tails which then hung back down over the side of the face.

Cow-tails were, indeed, an extraordinary feature of this costume, and a physical proof both of the nation's wealth in cattle and the number that must have been slaughtered on a daily basis. Any one warrior's costume required dozens of tails, called *amashoba*, stripped away from the bone, the hide cut into strips and the hair fluffed out. Each tail was bound to thongs to provide a dense bushy mop of hair which was tied principally around the arm, above the elbow, and above the knees. Sometimes similar ornaments were also fixed around the ankles and wrists. A dense curtain of tails, stitched to a hide necklace, was worn around the body, so as to hang to the waist at the front and all the way to the knees at the back. When fully dressed in all this panoply, the warrior was a spectacular sight, and hardly any part of his body was exposed. As a result, European travellers often found it difficult to recognise even individuals they knew well when they were fully dressed. According to the traveller David Leslie, writing in the 1850s:

> During the day the troops dancing in full war dress, showed one the maximum native ideas of greatness and splendour. It was actually impossible to distinguish one chief from another, so covered were they with skins and feathers – a kilt of monkey and cat skins round the waist, their breast and back covered with white ox tails, on their head a sort of cap with lappets of monkey skins, and as many ostrich and crane feathers as they could manage to stick in.[47]

Robert Samuelson, the son of a missionary who grew up in Zululand, often saw large numbers of men in full costume going up to attend the king; their dress must have been hot and uncomfortable, and the weight of the cow-tail necklace chafed around the neck, but although it looked cumbersome, it did not inhibit their movement. On one occasion he

asked the chief leader if his men did not find it a hindrance in their movements to carry so many things and wear so many ornaments, for these fellows
were attired with all kinds of beautiful plumes and skins, and carried large
shields and brightly burnished assegais in addition to sticks. The leader
smilingly replied, 'You will soon witness that these are not encumbrances.'
Soon after they marched off, and as they started ascending a rise, about 300
yards off, the leader gave out a ringing order, and the whole regiment
charged up the hill, moving like a whirlwind, and they were out of sight in a
moment. It was a grand sight.[48]

The numbers of pelts and feathers needed to supply an army in excess of
25,000 men boggles the imagination, especially as the items themselves
would be subject to natural wastage, and would presumably have been
replaced at regular intervals. Bishop T.C. Wilkinson attended the annual
umKhosi, or first fruits ceremony, at kwaNodwengu in January 1871, and
witnessed the uThulwana *ibutho* in all their splendour. His account gives
some clues as to how valuable were the pelts and feathers which made up
their costume:

This morning the crack regiment, composed entirely of chiefs, and dressed
far more magnificently than any of the rest, marched into camp. The Prince
Cetywayo, the heir to the Zulu throne, is in this regiment. When it arrived,
the king, wearing my beautiful rug, was wheeled out of his enclosure in a
carriage into one of the great circles, which I have described, surrounded by
military huts. Round him sat his great ministers and courtiers, ourselves
amongst them. The regiment of chiefs formed in a semi-circle – the Prince
Cetywayo in the centre – and went through all kinds of savage manoeuvres.
The dresses of many of these chiefs Mr Robertson estimates at £30 value; at
least, the magnificent feathers and ornaments would fetch this sum in
Europe.[49]

Henry Fynn was of the same opinion, noting that the *insimba* kilt alone
'generally contain from 15 to 20 skins in a dress, sometimes 50 or 60,
putting an astonishing value on them, which, if it is ever offered, will not
induce one to part with it'.[50]

Some of the component items were to be found in Zululand – blue
monkeys, for example, could still be hunted in quantity in the Nkandla
forest in Cetshwayo's reign – but the amount needed by the *amabutho*
outstripped Zululand's ability to supply them. Indeed, the increasing
numbers of white hunters who operated in Zululand from the 1850s further
reduced the natural wildlife, gradually driving it into the most inaccessible
parts of the kingdom. The solution adopted by the Zulu kings was to
demand pelts and feathers as part of the tribute supplied by subject

chiefdoms. This particularly applied to the Tsonga groups around St Lucia Bay, on Zululand's northern coastal strip, where natural conditions and less intensive human settlement combined to provide a seemingly inexhaustible supply of skins. Bikwayo kaNoziwana was an *induna* appointed by Cetshwayo to oversee the extraction of this tribute, and his account makes clear the enormous extent of Zulu demands:

> We used to go for genet skins for the warriors' dancing girdles; blue monkey skins for the strips worn at the side of the face; leopard and otter skins for the warriors' headbands; blue cloth to be worn by the king's isigodhlo; large red beads, and lion and leopard claws worn by chiefs; elephant tusks (for the king would send them on to Europeans); rhinoceros horns for making snuff boxes of the type carried in the ear lobe ...; beads; calabashes, gourds, etc.; beer baskets, food baskets, ubusenga rings, ornamental sticks and knob-sticks, and many other articles – ostrich feathers, and umampabane beads worn by chiefs....[51]

On one occasion, Bikwayo mentions that the Tsonga king, Noziyingili, collected 600 pelts as one payment of tribute. On another, shortly before the 1879 war, Bikwayo was sent to Mzila, the king of the Shangane people who lived along the lower Zambezi in Mozambique; he returned with 'skins of blue monkey, genet, leopard, and otter, and gunpowder, caps and lead.' No doubt the earlier kings pursued a broadly similar policy; Isaacs mentions that he gave Shaka 'a quantity of peacock feathers which he wanted for his warriors'.[52] Since the trading community at Port Natal were effectively white *izilomo*, who owed their privileged position there to the king, this was exactly the sort of tribute expected of them. Shaka, however, was not impressed with peacock feathers – 'he rather received them with indifference, and thought them not at all suited to his warriors, for whom he intended them'. Interestingly enough, Shaka is said to have been receiving tribute from a group of messengers from the amaMpondo people of southern Natal, with whom he had recently terminated hostilities, when he was attacked and assassinated.

Having obtained these skins from outside the kingdom, Ndukwana kaMbengwana describes how the kings distributed them:

> Dancing dresses of animal skins were distributed; genet-skins and blue money-skins were also presented by the king to izilomo. Izikhulu also wore these skins. Ordinary men also wore these. It was not necessary for the king to give an isilomo more than three skins. That quantity was not enough, but it would indicate the king's permission having been given, and the isilomo might then go to his umnumzana and report the fact, and he would give a beast to go and buy more dancing dresses.[53]

As with spears, the king's favour in the question of uniform was more important than the actual pelts or feathers given away. He could not hope to give away sufficient pelts for all his warriors, but the *izilomo* might be allowed to wear items forbidden to ordinary warriors, or be given pelts of particularly fine quality. A freshly *buta'd ibutho* might be given a supply of pelts and feathers in the required combination to start it off. It was no doubt easier to provide some items – such as the crane feathers worn sparingly by the men of the married regiments – than others. The majority of the ordinary warriors nonetheless apparently had to provide the bulk of their uniforms themselves. Although such ceremonial dresses were treated with respect in honour of the king's bounty, the fact that they were expensive doubtless also explained why they were safely stored away in private huts, and carried to the muster rolled in mats by *udibi* boys.

Tokens of authority

Certain items of dress were prohibited to commoners without the king's permission. Foremost amongst these was leopard skin, which had associations of royalty, and which none but men of rank were allowed to wear. If a leopard was killed by men out hunting, or because it had been attacking stock, the body was taken first to the *umnumzana*, who was obliged to send either the corpse, or, if that were impractical, the pelt and claws, to the district *izikhulu*. 'No one killing a leopard would keep it for his own use,' recalled Ndukwana.[54] It was the prerogative of the *isikhulu* and his sons to wear the pelt, which they did either as a wide collar, falling down over the chest and back, or occasionally as an *ibeshu*. This prohibition of wearing leopard skin did not, however, extend to the leopard skin headbands worn by ordinary warriors. Similarly, lion pelts were considered to be the property of the king, and were sent to him if one were killed, although they do not appear to have been worn to any significant extent.

Various other items denoted rank and status. Leopard claws were used together with large red beads to form a necklace which only men of the highest status were permitted to wear, and the feathers of the scarlet lourie (*iGwalagwala*) were considered a sign of royalty. These were short feathers, perhaps six inches long, crimson and dark green in colour; they were carefully split along the vein, twisted, and tied together to form a bright, crinkly bunch, which was attached to the headband, either at the back of the head, or on either side. Great men were entitled to carry them by birth, but ordinary warriors might be granted permission to wear them, either individually as a particular distinction, or as part of the costume of an entire *ibutho*. It is said that the uMbonambi *ibutho* were allowed to wear them,[55] and this may have been because they were recognised as having been the heroes of Isandlwana, the first to reach the British tents.

Since the social hierarchy of civilian life continued into the military sphere, there were no very clear badges of military rank, but whereas the basic components of ceremonial costume were common to all, it was still possible to tell a man's status by the number of such prestige items he wore. A description by Henry Francis Fynn of King Shaka's war dress provides an excellent portrait of the sort of regalia worn by a senior Zulu commander. Shaka was the only Zulu king regularly to command his army in the field; although under other circumstances a number of dress items were reserved for the king's exclusive use, this particular costume was typical of the men of the highest rank:

> Round his forehead he wore a turban of otter skin with a feather of a crane erect in front, fully two feet long, and a wreath of scarlet feathers, formerly worn, only, by men of high rank. Ear ornaments made from dried sugar cane, carved round the edge, with white ends, and an inch in diameter, were let into the lobes of the ears, which had been cut to admit them. From shoulder to shoulder he wore bunches, five inches in length, of the skins of monkeys and genets, twisted like the tails of these animals. These hung half down the body. Round the ring on his head were a dozen tastefully arranged bunches of loury feathers, neatly tied to thorns, which were stuck in the hair. Round his arms were white ox-tail tufts, cut down the middle so as to allow the hair to hang about the arm, to the number of four for each arm. Round the waist, there was a kilt or petticoat, made of skins of monkeys and genets, and twisted as before described, having small tassels round the top. The kilt reached to the knees, below which were white ox-tails fitted to the legs so as to hang down to the ankles. He had a white shield with a single black spot and one assegai. When thus equipped he certainly presented a fine and most martial appearance.[56]

By 1879, it was rare for such splendid costume to be worn on anything but the *umKhosi* festival. Nevertheless, the rules pertaining to the *amabutho*'s ceremonial regalia were so well known that, according to Robert Samuelson, 'Should a member of a regiment be found not properly attired he would be asked by his comrades, "Where do you come from?", and be set on and thrashed with light sticks, and sent home in disgrace.'[57]

NOTES

1. Account of Ndukwana kaMbengwane, Webb and Wright, *JSA* 4.
2. Account of Mtukwa Mtetwa, whose father was present at the battle. Notes on the shield colours of the *amabutho* compiled by the Bantu Affairs Commissioner, Nongoma, for the Department of Bantu Administration, 1961. Possession of Mr S.B. Bourquin.

3. For a list of the different shields and their functions, see R.C. Samuelson, *Long, Long Ago* (hereafter *LLA*), Durban, 1929.

4. See Gibson, *Story of the Zulus*.

5. Fynn, *Diary*.

6. Samuelson, *LLA*. There are a number of references in the extensive literature of the Anglo-Zulu War, from both British and Zulu sources, to the effect that the Zulus preferred 'small shields' *ie* smaller than the *isihlangu* by that time.

7. Account of Mayinga kaMbekuzana, Webb and Wright, *JSA* 2.

8. Gardiner, *Narrative*.

9. See for example account of Mangati kaGodide in Webb and Wright, *JSA* 2, and Mpambukelwa kaCangasa., ibid, 3.

10. Daphne Child (ed.) *The Zulu War Journal of Colonel Henry Harford, CB*, Pietermaritzburg, 1978.

11. Fynn, *Diary*.

12. Account of Mtshapi kaNoradu, Webb and Wright, *JSA* 4.

13. Isaacs, *Travels and Adventure*.

14. Account of Lunguza kaMpukane, Webb and Wright, *JSA* 1.

15. Account of Madikane kaMlomowetole, Webb and Wright, *JSA* 2.

16. Isaacs, *Travels and Adventure*.

17. Cetshwayo's evidence, Webb and Wright, *A Zulu King Speaks*.

18. Account of Mayinga kaMbekuzana, *JSA* 2.

19. See A.T. Bryant, *Zulu-English Dictionary*, Pietermaritzburg 1905.

20. Account of Lunguza kaMpukane, Webb and Wright, *JSA* 1.

21. F. Fynney, *The Zulu Army and Zulu Headmen. Published by Direction of the Lieutenant-General Commanding* (hereafter *TZA*), Pietermaritzburg, 1878.

22. Account of Mpatshana kaSodondo, Webb and Wright, *JSA* 3.

23. Account of Mtshapi kaNoradu, Webb and Wright, *JSA* 3.

24. A.T. Bryant, *The Zulu People*, Pietermaritzburg, 1949.

25. Dunn, *Cetywayo and the Three Generals*.

26. Quoted in Colenbrander, *Zulu Political Economy*, in Duminy and Ballard, *New Perspectives*. Colenbrander's paper gives a perceptive insight into the crisis in resources which plagued the kingdom in the 1870s.

27. Account of Mpambukelwa kaCangasa, Webb and Wright, *JSA* 3.

28. Fynney, *TZA*.

29. The author has had access to a number of shields either recovered from the battlefield at Rorke's Drift, or looted from the oNdini *ikhanda*, where the uThulwana were quartered.

30. Gardiner, *Narrative*.

31. Ibid

32. Account of Lunguza kaMpukane, in Webb and Wright, *JSA* 1.

33. Isaacs, *Travels and Adventure*.

34. Account of Mayinga kaMbekuzana, Webb and Wright, *JSA* 2.

35. Bryant, *The Zulu People*.

36. Mitford, *Zulu Country*.

37. Account of Ndukwana kaMbengwana, Webb and Wright, *JSA* 4.

38. Account of Baleni kaSilwana, Webb and Wright, *JSA* 1.

39. See, for example, Baleni kaSilwana's account of the burial of King Mpande in Webb and Wright, *JSA* 1.

40. See *'Kill Me in the Shadows'*; *The Bowden Collection of Anglo-Zulu War Oral History*, edited

by Ian Knight, in *Soldiers of the Queen*, the Journal of the Victorian Military Society, No. 74, September 1993. The Bowden Collection forms part of the collection of the Natal Museum, Pietermaritzburg.

41. Account of Mandlakazi kaNgini in Webb and Wright, *JSA* 2.
42. Isaacs, *Travels and Adventure*.
43. Field Marshal Sir Evelyn Wood, *From Midshipman to Field Marshal*, London, 1906.
44. Catherine Barter listed 'brass wire' amongst the trade goods she and her brother took into Zululand during Mpande's reign. *Alone Among the Zulus*.
45. Isaacs, *Travels and Adventure*.
46. Samuelson's *LLA* provides a description of the various items of nineteenth-century Zulu regalia. The 1974 reprint contains a number of Samuelson's newspaper articles which were not included in the original edition.
47. Leslie, *Among the Zulus and Amatongas*.
48. Samuelson, *LLA*.
49. Quoted in *Soldiers of the Cross in Zululand*, by 'E. and H.W.', London, 1906.
50. Fynn, *Diary*.
51. Account of Bikwayo kaNoziwana, Webb and Wright, *JSA* 1.
52. Isaacs, *Travels and Adventure*.
53. Account of Ndukwana kaMbengwana, Webb and Wright, *JSA* 4.
54. Ibid.
55. Samuelson, *LLA*.
56. Fynn, *Diary*.
57. Samuelson, *LLA*.

CHAPTER 4

The Sacred Coil of the Nation

In January 1871, the Reverend T.C. Wilkinson travelled at King Mpande's invitation to KwaNodwengu, the king's *komkhulu*, or 'great place', in the heart of Zululand, to witness the annual *umKhosi* ceremony. Wilkinson had been appointed the first Anglican Bishop of Zululand – an appointment bordering on the presumptuous, given the country's independent standing – and it was to be Wilkinson's first introduction to his prospective flock. Had he realised it, it was hardly a fortunate omen that he was invited to attend the *umKhosi*, the harvest festival which ushered in the first fruits of the season, since the ceremony was a demonstration of all that made the Zulus impervious to Christian evangelism; it was an expression of the nation's strength and purpose, a festival of national rejuvenation, in which the kingdom came together to reassert its sense of collective identity, to praise the ancestral spirits and to reaffirm its loyalty to the king. Nevertheless, Bishop Wilkinson's description of his journey is full of a sense of wonder at the spectacle of what was to prove one of the last great gatherings of its kind. By 1871 Mpande's long and patient struggle to rebuild the prestige of the monarchy was nearing its end, and the kingdom seemed, superficially at least, as wealthy and powerful as it had been in the early years. Yet Mpande had only a year or so to live, and the gatherings of Cetshwayo's reign were overshadowed by internal divisions and by growing tension with the British. Perhaps, even then, Wilkinson realised that he was witnessing the golden twilight of the Zulu kingdom:

> We passed through a beautiful country full of flowers and flowering shrubs. There had been rain, and the whole air was scented like an English conservatory. The yellow and pink mimosa trees were in full bloom, jessamines of all kinds, fuchsia trees, orchids hanging down from the branches, gardenias &c. All the way as we came we passed groups of warriors trooping to the king's place, all dressed in their very best – spears, shields, plumes, tiger [sic] and leopard skins covering their bodies. Wherever the eye ranged across the hills it met companies of these warriors, all converging to one focus, the king's place. Out of bushes, from behind rocks, out of gorges and beds of rivers, they came and went singing their wild war-songs, and tramping as only these people can tramp; formidable-looking fellows enough, and formidable, indeed, if they chose to be your enemies.
> About 3 p.m. we reached the top of a hill overlooking the valley in which

123

the king's place is situated. In the centre of this valley lies the king's kraal, or town; all around for miles lie large military kraals or barracks, enormous circles of huts – I measured one which was 320 yards across. They are, upon ordinary occasions, merely garrisoned with a hundred soldiers or so, but now crammed to overflowing; indeed, temporary huts of green branches are being everywhere constructed to accommodate the host, which is supposed to number 30,000, and all these the very flower of the country, magnificent men, few under six feet in height, and very models in shape....

... Altogether, it is a strange sight in a strange place. The continued roar and hum of voices throughout this vast camp of savages, which lasts late into the night as they sit round their watchfires singing their wild war-songs and relating the old traditions of their land – and then to feel that we are in the very midst (this is the centre) of Zululand, far removed from civilised governments, in the midst of these thousands of men, who might make mincemeat of us at small notice if they so pleased ... now most friendly towards us, feeding us at their own expense, showing us every attention and kindness....[1]

The word *umKhosi* itself is derived from the noun *inkosi*, meaning chief or king, and the ceremony itself, aptly described by one commentator as 'The King's Mass,[2] was a prolonged celebration of the concept of *ubukhosi* – the spiritual power and presence of the king. Its main purpose was to secure the blessing of the ancestral spirits on the new harvest – and by implication on the wealth and power of the kingdom in the coming year – by appealing, not to the ancestors of the clan chiefs who made up the nation as a whole, but specifically to the shades of the ruling Zulu élite. This was a confirmation of the elevated status the Zulu clan had enjoyed since the rise of Shaka, and was an effective demonstration of the way the royal house had come to monopolise the symbols of statehood. The *umKhosi* celebrated the crucial role of the king as the embodiment of the nation, the unifying force who held it together. His person was the sole medium of intervention with the great ancestral spirits, and it was into his keeping that the sacred objects which represented the Zulu concept of statehood were entrusted. The *umKhosi* was the only time outside the major military expedition that the army was regularly brought together in its entirety, and the rituals demonstrate like nothing else the overlap between the army's military and civilian roles, and its function as the mobilised manpower of the nation, gathered to pay homage to the king and all he represented.

The rituals of the *umKhosi*

The last full *umKhosi* festival was held by King Cetshwayo at the turn of 1877/78, and it is often difficult, now, to disentangle the sequence of events;

few Europeans witnessed the ceremonies in their entirety, and those who did seldom understood their true significance. The accounts of Zulu participants were often transcribed by outsiders years afterwards, and indeed, the exact order of ritual may have varied from one celebration to another. Nor was the timing fixed from one year to the next; the Zulus recognised the lunar month, which straddles its European counterparts, and, since the *umKhosi* embraced the full crop cycle from planting to reaping, the date of the ceremonies varied according to their progress.

It was given to the Cube people to set the cycle in motion.[3] The Cube enjoyed a close relationship with the Zulu kings, because Chief Zokufa had been a friend of Shaka's, and had allied himself with the kingdom, rather than having been incorporated by conquest. Their territory lay on the southern boundary of Zululand, in the hot, humid Nkandla forest, over-looking the Thukela valley, and it was generally believed that the planting season came to them first. In August and September they kept a close eye on the progress of the soil, and when they detected the first signs that the time was right, they sent to warn the king to begin the necessary preparations.

Before the major ceremonies could begin, the king himself needed to perform a rite that freed the soil from spiritual pollution, and made it safe for the crops. Known variously as *ukukota igeja*, 'licking the hoe', or *umkhosi igade*, 'the ceremony of the clod', this function was usually per-formed during the lunar month of *umFufu*, which straddles September and October. To ensure its success, the king's most trusted and powerful *izinyanga*, the 'doctors' who were trusted with the spiritual welfare of the people, were required to gather together a potent selection of *imithi* (sing. *umuthi*) – medicines – which reputedly included soil stolen from the fields of the nation's enemies. The purpose of these medicines was to ensure that no rival power could exert a malicious influence over the Zulu fields, and for them to be effective the *izinyanga* were expected to employ their powers to the full to make certain that they were collected and brought to the king in secret.

At each stage of the ceremonies, it was essential that the king opened himself up to the influence of the ancestral spirits. To prepare him for this, the *izinyanga* smeared his body with powdered medicines, known as *imithi emnyama* – black medicines – which preserved him from evil influences, and made him receptive to the spirit world. In this state, he was supposed to soak up so much of the collective power of his forebears that he entered a state of psychic rage, and commoners were afraid to look upon him. It was in this condition that he was required to 'lick the hoe'; the *izinyanga* pre-pared *umuthi*, including the samples of stolen soil, in a potsherd held over a fire, and when it was hot, the king was required to *ncinda* – to dip his fingers into it, and suck the liquid from his finger-tips. By doing so he ensured that the nation would be free from the supernatural influence of any enemy hoping to strike at the Zulus through their crops. The ceremony took place at dawn, so that the spreading rays of the sun would spread the power of the ritual across the king's domain, and bring confusion to his enemies. When it was over, it was necessary to return the king to his normal state, since the effects of mixing with his people whilst under the influence of black *umuthi* could be disastrous. The medicines on his body were carefully washed off, and replaced by 'white' medicines, *imithi mhlope*, which cleansed him of any potential contamination. So important were these rituals that the king was subjected to them at almost every stage of the *umKhosi* cycle.

The 'licking the hoe' ceremony was a small affair, conducted in private, but once it was over, the king gave orders for one or two of the younger *amabutho* to muster at his great place, in order to hoe his fields. These fields grew the mealies to feed the permanent staff quartered at the great place, and the true significance of the event was symbolic, since it confirmed the *amabutho*'s willingness to serve, and indicated to the nation that the time to plant was at hand. This was the *amabutho* as a labour-gang; they went out into the fields, chanting as they did so, and broke up the soil under the watchful eye of their *izinduna*.

The next month, October–November, was a time of waiting for the first signs of spring; it was called *uZibandlela*, the month when the paths, *ndlela*, are hidden by sprouting grass. In the following month, the nation looked for the first signs that the crops were pushing through the soil; November–December was called *uMasingana*, from *ukusinga*, 'to look for or scrutinise'. It was, however, strictly forbidden for anyone to harvest his crops before the king had performed the necessary ceremonies, and anyone found guilty of doing so was liable to be executed. Such an act was considered likely to compromise the blessing of the spirits, harm the king, and so open the entire nation to the risk of spiritual contamination.

The soul of the nation

The ripeness of the season was gauged by the condition of a particular plant which produced a small soft gourd known as the *uselwa*, and which grew in the hot, damp coastal belt. The royal *izinyanga* watched carefully its progress, and when it was ripe, messengers were sent to collect it, together with a wide range of ingredients that symbolised the unity of the nation, including sea-water and water from the country's greatest rivers. This, too, was a highly secret exercise, since the purity of the ingredients might be compromised if an outsider knew of their purpose. According to Mtshayankomo kaMagolwana, who took part in one of the last *umKhosi* ceremonies of Mpande's reign as a warrior of the iNgobama-khosi:

The gourd was fetched from Dhlokweni, where the Tukela enters the sea. It was fetched by the *izinyanga*, Nondo ka Sikakane and others. Seawater was also fetched; it was fetched on the same day. The water would bubble over and spill out. When they were crossing the rivers they would take water from each and fill the containers. They crossed the Amatigulu, iNyezane, uMlalazi, Mkukuze, Mhlatuze, and White Mfolosi. The *izinyanga* did not go near people's kraals when they were fetching the gourd. No one was supposed to set eyes on them as they went on their way. They took their own food with them. Indeed they were not seen. If someone came across them unexpectedly he would on no account say that he had seen them. They would arrive at the king's place after dark. They would not go in at the gate used by the cattle and the regiments, but would enter the upper end of the kraal through the opening used by the king, and prepare him for the ceremony. He would enter into a stage of rage.[4]

Nomguqo Dlamini, one of King Cetshwayo's *isigodlo* girls, remembered that these *izinyanga* also collected potent medicines representing the very essence of the Zulu, the soul of the nation itself:

These 'soul-substances' were found in the 'body dirt' of the populace, but especially that of the chiefs and the king himself. Tiny bits of grass against which the feet of passing multitudes had brushed on the country's footpaths, samples of thatch or scrapings from the wooden posts from doorways against which people had rubbed in crawling in and out of huts, and scrapings from any article with which friend or foe had been in physical contact, all of these contained the essence of the soul of the nation or a means by which the enemies of the nation could be suppressed.[5]

It was about this time, too, that the messengers were sent out to secure a bull – preferably a black one – from the herds of one of the king's enemies. The bull had to be fierce, since at the height of the great *umKhosi*, members of a selected *amabutho* were required to kill it, by hand and unarmed, in an act which symbolised the nation's triumph over its enemies. As Mtshayankomo put it, 'this bull would be fetched from foreign parts. It would be stolen from the grazing ground. It would be a fighting bull, pitch black in colour, a big, old one, that would rip out people's innards.'[6] Once again the *izinyanga* would use their full powers to help them travel abroad undetected, to steal the bull, and to bring it back unobserved to the royal homestead. Quite how practical such an exercise was in the 1870s, when the Zulu kingdom was hemmed in on two sides by colonial powers, remains obscure; certainly most Zulu accounts of the later *umKhosi* ceremonies suggest that the bull was usually stolen from adherents of the Swazi kingdom to the north, who must by then have been one of the few viable targets left to them.

When news reached the king that the *uselwa* gourds were maturing, he would consult with his senior advisers, and fix the date for the preliminary festival, the *ukweshwana*, the little *umKhosi*, also known as the *inyatelo*. This usually took place at the time of the full moon; the new moon was never a period for any auspicious undertaking, since it was a time of *umnyama*, literally blackness, when dark forces lurked perilously close to the mystical divide between the spiritual and everyday worlds. The main function of this first ceremony was for the representatives of the Zulu clan, the ruling élite, led by the king himself, to pay homage to his ancestors, and to appeal for their help in blessing the crops. This blessing was required in a tangible form; in a hot country plagued with periodic droughts, people, cattle and crops all depended on a plentiful supply of spring rain. Because the purpose of this ceremony was specific to the Zulu clan, it was not necessary that the entire nation attend. It was confined to the king, his most powerful and influential advisers, and his *izilomo*; the district *izikhulu* were not included. Similarly, only representatives from those regiments whose *amakhanda* lay close to the royal homesteads in the heart of the old Zulu territory were mobilised to take part in the ceremonies. They were not at full strength, since only a few companies were necessary, and these were always drawn from unmarried 'black' regiments alone, whose youth and vigour, uncomplicated by the muddying of the psychic waters which accompanied the married state, was considered 'pure'. Together the assembly represented the core of the Zulu kingdom – the Zulu clan itself, the heart of the nation. The first confirmation the nation had that the ceremony was imminent was when the selected *amabutho* were mustered and ordered to collect firewood in the Mfolozi valley for the coming rituals.

Praising the ancestral spirits

Before these could begin, the king once again prepared himself with the administration of black *muthi*, and he abstained from food until they were completed. The first ceremony required the killing of a bull by members of the *amabutho*; this was not the bull stolen from foreign fields by the *izin-yanga*, and which was required for the great *umKhosi* itself, but rather one selected from the king's own herds. It was, however, no less fierce than the stolen one, for if the bull proved weak and ineffectual, the symbolism of the event was lost, and the ritual lacked the necessary spiritual force. The selected warriors were not allowed weapons, and had to seize the bull by its horns and limbs and wrestle it to the ground. There are suggestions, however, that in the *inyatelo* ceremony a doctor was allowed to use a spear to deliver the *coup de grâce*. It was quite common, nevertheless, for warriors to be badly injured, or even gored to death. Occasionally, if the bull was too fierce, it might be hamstrung to prevent it breaking free, and eventually the

Probably the most accurate representation of warriors in action in 1879, advancing in open order, wearing only a few items of regimental regalia, and carrying a variety of firearms and *umbumbuluzo* shields.

Above: Seeing nothing but blood – a reconstruction of the hand-to-hand fighting at Isandlwana which suggests something of the raw experience of a Zulu battle. (National Library of Scotland)

Right: Ultimately, the traditional Zulu tactics of surrounding the enemy in the open proved outmoded in the face of the European weapon technology of the 1870s, as this engraving of the final attack during the battle of oNdini (Ulundi), 4 July 1879, implies.

Above: *Ukuhlomula*: although rather stylised, this representation of the death of the Prince Imperial in June 1879 is accurate in that it depicts the Zulu custom whereby the enemy dead are stabbed by each man who has fought against them. (Africana Museum)

Below: A clump of warriors cut down by British volley-fire at oNdini; in 1879 the Zulu army was acutely vulnerable to concentrated firepower.

Opposite page: In defeat, the Zulu warrior could expect little mercy from his enemy, as this engraving of an incident in the aftermath of Khambula suggests.

Left: 'The occupation of a military kraal'. The juggernaut of the British invasion rolls into an *ikhanda* during the latter stages of the 1879 war. Note the interpreter questioning women tending to a wounded warrior, left.

Opposite page, bottom: The end of it all: a dramatic rendition of British troops looting and burning King Cetshwayo's oNdini homestead, 4 July, 1879. (Rai England Collection)

Below: A charm necklace, consisting of small bags of lizard or snake-skin, containing medicine to ward off evil, and blocks of willow-wood, ritually burnt at the edges. Most warriors wore charms such as these into action; this particular example was from the collection of Lieutenant-Colonel Anthony Durnford, killed at Isandlwana. (Royal Engineers Museum)

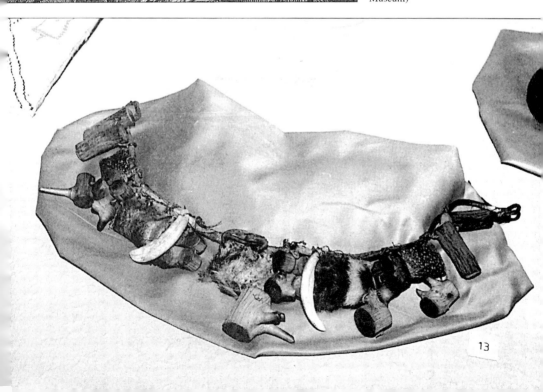

An *inyanga*; Zulu herbalists were able to treat a number of battlefield injuries, but were powerless in the face of the terrible wounds caused by bullets and shellfire in 1879. (Bryan Maggs Collection)

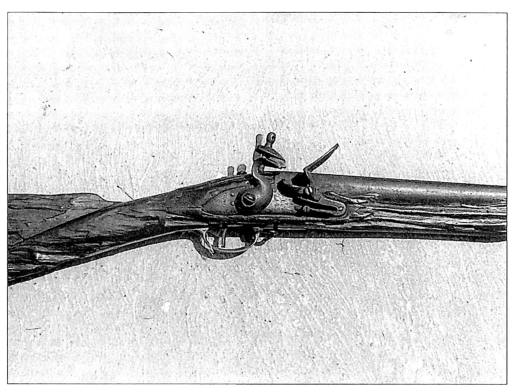

New technology.
Above: flintlock Brown Bess musket bearing the Tower mark, typical of the obsolete firearms carried by the Zulus in 1879. The wood on this musket has been damaged by termites. (Zululand Historical Museum, oNdini)
Below: A powder horn for use with a musket. (Keith Reeves)

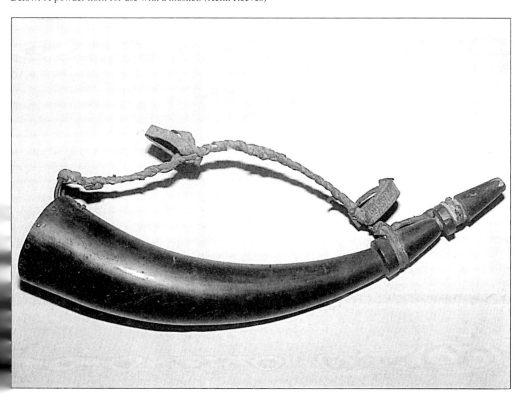

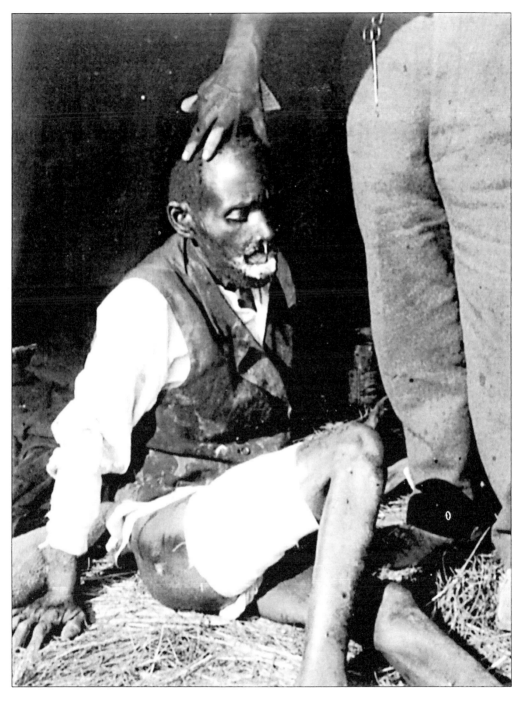

Three poignant photographs which demonstrate the futility of traditional Zulu tactics in the face of improving European weapon technology.

Opposite page, top: Zulu dead on the 1879 battlefield of Gingindlovu.

Opposite page, bottom: The 1884 civil war battlefield of eTshaneni, where Zibhebhu was defeated by a combined royalist and Boer force, still strewn years later with human remains.

Above: A rebel horrifically wounded in the face, arm and thigh by shellfire in the 1906 Bambatha Rebellion. (Photo from an original 1906 negative, by courtesy of Natal Carbineers Historical Centre/KwaZulu-Natal Museum Services)

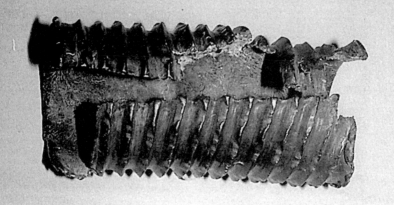

Left: Status symbols: brass *izingxotha* armbands, a highly prestigious recognition of services to the Zulu state. The damaged example has a gruesome story attached to it; it was apparently found on the oNdini battlefield early in the twentieth century. It has been damaged by shell-fire, and still contained human bones. (Natal Museum)
Above: The *iziqu*; the necklace of interlocking beads of willow-wood which was a symbol of courage in battle throughout the existence of the Zulu kingdom. (Killie Campbell Africana Library)

Left: An elderly Zulu who had fought with the uVe *ibutho*, photographed in the 1930s wearing the symbols of royal recognition; the *iziqu* necklace and *ingxotha* armband. (Natal Museum)

Above and overleaf: Two atmospheric studies of veterans of the Zulu King's army, photographed in the 1930s, both survivors of Isandlwana. The anonymous 'warrior' above wears the *iziqu* necklace. (Killie Campbell Africana Library)

A vetaran of the Battle of Isandlwana, Mapelu kaMkhosana Zungu, who fought with the iNgobamakhosi. (Killie Campbell Africana Library)

warriors would drag it to the ground and twist its neck until it snapped. They would then haul the carcass to the calf-pen and screened-off enclosure near the *isigodlo* at the top of the central space, which served as the king's private quarters throughout the ceremony. Any blood and offal spilt on the soil would be carefully gathered up by the *izinyanga*, and every particle of the dead animal collected in the calf-pen. There the *izinyanga* would remove the gall and other internal organs which were said to hold the strength and spirit of the animal. A great bonfire was built from the wood collected by the warriors, and the remaining meat was roasted on the fire, and given to those *udibi* boys who had accompanied their relatives to the great place. This had little to do with feasting, but rather was intended to dispose of the bull utterly, and to pass its strength into the coming generation. Only those lads who had not yet reached puberty were given the meat – those who had were considered impure – and they were expected to devour the entire carcass. This could be a lengthy and uncomfortable process, according to Mtshayankomo:

> The bull was eaten by the young boys, those who had not yet reached puberty, the carriers of mats and blankets. Older youths, those who had reached puberty, did not eat it. These younger boys were called into the enclosure of the isigodhlo, where the king was nqwamba'd [dressed by the *izinyanga*] and the bull burnt. The king was treated with protective medicines. He did not partake of any food until the next day; he took only medicines. The boys were not allowed to leave; they were shut up in the king's washing enclosure until the next day, without being allowed to defecate or urinate. At dawn the bull would still be burning. The fire was fed continually and the bull was burnt, the flames crackling. Strips of meat as long as one's arm were continually cut off. It would burn for two days, that is, for a day and a night.... On the third day the burning would be over.[7]

The body-parts carefully removed by the *izinyanga* were added to the powerful medicines they were preparing to purify the king and, through him, the nation as a whole. They were medicines of the greatest supernatural potency, and the implications should they fall into the wrong hands were appalling. For this reason, no part of the bull escaped the *izinyanga*'s attentions, since even the smallest speck of blood might be taken by a potential enemy and used by rival *izinyanga* to attack the king. Physically, these medicines were a dark, murky liquid, and when they were ready, the *izinyanga* took them to the main entrance of the great place. Here the king, still smeared with black medicines, *ncinda*'d as he did when 'licking the hoe', dipping his fingers into the liquid, then sucking it off the tips into his mouth. This time, however, he was obliged to *cintsa*, to turn to the sun and spray out the liquid between his teeth, thereby effusing its powers through the sun's rays. Lunguza kaMpukane witnessed King Dingane performing this part of the ceremony:

> The ncinda'ing was done with both hands and was continued after the king left the isigodhlo and went into the cattle kraal. The potsherd with the medicine would be carried by Ngungwana, the doctor, by means of pincers or holders. The king would walk straight ahead into the kraal as if towards the gate at the bottom and proceed say 50 or 60 yards, then turn back, ncinda'ing constantly with both hands, and spitting out. Ngungwana would walk a pace ahead on the right of the king, turning towards him with the sherd as he walked. The sherd was like a little pot of clay, as big as a soup plate.[8]

While the king was undergoing the *ncinda* ceremony, the assembled warriors were led off towards the graves of the king's ancestors to beg for rain. The early chiefs of the Zulu – Shaka's father Senzangakhona, his father Jama, and his father Punga, and others including the supposed progenitor of the clan, Zulu himself – were all buried in a comparatively small area, along the valley of the Mkhumbane stream, close to King Dingane's eMgungundlovu residence, and south of the White Mfolosi river. Their graves were marked by trees planted over them, and the area had such strong associations of royalty that it was known as *emaKhosini* – the place of the kings. It was the sacred heart of the Zulu kingdom, and the *amabutho* marched around the graves in turn, taking with them a herd of black cattle from the royal herds. At each grave the *izimbongi* – the royal praise-singers whose duty it was to declaim the long praise poems which celebrated each king's great deeds – shouted out the appropriate praises. They were joined now and then by some of the king's closest friends and most powerful advisers, representing the king himself. Many of the homesteads associated with the old Zulu chiefs still survived, although they had been moved and rebuilt many times since, and at each of these the *amabutho* sacrificed cattle to the memory of their former occupants. The warriors, carrying only small *ihawu* shields and sticks, danced and sang the national song, the *ihubo*, at each halt along the pilgrimage. So powerful was this ceremony to those who took part that they fully expected an immediate indication of the ancestor's benevolence, as Mtshayankomo explained:

> The men who drove [the cattle] went dressed in the finery which they wore at the time of the umkosi. Only their ox-tail decorations were left in the huts. They were not worn as they would get wet. There was no thunder; only a drizzle fell. When they left the sky was clear; there were no clouds, for it was very dry ... [later] we got wet in the rain, but it had not yet begun to fall in

the rest of the country; it had not yet reached Nodwengu [Mpande's homestead] either. As we were about to cross the White Mfolozi the rain caught us.[9]

Finally, the army returned to the great place, to find that the king had been cleansed of the medicines taken that morning. The *amabutho* were then presented to the king, and it was at this point that he first gave clues that he had allowed one or more of the *amabutho* to *tunga*, to sew on the headring prior to being allowed to marry. He announced the names of the female *amabutho* who were directed not to cut their hair; this was a clear indication that they would soon be told to put on the married woman's top-knot. This was not, however, final permission to marry; that would have to wait until the great *umKhosi* itself. The announcement was the last formal act of the *inyatelo* ceremony, and the regiments were allowed to disperse. Those *amabutho* who expected permission to marry at the main ceremony also ceased cutting their hair, since when it was long, it was easier to bind into the *isicoco*. There were, in any case, many preparations to be made ready for the great gathering itself.

The great *umKhosi*
The final stage of the proceedings, the great *umKhosi*, took place anything from a few days to a few weeks later. It was usually held at the end of December or in the beginning of January, in the month of *uNtlolanja* – which translates, rather intriguingly, as 'the dog-copulating moon'. Once the king had decided the date, messengers were sent out to the *izinduna* in command of the district *amakhanda* to order them to assemble their regiments. Those *amabutho* whose headquarters were situated close to the king's homestead would use it as a base throughout the ceremony, but those whose *ikhanda* was further off would have to erect temporary huts nearby. These were the grass huts noted in such profusion by Wilkinson. This muster was to be the grand review of the army; it was the one time when each of the regiments turned out in their full regalia. No warrior could afford to appear poorly dressed before the king, and the regalia itself had been carefully cleaned and repaired well in advance. In theory, the entire male population of the nation was required to attend the ceremony. In the early days of the kingdom this may indeed have been the case, but by the 1870s there were many who felt themselves exempt from the summons. A number had legitimate and pressing business at home, some were undergoing a form of ritual that made them unfit to enter the king's presence, while others simply stayed at home because their district chiefs took the opportunity to demonstrate something of their independence. There were those, too, who attended part of the ceremony, but did not wait for its

completion before returning home. Nevertheless, the great *umKhosi* was still an extraordinary spectacle, and the figure of 30,000 people in attendance, suggested by Wilkinson, was not an exaggeration. Excitement throughout the kingdom was intense. Nomguqo Dlamini recalled the atmosphere at the royal homestead during the preparation:

> The days went by with practising. Wood was being collected for brewing beer. A colossal amount of germinated sorghum grain was ground as malt. Now everybody knew on what day the festival would take place. On the day before the feast the young men crushed the fibrous plants and the older men wove them into a garment for the king.[10.]

Mtshayankomo's description of the gathering in which he participated is no less impressive than that of Bishop Wilkinson:

> [The warriors] would go and wash their ox-tail decorations, repair them, and put them in good order. New ox-tails would be cut, and shields would be repaired. The new moon had appeared, and had now become full. When it was full, all the peoples from the distant parts of the country set off, like the Mdhlalose and the people of Mapita, the Mandhlakazi. They came dressed in their finery, with girls carrying grass mats on which their ox-tail decorations were placed. When the umkosi was over the ox-tails were placed back on the mats, for they used to cause severe chafing to the wearer's neck. They would arrive with them at their various amakanda in the vicinity of Nodwengu, and hang them up in huts....
>
> The men from Siklebeni, Ngwegwe, Dukuza, and Nobamba would arrive on the day the umkosi began, travelling in columns. The country was white with people coming in. These were the first to arrive at the king's place. Then came the people from Gqikazi, on the other side of the Black Mfolosi river. Then came the people of Mfefe, with Hamu, all of them, dressed in their finery. Then came the abaQulusi, also from far off. Then the people from ekuBuseni (an umuzi of Mpande's), and the Mbelebele. Then came the people from emaNgweni, down-country, together with the people of Somkele ka Malanda. They arrived to find the assembly (umkosi) forming and the place filled with people....
>
> Women carrying food had arrived. the girls were in their regiments; they went in columns to all the amakanda.... Young wives, too, had come to attend the umkosi. There remained only at home those who were looking after the cattle and children; only a few remained ... [the girls] too had wanted to see the regiments, and the king, and the young men. They did not want simply to hear about the umkosi from other people. A great crowd would gather at the gate of Nodwengu; people came from every path. That is how it was.[11]

Even the trader David Leslie was struck by the carnival atmosphere. 'The whole countryside,' he wrote on witnessing the ceremony in the 1850s, 'was full of people, and the noise, day and night, was incessant – chattering at night and dancing during the day. At night the fires on the hill, and the figures of the natives passing the light, imparted a weird-like character to the scene which would have made a famous study for a Gatti or a Van Schendal.'[12]

The ceremonies began late in the afternoon of the first day, with a great parade of the army. Traditionally, this took place in the cattlefold of the *komkhulu* itself, at kwaBulawayo, then Dukuza in Shaka's day, eMgungundlovu in Dingane's, and kwaNodwengu in Mpande's. Cetshwayo broke with tradition, however, in that he held the ceremonies not at his own great place, oNdini, but in the Nodwengu *ikhanda*. This, too, was on the Mahlabathini plain, opposite oNdini, though it had been moved to a fresh spot after Mpande's death. It is not quite clear why Cetshwayo chose this site in preference to his own *komkhulu*, but it seems that he wished to imply a continuity of custom from his father's time, perhaps to offset the dangerous division that greeted his succession.

The great muster

When the army was fully mustered, it was an extraordinary and impressive sight, to Zulus as well as outsiders. The central enclosure of the great *ikhanda* was so packed that hundreds of observers were left outside the gate. The regiments formed a circle in strict order of seniority, with the 'white' regiments at the top, near the *isigodlo*, and the 'black' at the bottom, near the gate. Mtshayankomo again:

> All the 'black' regiments, the younger ones, were ordered to stand back. The 'white' ones, whose members wore crane feathers in their headbands, were brought forward closer to the king; it was these who encircled him. The black ones stood back, making way for the Tulwana. After this no other regiment was allowed in. We Ngobamakosi and Kandempemvu were outside.[13]

With so many regiments gathered together, the excitement was such that stick fights frequently broke out. Indeed, according to Ndukwana kaMbengwana, 'the umkosi was invariably characterised by quarrelling and fighting among the different regiments, when indunas used to interfere and strike among them with sticks right and left'.[14]

Into this excited gathering stepped the king, shouting '*Ima! Ima! Ima!*', 'Stand!', and dancing about. Such was the press of people that, according to Mtshayankomo:

... he could not be seen. He cried, 'Ima!' The Seketwayo, Masipula, Godide and all other izikhulu who had been standing with him moved off, crying 'They hate him! They hate the king!' They sang this. Then the Tulwana, the last of the 'white' regiments, moved off. The 'black' regiments cried, 'They hate him! They hate the king!' They hate Punga and Mageba!' Then the white regiments cried in their turn, 'Ima! Ima!' This meant that the king should continue to reign. This practice was not simply in Mpande's; it had existed in the time of his elder brothers, and before them. It was the practice under all the kings.[15]

As the king danced, the warriors encouraged him by singing the *ingoma*, the mournful song, sung only before the king, praising his ancestral spirits. At last the king signalled an end to the proceedings by walking off towards the *isigodlo*, and the warriors shouted after him the royal salute, *'Bayethe!'*

Nomguqo Dlamini described how that night passed in the *isigodlo*:

> Not one of the girls slept on that night. In rival sing-song we contended for the king. Each regiment [of girls] tried to get hold of him. We surrounded him, like bees congregating around their queen; we called out to him, attempting to lead him to our way. He was then in the wives' section of the isigodlo. Soon after he withdrew to his hut and was not seen again until the following morning. But this did not stop us from calling out to him in our song, 'Come, Oh King, come here to us.'
>
> Throughout this night a light was kept burning in the hut harbouring the magic coil. At sunrise the king emerged from his hut, his face painted in three colours, the right cheek white, the forehead red and the left cheek black. He was wrapped up in a greenish covering made of fibre. His whole body from head to toes was enshrouded by it; only his face showed. He looked like a big tree, nay, a monster. From all quarters he was assailed with shouts, 'Come here, come this way, Oh King!' How we did shout when, at sunrise, he emerged from the hut, the sacred spear, the inhlendla, in his right hand! The crescent-shaped blade of the spear, resembling the new moon, gleamed in the rays of the early morning sun....[16]

This bizarre costume, consisting of green rushes known as *imizi*, consisted of a skirt and cape which hid the king's body from view, as Lunguza recalled:

> ... umhlahle grass was gathered and prepared for plaiting. It was plaited into strips which were put around the neck, so that they fell about him on all sides. The arms were hidden from view; also the body. The king would then be brought forth into the open. He did not wear any feathers and had nothing in his hands. The head had nothing on and was visible; the feet were

visible. The grass tassels extended to slightly below the knees, leaving the legs visible.[17]

The purpose of the costume remains obscure, but it was presumably intended to stress the agricultural nature of the ceremony. Lured out of his seclusion by the cries of his subjects, the king walked slowly out of his private quarters to greet them. The *isigodlo* girls accompanied him, singing and dancing, from his hut, but left him at the fence of the royal enclosure. He went through alone, into the calf-pen, then out into the great cattle enclosure, where the vast concourse was once again waiting for him. He walked slowly through them towards the main gate of the homestead, where the *izinyanga* were again awaiting him, with specially prepared medicines on a postsherd. Once more he *ncinda'*d, sucking up the *umuthi*, then *cintsa'*d it towards the sun, to the accompaniment of a tremendous shout from the onlookers.

Now was the time for the *uselwa* gourd. The *izinyanga* brought forward a container full of them, and the king took them one at a time, rushing forward to hurl them on to the shields of the nearest warriors, so that they burst into fragments. Attendants immediately gathered up the pieces, to prevent them falling into the hands of evil-doers. Nathaniel Isaacs, who recorded his adventures as King Shaka's court in a style that varied from the sceptical to the lurid, witnessed this part of the ceremony during the early days of the kingdom. King Shaka, he said, was

> decorated with herbs and corn leaves, and bedizened with beads and bangles, surrounded by his warriors and attended by a great number of boys, [he] performs a ludicrous ceremony, and announces his permission for them to eat the new crop. Standing at the head of the kraal, he runs backwards and forwards three times towards the warriors, followed by the boys, whistling as loud as they are able; each time throwing a calabash, as indicative of his command for them to garner and eat of their new food. The person on whom the calabash may fall conceives himself to have been favoured by its touch, and exults not a little at his singular good fortune at being thus honoured....[18]

Killing the bull

The king having completed his part of the ceremony, he retired to the *isigodlo*, as it was now time for the youngest *ibutho* to kill the black bull which had been secured by the *izinyanga* from an enemy's cattle-fold. This time, the bull was to be killed in front of the entire nation, and it required no little courage on the part of the selected *ibutho*. Mtshayankomo described what happened when the duty fell to the iNdlondlo, perhaps at the very ceremony Bishop Wilkinson had attended:

They caught a black bull. It too was from foreign parts, only the king knew where. When the bull ripped out men's innards the king called to the Mbonambi regiment 'Go and help!' They went and headed it off in front, standing in a densely packed mass. A bull that did not gore was not fetched. Its horns were as sharp as awls – like thorns. It would impale anyone. In my opinion its horns were deliberately sharpened.

The bull would then be carried up to the top end of the kraal. The men would break into a chant.... They walked very slowly, scarcely moving. They held it by all four legs. When it had been skinned it was carried into the king's washing enclosure, where it would be burnt, and where no one was allowed to go in. They would put it down and leave. The izinyanga then chopped it up and put it on the fire.[19]

The trader David Leslie watched the struggle when the uThulwana *ibutho* participated in the ritual at the end of 1866:

The bull – which on this occasion was a fine three-year-old – is turned out, and the men throw themselves upon it like ants. It accepted their embraces quietly for a while, until finding that something more than a joke was intended, it commenced to kick and plunge furiously. Three or four got kicked and gored; but it was of no use, for despite of its tremendous exertions, they at last fairly choked it, shouldered it off to the kraal, and then burned it.[20]

Once the bull had been burnt – and it is not clear whether on this occasion the pre-pubescent boys were required to eat the meat – the ash was carefully collected together, since it was needed later in the ceremony. The medicinal parts were, with other *muthi* from the ceremony, including the 'soul-substances' of the nation, then added to the *inkatha yezwe yakwaZulu* – the sacred coil of the nation.

The *inkatha*

Since the *inkatha* (pl. *izinkatha*) was one of the most sacred symbols of Zulu nationhood, it is worth describing in some detail. It apparently consisted of a coil of grass rope – representing the entwined and indivisible fortunes of the people – wrapped round with a python skin. The *inkatha* was not unique to the Zulu, and both the chiefs of each of the neighbouring peoples, and of the component clan within the Zulu kingdom, had their own *inkatha*. The Zulu *inkatha* was supposed to date at least from the time of Senzangakhona. King Shaka, in due course, had carefully secured particular items of psychic potency from each of the clans he had conquered or fought against, adding them to the Zulu *inkatha* until its supernatural power was such that it held the entire nation together. Shaka had appointed his father's fourth wife, Langazana, as the guardian of the *inkatha*, a post she held throughout the life of the kingdom – she outlived the *inkatha* itself, dying in 1885, five years after the British had devastated the nation. Langazana was attached to the esiKlebheni royal homestead, and it was here that the *inkatha* was kept – in the *umsamo*, the sacred part at the back of a special hut known as the *eNkatheni*, which was situated in the depth of the black *isigodlo*. Presumably it was moved on occasion, however, so that it could be used at the *komkhulu* of the various kings who held the *umKhosi* ceremony. Nomguqo Dlamini saw it at oNdini just before the Anglo-Zulu War:

> Right in the centre of the black isigodlo was situated a most sacred shelter called eNkatheni – a hut containing Cetshwayo's personal inkatha and the nation's inhlendla, a ceremonial barbed assegai.... The common people were not permitted even to mention the inkatha. Talking about it was taboo as the singing of certain national songs, which were sung only in the presence of the chiefs. Only on the occasion of great feasts was the inkatha brought into the open. A venerable old woman was appointed as guardian. The king went into this hut when he wished to discuss matters of national importance, or when the great feasts were being celebrated.... We girls were sometimes naughty, surreptitiously peeping into the hut to see what was going on inside.
>
> The magic coil of the inkatha was so big and wide that the king could squat on it. It was intertwined with grass and wrapped round with some new cloth. Its contents symbolised the unity of the nation and all the values associated with the king's ancestors. The properties and magic powers of wild animals embodied in this coil were transferred through it to the people. Shaka greatly strengthened the power of the inkatha. He subjected a large number of tribes but formed them into a united people by collecting bits from the izinkatha of vanquished tribes and particles from the bodies of slain chiefs and embodying them in his own coil.[21]

The king spent the second night of the great *umKhosi* in the privacy of the *eNkatheni*, soaking up the mystical emanations which arose from it, attended only by one of the *umdlunkulu* girls. The next morning, before dawn, he left the *isigodlo*, accompanied by the *amakhosikazi*, the royal queens. These included not only his own wives, but the royal widows who commanded the *izigodlo* of the regional *amakhanda*. The procession made its way down to a nearby river, and as it did so the *izinduna* hastily roused the *amabutho*, and ordered them to follow on. The regiments streamed out of their shelters, forming a chanting procession behind the king and his household. It was time for the final part of the ceremony, the ritual bathing in which the king and his warriors cleansed themselves of the influence of the medicines with which they had been in contact throughout the ceremony. Mtshayankomo recalled the excitement of the moment:

The king would then go out by the gate, the one used by us regiments, the ordinary people, and by the cattle. It was not known where he was going to wash. We called continuously as we went out through the gate, following him. He went out ahead of us, with the amakosikazi, a dense crowd of them from all the amakhanda, those who no longer bore children, those who came to the umkosi. The king went out with the amakosikazi alone.[22]

The king and his entourage made for a spot on a nearby river bank already selected by the *izinyanga*. When he reached it, the king threw off his costume of reeds – it was immediately gathered up to be burnt – and stepped into the waters. The warriors, meanwhile, were marched further downstream, where they, too, were ordered into the water. The king carefully washed off every trace of the remaining black medicines, whilst the *izinyanga* emptied the ashes of the bull into the current above him. The ashes flowed around the king, splashing against his body, and the current carried them on down to where the warriors were also washing. When the king was clean, he climbed out of the river, and the *izinyanga* administered white medicines to clear away the last effects of the black ones. He now put on his ordinary regalia and made his way back to the *isigodlo*.

By the time the warriors had washed and marched back to the *komkhulu*, the king was ready to greet them. At last the rituals were complete, and the assembled nation had crossed the psychic minefield without mishap. The spirits had been appeased, the unity of the nation ensured, and the harvest blessed. Now there only remained the king's announcements, and further dancing.

At last, the king confirmed the names of the *amabutho* he would allow to marry. 'The form of Juba was this,' recalled Ndukwana: 'A man, deputed for the purpose, would step forward, praise the king again and again i.e. at considerable length, and then, still shouting out, say, "He declares, let such and such a regiment put on the headring." '[23]

After this, the great gathering began to break up. Those *amabutho* whose *amakhanda* were situated near the *komkhulu* stayed to spend another night dancing, but the rest, who lived further off, began to slip away that evening. By dawn the next morning the crowd had dispersed, and the routine at the great place began to return to normal.

For the most part, the weeks after the *umKhosi* were happy ones. Herdboys were allowed to play flutes made from reeds as a sign that the harvest was blessed, and the countryside echoed to their whistling times. The lucky warriors given permission to marry wandered the countryside sporting their new headrings, searching out brides. It was not always, however, such a happy time for the girls in the female guilds to whom they had been appointed, as Mtshayankomo explained:

A girl putting on the top-knot [ie in preparation for marriage] would cry, for she knew that she could no longer go with her lover; she was bound to take a headring from among those men who were putting on the headring. Their mothers too would cry; they would cry at the river. They would cry for their daughters, whose lovers had not received the order to put on the headring. There would be great lamentation. Some people would take their daughters and cross the river to the white people's country. This is what caused people to cross over. This is what destroyed the country.[24]

In a male dominated, patriarchal society, such tensions were inevitable, and the level of state control implicit in the *amabutho* system inevitably produced casualties. A poignant account by Ndukwana suggests not only the individual heartbreak involved, but echoes Mtshayankomo's view that those thwarted in love had to make a direct choice between their allegiance to the king, and the possibility of refuge in colonial Natal:

What used to happen was this. As soon as any set of girls was jutshwa'd [ie told off to marry], those of them who did not wish to marry men they did not care for would bring their sleeping mats to their respective lovers, for the purpose of saying good-bye to them. She had come to say good-bye to her lover, for she had been ordered to marry, and would now be separated from him. If a young man wanted to sacrifice the girl's love in preference to undergoing expatriation or banishment (which flying to Natal meant), he would endeavour to evade his sweetheart by, as soon as he heard the order ... proceeding straight to the king's kraal, and staying there, and so avoiding a painful parting with his sweetheart.... All along the Zulu–Natal boundary [those who opted to flee] would be killed if caught, for they had, by flying in this way, turned themselves into vagrants. . . .

Despite these harsh methods, the Zulu kings never did manage entirely to prevent the trickle of refugees into Natal, which thereby continued to undermine their authority. Yet, on the whole, the system fulfilled its objectives successfully for sixty years, and the bonds between the king and his subjects, embodied in the *umKhosi* ritual, were strong. As Ndukwana put it, 'All men had great affection for their king. It could not be otherwise for they were bound together.'[25] Indeed, it might be more truthful to suggest that it was the system's very strength which aroused the British hostility towards it, and thereby brought about the destruction of the country. Yet the British found to their cost just how deep lay the Zulu attachment to it, for through the *amabutho* the Zulu resisted their intervention until they were prised from their king by force alone.

NOTES

1. Quoted in *Soldiers of the Cross in Zululand*.
2. Samuelson, *LLA*.
3. Bryant, *Zulu People*.
4. Account of Mtshayankomo kaMagolwana, Webb and Wright, *JSA* 4.
5. Filter and Bourquin, *Paulina Dlamini*.
6. Account of Mtshayankomo kaMagolwana, Webb and Wright, *JSA* 4.
7. Ibid.
8. Account of Lunguza kaMpukane, Webb and Wright, *JSA* 1.
9. Account of Mtshayankomo kaMagolwana, Webb and Wright, *JSA* 4.
10. Filter and Bourquin, *Paulina Dlamini*.
11. Account of Mtshayankomo kaMagolwana, Webb and Wright, *JSA* 4.
12. Leslie, *Among the Zulus and Amatongas*.
13. Account of Mtshayankomo kaMagolwana, Webb and Wright, *JSA* 4.
14. Account of Ndukwana kaMbengwana, Webb and Wright, *JSA* 4.
15. Account of Mtshayankomo kaMagolwana, Webb and Wright, *JSA* 4.
16. Filter and Bourquin, *Paulina Dlamini*.
17. Account of Lunguza kaMpukane, Webb and Wright, *JSA* 1.
18. Isaacs, *Travels and Adventure*.
19. Account of Mtshayankomo kaMagolwana, Webb and Wright, *JSA* 4.
20. Leslie, *Among the Zulus and Amatongas*.
21. Filter and Bourquin, *Paulina Dlamini*.
22. Account of Mtshayankomo kaMagolwana, Webb and Wright, *JSA* 4.
23. Account of Ndukwana kaMbengwana, Webb and Wright, *JSA* 4.
24. Account of Mtshanyankomo kaMagolwana, Webb and Wright, *JSA* 4.
25. Account of Ndukwana kaMbengwana, Webb and Wright, *JSA* 4.

CHAPTER 5

Drinking the Dew

The great *umKhosi* ceremony was not held as usual in January 1879. Tension had been mounting with British Natal since July of 1878, when Chief Sihayo's impetuous sons had crossed the border and dragged back two of their father's runaway wives, executing them – as the outraged settlers noted with alarm – within sight of the mission station at Rorke's Drift. King Cetshwayo was astute enough to realise that the fuss the British were making about the incident masked a deeper motive, but neither he nor his councillors could decide how best to placate them. This was hardly surprising, since the British wanted nothing less than the destruction of the Zulu state apparatus. It was a dilemma which placed the king on a precarious high-wire, balancing a genuine desire to resolve the crisis peacefully with the need to maintain his own power and credibility within the kingdom. While many senior *izikhulu* urged the king to appease the British and surrender Sihayo's sons, Cetshwayo could only do so by betraying a royal favourite. Moreover, the mood among the *amabutho* – Sihayo's senior son Mehlokazulu held a command in the iNgobamakhosi – was increasingly truculent, and would countenance no surrender to the British demands.

This tension found expression in a number of false alarms as 1878 wore on. In September the king ordered the population along the border to stage a ceremonial hunt, driving through the Ncome, Mzinyathi and Thukela rivers to the sea. Whereas Cetshwayo's diplomatic exchanges with the British assured them of his desire to smooth over the rift, the hunt was a clear demonstration that, if pushed, he was prepared to defend his borders by force. Several times towards the end of the year, various *amabutho* were summoned to their *amakhanda*, particularly those, like KwaGingindlovu, which were sited near the borders, only to be released again when the immediate mood of crisis passed. Although the majority of the warriors were eager to obey the summons – indeed, the truculence of the younger *amabutho*, who were full of bravado and clamoured for the chance to fight, made it increasingly difficult for the pro-peace party to appease the British demands – these false alarms sapped morale, and some warriors grumbled that they would only muster again if war were truly imminent. The situation was exacerbated by a severe drought and the resultant scarcity of food throughout the kingdom as the year drew to a close; many warriors

157

suffered badly from hunger during their time in the *amakhanda*, since there was simply not enough food to feed them.

At the end of 1878 the king appointed a date in the second week of January as the start of the great *umKhosi* ceremony. By then, however, it had already been overtaken by events. On 11 December British representatives had met the king's envoys on the border, and presented an ultimatum demanding not only the surrender of Sihayo's sons, but the disbandment of the Zulu army itself. It was a demand with which no Zulu king could comply without dismantling the kingdom, and the British knew it; their troops were already mustering on the borders to invade Zululand. When the king called up his army in January, then, it was not to perform the *umKhosi*, but to undergo the rituals necessary to prepare it for war.

The Zulu army could be mustered with remarkable speed whenever the need arose. The king's messengers were sent out to the *izinduna* commanding the district *amakhanda*, who then set about summoning all the warriors in their district. According to Mpatshana kaSodondo, a warrior in the uVe *ibutho*, the youngest regiment to fight in 1879:

> The order will be instantly dispatched by the various izinduna to all belonging to their respective commands, the utmost expedition being used to get men to mobilise, for fear lest the king will send and kill them, or 'eat them up' for being dilatory – for failing to hurry up men and come forward. Then all under him will have the same fear, hence there is celerity of movement throughout the entire organisation.[1]

Nor was this threat an idle one, since the king occasionally found it necessary to make a demonstration by punishing some who had been too slow to respond. The trader Leslie was visiting the then Prince Cetshwayo in 1866 and witnessed such an incident when one *ibutho* arrived late at a muster:

> Cetshwayo saw them coming in the distance, and instructed about a thousand men to go outside the gate, make a lane for them to pass through, and when they were in to close the entrance. Up they came, very unsuspiciously, shouting and clashing their shields and assegais in honour of the Prince; but directly they got within the gate it was closed, and one of the captains coming forward simply said, 'Why are you late? Beat them!' Immediately all the others who were in the kraal fell upon them and did beat them with a vengeance. The poor fellows made no resistance, but only guarded themselves as well as they could, and tried in every way to escape. The noise and clatter of sticks – they did not use assegais – was tremendous, and broken heads were going freely. At last they managed to get out, and were chased all over the country – 'they scattered like a herd of wilde-beeste when a lion

makes his sudden appearance in their midst', as a Zulu described the stampede.[2]

Such demonstrations were no doubt rare, but they made their point. The process was, in any case, assisted by the remarkable speed at which information could be passed around the country. The king's messengers regularly covered large distances at an economical jogging pace which they could sustain throughout the day, and each regional *induna* was expected to know his district intimately and to be able to communicate quickly and efficiently with its inhabitants. It was common practice to spread important news by shouting from hilltop to hilltop; lacking written communications, the Zulus were accustomed from youth to hailing one another at surprising distances, stretching out the syllables of important words so that the sound rolled and echoed around the valleys, especially on a still day. Harry Sparks, a trooper in the Durban Mounted Rifles, was privy to an effective demonstration of this; he was on picket duty near the mission station at Eshowe, in the coastal belt, on 26 January 1879 when he heard Zulus shouting to one another from neighbouring hilltops that they had won a great victory.[3] They were referring to Isandlwana, and the battle had taken place four days before – the first the garrison at Eshowe knew of it was therefore from their enemy. It was several days before they received an official dispatch by runner from the border.

The king was kept fully informed of the progress of the muster. All of those warriors living within fifteen miles or so of the king's great place were expected to report directly to it within twenty-four hours. As they arrived, the *izinduna* sorted them into their respective regiments, and those whose *ikhanda* lay close by were directed to occupy it. The remainder were appointed a sheltered spot nearby, often a valley or a donga, where they were told to build temporary grass huts. Over the next few days, they would be joined by those from the outlying districts, who had already been formed into regimental order at the regional *amakhanda*. Once the muster was complete, the entire army was called before the king, and the necessary doctoring ceremonies began.

The doctoring ceremonies contained a number of elements in common with the *umKhosi* rituals, and their purpose was broadly similar; to ensure by psychic means the strength, unity and invulnerability of the nation. Before so important an undertaking as a military expedition, it was crucial that the king and his warriors be free from any negative spiritual influences, including any supernatural efforts which the enemy might have made to thwart them. The doctoring ceremonies were therefore intended to purify the warriors, to bind them to one another spiritually, and to their king. To this end, they were required to undergo a series of rituals *en masse*, each involving the most potent forms of supernatural medicines, known as *imithi*.

Doctoring the army

The king's most senior war-doctors had been busy while the army gathered, collecting together the necessary ingredients for their purifying and fortifying medicines. When the army was fully assembled, it was marched to a specially chosen spot – in 1879 it was on the eNtukwini stream, near the point where it flows into the White Mfolozi – where the warriors were required to undergo a ritual in which each had to swallow medicine, then regurgitate it into a specially prepared hole. Each hole was about eighteen inches wide and seven feet deep, and the warriors were summoned up in small groups. The doctors, who had bowls of liquid medicine sitting on their own *inkatha* coils nearby, required each warrior to take a sip of the liquid and then vomit into the hole. Mpatshana, who underwent this ceremony, described it in graphic detail:

> ... after taking a mouthful or two of the medicine in great pots (izimbiza) and woven baskets (izinqabeto) nearby, [the warrior] proceeds to vomit – of course prior to having had any food that day. There may be three or four pots. Two, three or four may go up to this hole at one time. There is naturally a desire to quickly finish, and have done with the vomiting, but the doctors will not allow crowding. These, two of them, stand on either side of the hole and see that everyone conforms to his instructions. Here and there the stick may be used on men who have merely pretended to drink the medicated water and therefore are unable to vomit into the hole as required. And so the vomiting goes on practically all day long.[4]

Presumably the medicines contained an effective emetic, but Ndukwana added that it was often necessary for warriors to induce themselves to vomit by putting their fingers down their throat.[5] The purpose of this ceremony was to cast out impurity, and at the same time bind the warriors together by their shared drinking of the medicine. Once the ceremony was completed, the doctors used twists of grass to remove samples of the vomit – which thereby constituted the very essence of the nation under arms – to add to the national *inkatha*. The holes were then filled in, and all traces of it carefully obscured, lest any enemy discover it. Most of the army was required to wait until the entire ceremony was completed, the warriors squatting down on a slope nearby until all of them had had their turn, but a chosen *ibutho*, who had been led forward to vomit first, was marched back to the king's *komkhulu*. Here the men were required to kill a black bull in the same way as at the *umKhosi* ceremony.

Like the *umKhosi* ceremony, the doctoring of the army usually took place at the *komkhulu* itself, although in 1879 King Cetshwayo once again staged the ceremonies at kwaNodwengu. They took place over several days, ending on 17 January. The black bull was once more wrestled to the ground and killed, and the *izinyanga* stripped off the hide, then cut up the flesh into long strips, known as *umbengo*, which were roasted over fires of specially collected mimosa wood, and smeared with the black *umuthi* powders. By the time this had been achieved, the rest of the army had returned from the vomiting ceremony.

The troops were now formed up into an *umkhumbi*, a circle, with the *izinyanga* in the middle, and the doctors began tossing the strips of roasted meat up into the air, among the warriors. As the meat landed in the crowd, each warrior was supposed to seize it, bite off a piece, then fling it back over his head. He was required to chew the piece in his mouth to extract the full worth of its medicinal juices, then spit it out. If at any time the *umbengo* strip fell on to the ground, its power was thought to dissipate immediately, and to be useless. To ensure that each section of the army had an equal chance, the king's attendants opened paths for several doctors to plunge directly into the throng, tossing out strips as they went. The excitement among the warriors was intense, but the experience could be a trying one, as Mpatshana explained:

> ... many of the troops are extremely hungry and even emaciated, [and] they sometimes swallowed the piece bitten off, although it is quite contrary to custom and the requirements of the ceremony to do so ... it not infrequently happened that the forbidden meat was picked up and voraciously consumed during the excitement going on round about.... During the eating of the meat-strips ceremony, several of the half-starving, and weak men may be seen to fall forward, fainting on account of the exertion and heat caused through being in the midst of so large a concourse violently contending for the meat-strips. These will perhaps pitch forward, shield and assegais falling clatteringly from them, and thereafter be helped by their friends or relations to some place where they can recover.[6]

Whilst the warriors underwent the ceremony of the meat-strips, the king himself was ritually cleansed by his doctors at his enclosure at the top end of the great cattle-kraal. Once the warriors had observed these rituals, they were considered to have entered a different state of spiritual being from that of their daily lives. They were prepared to combat the dark spiritual forces, *umnyama*, which might be unleashed by their impending encounter with violent death on the battlefield; but as such they were both vulnerable to ritual pollution themselves – which might destroy the effect of the medicines

– and a source of potential contamination to those who had not undertaken the ceremonies. As a result, they were required to abstain (*ukuzila*) from the normal activities of civilian life until such time as they returned from campaign, and had undertaken further cleansing ceremonies. In particular, they had to refrain from any intimate contact with women, and this prohibition was so strong that any women who brought food to their husbands or brothers in the *amakhanda* left it there and departed without direct contact with their menfolk. Indeed, during this period women felt it was quite safe to walk about the country unescorted, as in theory all of the nation's manpower had gone to the king, and none would dare to molest them once they had undergone the doctoring ceremony.[7] Even those *amabutho* whom the king might appoint to his personal bodyguard, and who did not necessarily see action, were considered under the same ban.

Spiritual preparations

The importance of these rituals to the Zulu-speaking peoples cannot be overstated. Since the shadow-world existed in such close proximity to daily life, it was crucial that the blessing of the ancestral spirits be secured before embarking on a campaign. Moreover, the precautions to ward off evil influence were a practical consideration, as important as ensuring that warshields had not been damaged by rats, and that the spears were securely hafted and honed. The Zulu perception of combat was coloured by an implicit belief in the success or otherwise of such medicine. According to Nomguqo Dlamini, one of King Cetshwayo's *isigodlo* girls, for example, when runners brought news to the king that battle had been joined at Isandlwana, the king retired to the hut that housed the sacred *inkatha*, and squatted over it. It was believed that by doing so he could concentrate its immense power behind his warriors and ensure victory, but:

> Fleet-footed messengers kept coming in with hurried reports about the progress of battle. When the king heard that his regiments were heading towards victory, he began to leave his seat on the inkatha every now and then. But the mothers scolded him on that account. In the end it did not help very much; the warriors returned from battle carrying the fury of war on their backs. They were covered in blood and tied up their wounds with grass.
>
> When it became known that a large Zulu force had failed to overwhelm the small British garrison at Rorke's Drift, the mothers reproached Cetshwayo severely. They put the blame on the king for not having occupied the inkatha uninterruptedly.[8]

When the troops were reviewed after the battle, an *induna*, Sitshitshili kaMnqandi, blamed the heavy casualties the Zulus had suffered on the senior commanders, who had allowed the attack to develop without the customary last-minute doctoring. 'The army has been ruined, Nkosi,' he claimed. 'The *izinduna* ruined it. They sent it into battle. It was not sprinkled with medicines or treated with medicinal fumes. We simply went forward to fight by ourselves.'[9] Conversely, when, on 25 June, Zulus of the Cube chiefdom, living along the middle reaches of the Thukela, made a successful raid across the river, burning a number of homesteads belonging to Natal Africans and retiring unmolested, the Zulus credited this success to the skill of a war doctor who had managed to summon a dense mist to hide their movements. According to Mpatshana:

> There had been sunlight on that day, but as the impi went forward a thick fog spread all over that part, and in this fog the impi went from kraal to kraal, killing people, finding them in their respective kraals. After finishing what they wanted to do, they returned and, after re-crossing into Zululand, the mist cleared. It was the Cubes who are said to have caused this mist....[10]

This supernatural ascendancy in warfare, known as *ithonya*, could, of course, work both ways. In April 1906 the rebel chieftain Bambatha was thought to have had good *ithonya* when he ambushed a party of Natal troops in the Mpanza valley. When, however, his own forces were caught at the mouth of the Mome gorge on 10 June by colonial troops who had made an extremely difficult approach across steep country in the dark, Bambatha's failure to detect them was explained on the grounds of the superior *ithonya* employed by the whites. Bambatha had failed to post sentries and had ignored a warning from a boy who had seen the troops approaching – sure signs that his eyes had been closed by supernatural means.[11]

Zulu history is littered with references to signs and portents which are thought to have influenced the outcome of particular battles. During his great campaign against the Ndwandwe in about 1818, for example, the wind lifted a crane feather out of King Shaka's headdress and tossed it on the ground. One of his *izinduna* complained that this was a bad omen, but Shaka insisted that it meant he would strike his enemies down; and so he did.[12] Rather better known was the Zulu reluctance to join battle on 22 January 1879, the day before the night of the new moon. This was a time when the forces of *umnyama* were dangerously close to the surface of ordinary life, and therefore a dangerous time to embark upon a battle; curiously enough, circumstances combined to force the Zulus to give battle on three separate fronts. Although the day brought the Zulus their most spectacular victory of the war, such was the calamitous cost that many found it difficult to distinguish it from a defeat.

'I shall surpass you'

Once the ceremony of the meat-strips was complete, usually on the following day, the king called out several of his regiments in pairs. These were young regiments who followed closely on each other in age, were often called up together, and were therefore considered *phalane*, linked together. 'I summon you,' said the king, 'so that I may see what you will do on the day you see the enemy.' This was the cue for the two regiments to challenge (*xoxa*) one another, to stoke up existing rivalries and channel them into battlefield aggression. In 1879, Cetshwayo pitted the iNgobamakhosi against the uKhandempemvu and, a few days later, the uNokhenke against the uMbonambi. It was considered undignified for regiments to challenge one another if the age difference between them was too great; the older men would be offended by being partnered with boys, and might refuse to challenge them, as once the uDloko refused to *xoxa* the younger uKhandempemvu.[13] The regiments sat on either side of the great enclosure in the centre of the *ikhanda*, and individuals stood up freely, dancing and shadow-fighting in front of their colleagues, and challenging individuals in the ranks of the *ibutho* opposite. Mpatshana again:

> A man of the Ngobamakosi lot got up and shouted 'I shall surpass you, son of So-and-so. If you stab a white man before mine has fallen, you may take the kraal of our people at such-and-such a place' (giving the name); 'you may take my sister, So-and-so' (giving sister's name). Having said this, he will then start leaping about (giya'ing) with his small dancing shield and a stick (for assegais are not carried on such occasion in the presence of the king, for it is feared that the troops may stab one another with them). The other who had been addressed may now get up and say, 'Well, if you can do better than I do, you will take our kraal (giving the name), and my sister (giving the name).' He will then giya. Whilst the giya'ing goes on, he is praised by those of his regiment, and, if the man happens to be known to the king and is trusted (temba'd) by the king, the king will hold out his arm towards him, pointing the first or first two fingers at him, and shaking them and the hand approvingly.[14]

An open challenge required an answer as a matter of honour, and anyone who failed to take it up was regarded as a coward, and treated with contempt by his colleagues, unless he redeemed himself in the coming fight. In fact, the wagers laid at this challenges were symbolic rather than literal, and, although the king called up the same regiments again after the fighting, to hear how well they had lived up to their boasts, the bets were discreetly forgotten, and no property actually changed hands. It was quite common, however, for these challenges to be recalled in the heat of battle, sometimes with devastating effects to the enemy.

The introduction of firearms

In 1879 the doctoring ceremonies were presided over by an anonymous Sotho doctor, who may have been employed by Cetshwayo because the Sotho were believed to be more skilled in the use of firearms than the Zulu. Certainly, he paid particular attention to the guns in the *impi*. The Zulus had been accustomed to the idea that Europeans fought with firearms since the first whites had arrived in the 1820s. Both Shaka and Dingane had been intrigued by the possibilities afforded by these weapons, and insisted the whites demonstrate their effectiveness, using cattle, shields, birds and even an elephant as targets. Nathaniel Isaacs described one such demonstration:

> The king [Dingane] sent for me this morning to fire at a tree, that he might see the force of the bullet. The tree I selected was not very hard; I fired with my fowling piece at a distance of thirty paces, and the ball penetrated nearly half through it; but on firing with my musket at the same distance, the ball went quite through, and could be heard after it had passed, which astonished the ignorant Zoolas, who ... were unanimous, however, in declaring it would be impossible to fight against such weapons. The king had often asked me for a musket, and did so again today....[15]

That early contact with firearms provoked considerable discussion amongst the Zulu commanders as to their worth; according to Henry Fynn, Shaka was not overly impressed. He argued:

> The shield, if dipped into water previous to an attack, would be sufficient to ward off the effect of a ball fired when they were at a distance, and in the interval of reloading they would come to close quarters, when we, having no shield, would drop our guns and attempt to run, but, as we were unable to run as fast as his soldiers, we must all inevitably fall into their hands.[16]

Dingane was of the same opinion: 'When the white people discharge their muskets,' he told Isaacs, 'we could go in and spear them before they reloaded.'[17] When Fynn pointed out to Shaka that European troops fired volleys by ranks, so as to overcome this problem, Shaka remarked that

> 'losing a few men by the first discharge would be nothing to him who had so many'. We now showed him the position of the square, one of us kneeling in front, and the other two in their respective positions, which proved to him that, according to the system of firing in that manoeuvre, the position was invulnerable to an irregular force. He saw it, but his warriors being inclined to flatter his military genius, observed that by charging in a body, in the way to which they usually resorted, especially under his bold and judicious

command, they thought it would more than overbalance the strength of our position, and the force of our arms.[18]

This is a curiously prophetic exchange, which encapsulates the respective strengths of the European and Zulu fighting techniques in exactly those terms under which they would be put to the test sixty years later. On occasion, when the British were caught in scattered formations, Shaka's instinct would prove correct; nevertheless, this overconfident view failed to take account of the extent to which European technology improved over half a century. It was the Zulu nation's tragedy that in 1879 the British were no longer using the slow, cumbersome and inaccurate Brown Bess with which Fynn and Isaacs had been armed, and the cost in lives wasted in trying to overwhelm them would be unbearable.

Nevertheless, firearms did have an obvious appeal to the Zulu. Even in the early days, both Shaka and Dingane pressed their white clients into action, adding small groups of gunmen to their conventional armies. Isaacs described the unnerving effect on friend and foe alike when he first took part in a Zulu punitive expedition:

In front of us we saw a small party of about fifty [of the enemy], whom we attacked and defeated. The report of our muskets reverberated from the rocks, and struck terror into the enemy; they shouted and ran in all directions, and the Zoolas were observed all lying on the ground with their faces under, and their shields on their backs, having an idea that, in this position, the balls would not touch them. This singular movement of the Zoolas had a terrific effect on the enemy, who, on seeing the others fall at the report of the musketry concluded they were all dead, and ran off to avoid coming into contact with us.... [19]

Such a reaction prompted Dingane to remark that the noise and smoke produced by firearms was enough to overcome the Zulus, regardless of any casualties they inflicted. In fact, however, this understandable confusion did not last long. Even in Isaacs's skirmish the enemy recovered themselves enough to return to the attack, wounding Isaacs in the back, and by the time of Shaka's great battle against the Ndwandwe at Ndolowane in 1826, Fynn reports that the shots fired by his musketeers provoked no response from the enemy beyond a sullen growl of defiance. Indeed, by the time the first war against whites armed with firearms had broken out – Dingane's war against the Voortrekkers, 1838–40 – the Zulus seem to have developed techniques designed to deal with them. In a series of battles early in the war, the Zulus were not only undaunted by firearms, but overcame them, notably at the battles of the Thukela and eTaleni, both fought in April

1838. At the battle of the Thukela the Zulus braved the heavy fire to rout a large force, consisting of white settlers from Natal and their retainers, who were fighting on foot but armed with firearms and well trained. At eTaleni, the Zulu tactics seem to have been designed to counter the manoeuvrability of the Boer commandos, who were lured into rough country, then attacked by warriors carefully hidden in the grass. The Boers scattered, and, unable to concentrate their firepower, were driven off with significant casualties. Only when the Boers were able to combine their firepower with an impenetrable barricade, as at Ncome/Blood River in December 1838, where their wagon-laager kept the Zulus at arms' length and allowed the Boers to reload unmolested, were the Zulus overcome.

It is interesting to note that Zulu tradition suggests that it was King Dingane who reintroduced throwing spears, and this may have been a counter-measure against firearms. Both Fynn and Isaacs talked of demonstrating their firearms at only thirty or forty yards' range and, indeed, their smooth-bore muskets – the old Brown Bess of the Napoleonic Wars – were scarcely accurate beyond that. Since a well-aimed spear could reach that distance, any fighting conducted at such a range at least allowed the Zulus the chance to reply.

The gun trade

As Isaacs suggests, King Dingane was nonetheless anxious to obtain firearms for his army, and the first muskets were imported into Zululand during his reign.[20] The missionary Gardiner noted sorrowfully that Dingane persistently asked him to teach the use of firearms rather than the word of the Lord.[21] There are suggestions, indeed, that Isaacs may have set up a clandestine gun-running business, working in partnership with American traders and importing the weapons through Port Natal. They were poor-quality weapons, however, and the numbers were small; it was not until King Mpande allowed hunters and traders access to his kingdom in large numbers in the 1850s and 1860s that guns became an increasingly important element, not only of military thinking, but also of political power. As with all prestige goods, the Zulu kings attempted to control the firearms trade, since a royal monopoly of guns reinforced the power of the king in a very real sense. Mpande sometimes demanded firearms as the price of a concession to trade or hunt in his kingdom,[22] although many Natal hunters were reluctant to agree to this – such an exchange not only risked their personal security, it also raised the possibility of an armed body of African hunters emerging to challenge their commercial interests – others were less scrupulous. Nor was the king able strictly to enforce his monopoly; as early as 1854, the hunter Baldwin commented that one chief 'made me a present of a small pair of tusks, and tried hard to bargain for one of my guns, offering me five splendid tusks worth ten times as much as the gun'.[23] The famous 'White Chief of the Zulus', John Dunn, who thrived under the patronage of Cetshwayo from the 1860s, was useful precisely because he afforded easy access to European commodities. Even after his victory over his rival Mbuyazi at 'Ndondakusuka in 1856, Cetshwayo was acutely sensitive to challenges to his role as heir apparent, and he needed firearms to bolster his position. Dunn, arguing that by strengthening one faction he was reducing the risk of further internecine conflict, secured permission from the Natal authorities to import firearms in large quantities through Portuguese Mozambique in the north. Zulus who witnessed the trade recalled that Dunn used to bring guns to oNdini by the wagon-load.[24]

It is difficult to be precise about the number of guns in the Zulu kingdom by the time of the war against the British, but they undoubtedly numbered thousands. Between 1872 and 1877, 60,000 guns were legally imported into Natal, 40,000 of which were re-exported, 20,000 of them to Mozambique. As tension mounted, the numbers increased; Portuguese officials admitted that between 1875 and 1877 20,000 guns, including 500 breech-loaders, and 10,000 barrels of powder were imported into Delagoa Bay. Most of this was destined for the African trade, the greater proportion for the Zulus.[25] One report of August 1878 suggested that there were as many as 20,000 stands of arms then in the country, of which 500 were modern, good-quality breech-loaders, 2500 were recent percussion models, 5000 were older percussion weapons, and the rest were obsolete muskets. Certainly, increased availability was reflected in a drop in the price: a good double-barrelled muzzle-loader, when first introduced into the kingdom by John Dunn, cost the princely sum of four head of cattle but by 1878 fetched only one. At the same time a percussion rifle, such as the British Enfield, which had been standard military issue only a decade before, could be bought in Zululand for as little as a sheep. As the commercial demand for firearms became increasingly sophisticated, and technological improvements in the field of breech-loading mechanisms and metal cartridges led to an arms race among the major European powers, the outdated weapons, ranging from Napoleonic Brown Besses to the percussion model of the Crimean War era, were dumped cheaply on the world market, including Africa. Bikwayo kaNoziwana of the iNgobamakhosi, who was employed by Cetshwayo on missions to collect guns from Mozambique, listed no less than eight Zulu names for the types of gun he encountered, suggesting the extent to which such a variety had become commonplace.[26] By 1879 the majority of warriors in the king's army had access to some sort of firearm or another, and the king made a determined effort to ensure that his men were well armed. When the uVe *ibutho* paraded before him, he ordered: 'Lift up your guns.' We did so. 'So are there no guns? Each man with a beast from his place must bring it up next day and buy guns of Dunn.'[27]

As a result, both the king and his warriors were convinced that they would be able to match British firepower in the field. They failed to realise, however, the extent to which their weapons were inadequate for the coming contest. A report describing the guns taken by the British after the battle of Nyezane in January 1879 gives a revealing insight into the types of firearm available to the Zulus at the start of the war:

There were all sorts of guns. From Potsdam, from Danzig, Murzig, and Tulle, from 'Manchester, N.H., United States', etc. The majority, however, were Tower muskets. The foreign weapons are very ancient indeed; some of them manufactured in 1835. As far as I could make out by the inscriptions, the continental weapons were condemned army ones. The sights were the most extraordinary contrivances.[28]

After Gingindlovu – a battle which took place over two months after the Zulus had looted 1000 rifles and 500,000 rounds of ammunition from the field of Isandlwana – the British recovered a total of 435 guns from the Zulu dead. Just five were captured British Martini-Henrys; one was a revolver – presumably another piece of Isandlwana loot – four were double-barrelled fowling pieces, whilst the remaining 425 were all old muskets, either of British origin, with the Tower mark, or Prussian.[29] It should be remembered, too, that the Zulus were inevitably deficient in training, powder and ammunition. The hunting parties who roamed Zululand in the 1850s and 1860s had employed local Zulus, it is true, and some were more than competent shots; John Dunn, for example, had taught his friend Prince Dabulamanzi to be an excellent marksman. Such specialists were few, however, and most Zulus had only the haziest concept of range and the function of sights. The king attempted to remedy this by ordering selected *amabutho* to indulge in musketry practice at oNdini, but this was hardly enough to overcome their handicap. Good-quality powder was in short supply, although Cetshwayo employed Sotho specialists (the Sotho had been using firearms in large quantities since the 1850s) to make it for him. The quantity of raw powder was sufficient – the British blew up over a thousand pounds of it when they discovered it stored in a cave near emLambongwenya, north of oNdini, in August 1879 – but the quality was poor. Bullets were often home-made from any vaguely appropriate material, including stones; such projectiles had a decidedly unpredictable trajectory in flight, and were therefore highly inaccurate. They were known to colonial troops on the receiving end as 'pot legs', in the belief that they were cut from the feet of the three-legged iron pots traded so freely in the country; some probably were. Most Zulus were in any case able to use only the crudest means to measure out powder each time for the charge. To carry their arms and ammunition, most had to improvise equipment from belts or pouches bought from traders; surviving powder-horns are of such a similar design as to suggest that they, too, may have been manufactured in Natal specifically for the Zulu trade.

To ensure that the guns fired straight and true, the Sotho *inyanga* presiding at the great muster in January 1879 burnt some medicines on a potsherd, and called warriors forward to hold their guns muzzle-down over it, so that the smoke drifted up the barrels. Given the material he was working with to be effective his *ithonya* probably needed to be stronger than even he could have reckoned.

Final preparations

Once the major rituals had been accomplished, there was one further ceremony to be undertaken before the *impi* departed for the front. Henry Fynn witnessed it when performed for one of Shaka's punitive expeditions:

> [The troops] about 3000 in number, were mustered in the kraal, and being ordered to march out of the kraal, they ran in four divisions to the spot at which they were directed to halt, and there formed three sides of a square. A fire was made in the middle, and a pot containing a mixture of roots, plants and water were kept boiling. An inyanga, in his ceremonial dress, kept dipping an ox-tail frequently into the decoction. The men placed themselves in turn with their backs towards him, when he sprinkled them with the mixture, which was supposed to have the effect of giving them strength in war, and ensuring a good result.[30]

This medicine, known as *intelezi*, from the verb meaning 'to sprinkle', was believed to be particularly powerful. Although Fynn did not realise it, it often included more sinister elements than mere roots and plants. Mpatshana, who recalled undergoing the same ceremony in January 1879, clearly did not wish to look too closely into the *inyanga*'s bowl; 'I have noticed,' he remembered, 'the stuff burnt in the circle of men smelling like flesh, without thinking what flesh it could be'.[31] Often it was human flesh, for body parts taken from a fallen enemy were an extraordinarily powerful form of *umuthi*. By cutting off human flesh from an appropriate corpse (a practice known as *cwiya*), a skilled *inyanga* could render the enemy powerless. Those parts of the body which represented strength, courage and vitality were necessary for the operation; during the Zulu civil wars of the 1880s, Chief Zibhebhu kaMapitha's *inyanga* managed to acquire parts from the corpse of

a member of the rival royalist faction. These included a strip of skin, flayed
vertically from the centre of the forehead, tissue from the rectum, the penis,
bone from the right arm, and cartilage from the bottom of the breastbone.[32]
The symbolism of the penis need not be explained; material from the arm
was required to render the enemy's ability to strike powerless, whilst
material from the rectum was thought to create such fear that it provoked
diarrhoea. These ingredients seem to have been broadly the same in all such
incidents of mutilation.

   If human flesh was used in the doctoring ceremonies in January 1879, it
is not at all clear whose flesh it was, since it certainly did not come from a
white victim. However, it is possible that flesh was removed from the bodies
of some of the British dead after Isandlwana, for use in the later stages of the
war. The journalist Archibald Forbes, visiting the battlefield at the end of
May, commented that 'some [of the corpses] were scalped, and others
subject to yet ghastlier mutilations',[33] and although wild animals and the
elements had by then taken their toll, this description is highly suggestive.
Certainly parts taken from the bodies of men who had fought bravely, and
yet had been overcome, were an obvious source of spiritual power for the
victorious Zulus. When the war was drawing to a close, and the tide was
clearly turning against the Zulus, the need for powerful medicine was all the
more urgent. By the beginning of July 1879 the British had advanced to the
White Mfolozi river, and a final confrontation was imminent. On the 3rd
three troopers were killed in a skirmish on Mahlabathini plain, and their
mutilated bodies were found the next day, when the main British force
advanced on oNdini. Forbes, again, described their injuries – they were
'mangled with fiendish ingenuity; scalped, their noses and right hands cut
off, their hearts torn out, and other nameless mutilations'.[34] Allowing for a
little understandable exaggeration, this description is remarkably similar to
the account of mutilations later performed by Zibhebhu's *inyanga*.
Although the British were at first convinced that the men had been tortured
before death, there is no evidence to suggest that was the case; on the night
of the 3/4th there had been a doctoring ceremony, and the British, who
were camped several miles away, had heard, with unnerving clarity, the
songs chanted by the *amabutho*.

   Forbes's repeated reference to scalping is interesting, since scalping, in the
widely understood Native American sense of the word, was unknown
among the Zulus. Nevertheless, it seems that for some reason facial hair
from a dead European was considered a particularly potent form of *intelezi*
medicine. In 1906, at the beginning of the Bambatha rebellion, Bambatha's
troops successfully ambushed a party of colonial troops in the Mpanza
valley. The bodies of three white soldiers were left on the field; when they
were recovered, one, that of Sergeant Brown of the Natal Mounted Police,

was found to be missing the penis, left forearm and upper lip. Sergeant Brown had been noted for his particularly fine moustache; Bambatha's *inyanga* Malaza had taken it.[35]

If no body parts from a fallen enemy were available, one of his discarded weapons might serve a similar purpose. Mpatshana recalled that, during the civil wars, one of the *izinyanga* of the royalist faction acquired a spear abandoned in battle by a member of Zibhebhu's rival faction. The *inyanga* bent the blade and tied a gourd full of medicines into the curve. The spear was stuck blade-upright into the ground, and the assembled royalist forces were marched past it, chanting an appropriate incantation, each warrior touching the gourd lightly as he went. It was believed that this would cause Zibhebhu's spears to become blunt and ineffective.[36]

After the warriors had been spattered with their last medicine, they were addressed by the king or his officers. King Shaka regularly accompanied his forces on important expeditions, and, indeed, was probably one of the most talented generals in Zulu history. Even he, however, often gave the command of minor expeditions to trusted *izinduna*, and few of his successors ever took to the field. Kings Dingane and Mpande served their time in the *amabutho*, and accompanied expeditions as young men; they did not, however, take the field once they had become king. King Cetshwayo commanded his faction, the uSuthu, at the 'battle of the Princes', at 'Ndondakusuka, in 1856, but did not accompany his forces in 1879. His son, Dinuzulu, revived something of the Shakan tradition by leading his army into battle several times in the 1880s, but by then the world of the Zulu had greatly changed.

The king's instructions

In January 1879, Cetshwayo had decided a strategy in conjunction with his *ibandla*.[37] He knew that the British were invading in three separate columns, converging on oNdini. He had directed that men living in the north-western and coastal sectors of the country report to their local *amakhanda*, in order to harass the flanking columns. Although a portion of it was to be sent to support the coastal forces, the main Zulu army was to proceed to attack the British central thrust, which was coming from the direction of Rorke's Drift. The king entrusted command of his army to one of his most senior advisers, Chief Ntshingwayo kaMahole of the Khoza. He left almost all command decisions to the *izinduna* in the field, beyond asking that they should try to make one last attempt to negotiate a peaceful settlement before resorting to fighting. The king's advice to his warriors was simple; they were to advance slowly (so as not to risk fatigue) to avoid attacking the British in defended positions, and to drive them back into Natal, but not to cross the border themselves. Both the king and his warriors were confident that they would overcome the British quickly and easily provided they could catch them in the open; according to Sofikasho Zungu of the iNgobama-khosi, Cetshwayo told the assembled *impi*, 'There will only be one day of fighting, it will all be over in one day.'[38] This comment reflected not only the confidence born of years of military victory, but the fact that in truth the Zulu could not afford a prolonged campaign. They had no logistical infrastructure to support it, and neither could the warriors be spared for long from their civilian responsibilities. By choice, the Zulus preferred to embark on a campaign in the winter months – June, July, August – since the weather was cool, and there was no shortage of food stored in the grain pits. In 1879, however, it was the British who had made the first move, and Lord Chelmsford had deliberately chosen January in the hope that the need to harvest the ripening crops would sap the warriors' will to stay in the field.

Cetshwayo's instructions do not seem markedly different from those given to the expedition that Henry Fynn witnessed setting off in the 1820s. It is worth quoting this account at some length, since Fynn goes on to record some other interesting features:

A speech was made by Mbikwana in which he showed what the aggravating cause was that called for revenge, namely, the attempt on the life of their King. The order to march was given, and they were directed to spare neither man, woman, child nor dog. They were to burn their huts, to break the stones on which the corn was ground, and so prove their attachment to their King. The command was given to Benziwa, an elderly chief.

The force moved off in the following order:

The first division wore a turban of otter skin round the forehead, with a crane's feather, two feet long, erect on the forehead; ox-tails round the arms; a dress of ox-tails over the shoulders and chest; a petticoat (kilt) of monkey and genet skins made to resemble the tails of those animals; and ox-tails around the legs. They carried white shields chequered at the centre with black patches.... They each carried a single assegai and a knobbed stick.

The second division wore turbans of otter skin, at the upper edge of which were two bits of hide resembling horns; from these hung black cow-tails. The dress round the chest and shoulders resembled that of the first division, a piece of hide cut so as to resemble three tails hanging at the back. They carried red-spotted shields.

The third division wore a very large bunch of eagle feathers on the head, fastened only by a string that passed under the chin, trappings of ox-tails over the chest and shoulders, and, as the second division, a piece of hide resembling three tails. Their shields were grey....

The fourth division wore trappings of ox-tails over the chest and shoulders, a band of ox-hide with white cow-tails round the head, and their shields were black.

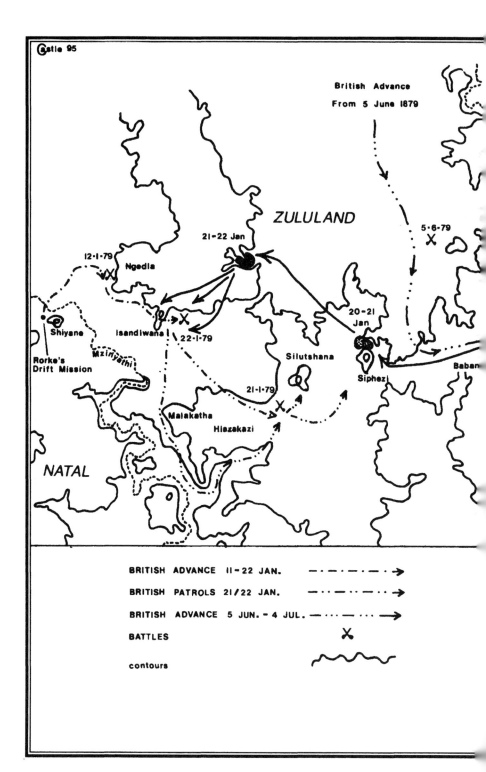

British Advance
From 5 June 1879

ZULULAND

21-22 Jan

5·6·79
X

12·1·79
X X   Ngedla

20-21
Jan

Shiyane

Isandlwana   22·1·79

Silutshana

Siphezi

Rorke's
Drift Mission   Mzinyathi

Babana

Malakatha   21·1·79
X

Hlazakazi

NATAL

BRITISH ADVANCE 11 – 22 JAN.   — · — · — · →

BRITISH PATROLS 21/22 JAN.   — · · — · · — · →

BRITISH ADVANCE 5 JUN. – 4 JUL. — · · · — · · · →

BATTLES   X

contours

The Movements of British and Zulu troops during the Isandlwana campaign, and the British advance of June–July 1979

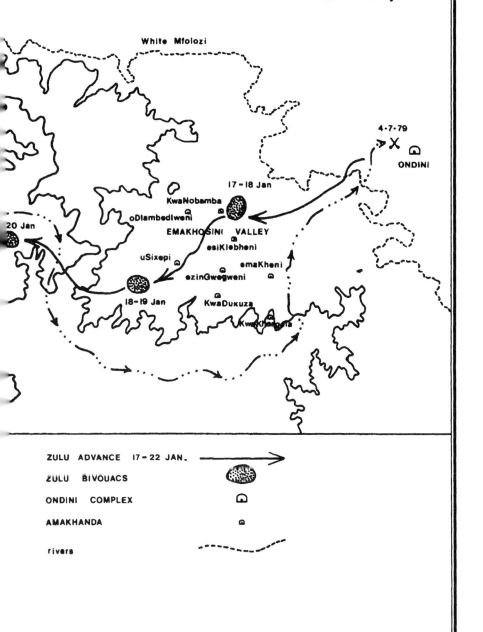

White Mfolozi

4-7-79

X

ONDINI

17 – 18 Jan

KwaNobamba

oDlambedlweni

EMAKHOSINI VALLEY

esiKlebheni

uSixepi

emaKheni

ezinGwegweni

18-19 Jan

KwaDukuza

20 Jan

KwaKhangela

ZULU ADVANCE 17 – 22 JAN.

ZULU BIVOUACS

ONDINI COMPLEX

AMAKHANDA

rivers

The force descended the hill in the direction of the enemy's country. They held their shields down at the left side – and, at a distance, very much resembled a body of cavalry. The first and third divisions marched off making a shrill noise, while the second and fourth made a dreadful howl.[39]

The 'shrill noises and dreadful howls' were undoubtedly war-cries. Each *ibutho* had its own cry or short chant which it uttered on setting off on campaign, and these often recalled some former glory. Among the uKhandempemvu, for example, one man chanted, 'It is not to be seen; the hornbill is not to be seen. Do you burn the whiskers of the buffalo? Do you burn them? We catch the rocks of the sky!', and the entire regiment chorused 'Catch! At the place of Hisi!'[40] This seems to have been an obscure reference to Zulu expeditions to southern Natal in the 1820s. Another recorded chant clearly shows the influence of the early battle of 1879. The iNgobamakhosi, for example, cried '*Iya! Iya! Iya! O ho, ho, ho*, the lightning of the sky. *Tshitshilizi, tshitshilizi*! This sky is dangerous!' – an apparent reference to the 'lightning of heaven', the British rockets the regiment first encountered at Isandlwana. The uMxapho's cry was 'Ha, ha, ha, ha! It dug! It dug! It dug! We buried it in the ground at Gingindlovu!', a sly comment on the entrenchments behind which the British sheltered in that battle.

War-dress

It is also particularly interesting to note that Fynn describes an army, actually moving off on campaign, still wearing its full ceremonial regalia. It is not clear, of course, whether it was actually worn into battle – perhaps it was packed away in sleeping mats after the first bivouac – but it does seem likely that more regalia was retained in action in Shaka's time than was later the case. By 1879, there are very clear indications that the full regimental regalia was not worn into battle; British reports suggested that when King Cetshwayo mustered his army in January, he ordered them to assemble without their regimental regalia, and ready for action.[41] It is not entirely clear why the practice of wearing it had fallen away; it did not hamper movement in the field, as descriptions of the *umKhosi* ceremonies demonstrate, but it was, as already noted, both fragile and expensive. Perhaps, by 1879, the various combinations of feathers and pelts were becoming so expensive to obtain, even through tribute, that it was widely accepted that to wear it into battle was unnecessarily wasteful. Certainly, British officers, who had been issued with pamphlets describing the full dress of Cetshwayo's regiments, were disappointed to find that the troops facing them in the field wore little more than their loin-coverings. At the battle of Gingindlovu on 2 April, Lieutenant Edward Hutton of the 60th Rifles noted that 'contrary to precedent, they did not wear their full war costume, but carried rifles, assegais, and small shields.'[42] An NCO of the 17th Lancers, commenting on the final stages of the battle of oNdini (Ulundi) on 4 July, noted 'the fellows we charged were all young men, splendidly-made fellows, and all stripped for fighting.'[43] Nevertheless, this practice was not universal, and another eye-witness at Gingindlovu noted 'their white ox-shields, the headdresses of leopard skin and feathers, and the wild ox-tails hanging from their necks.'[44] After Gingindlovu, the 91st Highlanders recovered sufficient items of Zulu costume to make a fair-sized trophy,[45] whilst after Rorke's Drift some attempt was made to identify the Zulu regiments who had taken part according to their headbands and feathers.[46]

Where accounts do suggest that regalia was worn in action, it is interesting to note that it seems to have been more prevalent among the more senior *amabutho*. It is the white shield regiments who wear 'wild ox-tails' at Gingindlovu, while the young men are 'all stripped for fighting', and of course the regiments who fought at Rorke's Drift were principally married men. Many factors no doubt affected how much costume was retained in action, and conservatism was one. The younger men – who made up most of the king's main striking arm in 1879 – wore very little. Nevertheless, there was probably considerable variation, even within a particular *ibutho*; it is quite possible that those who assembled at one *ikhanda* might have worn more than those who assembled at another, whereas warriors fighting in their own areas are likely to have worn more than those who had to travel further to the front. Senior commanders probably retained their crane- or lourie-feathers, and perhaps a cape of leopard skin, to indicate their rank. Personal choice itself was also a consideration. In general, light items, such as headbands and cow-tail leg or arm ornaments, were more likely to be retained than the complex components of the headdress. The heavy cow-tail ornaments worn about the body were uncomfortable, and probably discarded, although there are suggestions that a lighter variant, containing just a few tails, was sometimes worn instead.[47] Almost all warriors wore necklaces consisting of charms to ward off *umnyama* – small pouches of lizard-or snake-skin, containing *umuthi*, and blocks of willow wood, which had strong associations with victory, and which were carefully trimmed and burnt at the edges. Apart from these, it is probable that the majority of warriors went to war in 1879 wearing little more than the *umutsha* and *ibeshu* loin coverings.

Moving off

When the regiments finally moved off, they did so in a single column, in an order of march appointed by the king himself. To be in the vanguard was a jealously guarded honour, usually granted to one of the king's favourite younger *amabutho*. This regiment was said to have the right to 'drink the dew', to be in the forefront, though rival regiments, particularly those of about the same age, were keen to contest the honour, as Mtshapi kaNoradu of the uKhandempemvu explained:

> The regiments used to quarrel over their 'rights' to the dew. For if the foremost regiment was overtaken by one from further back, its members would want to start a fight, crying out, 'They are taking our dew!'.... It would be a serious matter if the dew were to be drunk by one of the regiments that marched behind. The foremost regiment would lose prestige in the eyes of the king; they would be regarded as weak-footed. 'Where were you, then, when those from behind came and took your dew? So you were tired out? Had you forgotten that the dew is yours?'[48]

It is interesting to pause and consider, for a moment, just how fast a Zulu army moved when on the march. Tales of the speed and stealth of which a Zulu *impi* was capable were legendary in Natal, even before the war of 1879. After Isandlwana they achieved almost mythic proportions: 'No one knows where the Zulu armies are,' wrote Second Lieutenant Baskerville Mynors, one of the British reinforcements sent out in March 1879; 'one day they are seen at one place, another at another; one meal lasts them for three days; and the bush they can creep through like snakes.'[49] In stories such as this lie the origins of the image of the indefatigable Zulu warrior who could 'run fifty miles, and fight a battle at the end of it'.[50] In fact, the available evidence suggests that, although extremely mobile by European standards, the Zulus seldom achieved such marathon distances, and certainly not in 1879. In the Isandlwana campaign, the main army left oNdini on the 17th and arrived in the Ngwebeni valley five miles from Isandlwana on the 21st – a distance of less than sixty miles. True, the king had specifically ordered the *amabutho* to march slowly, so as to preserve their strength for the coming fight, but this rate was not untypical. During the second phase of the war, for example, the main *impi* left oNdini on about 24 March, and reached Hlobane mountain, near Colonel Wood's camp at Khambula, about seventy miles away, on the 28th. Nevertheless, the army was clearly quite capable of averaging distances of over twenty miles a day with ease, and sustaining it for many days. This was a rate of movement that would have staggered their British opponents, who were tied to the pace of their transport wagons, and regarded half that as an acceptable day's march.

Moreover, the Zulu army was not tied to roads in the way that European armies were. Made up, as it was, of thousands of individuals who were accustomed to moving in the bush and veld in their daily lives, it could traverse open country with relative ease. Thornbush, steep hillsides and rocky outcrops which proved impassable barriers to white troops were no obstacle to the Zulus, who were therefore able to advance on their objectives by the most direct route. In the dry season they could cross rivers almost at will; in the summer months, when the water level was high, or in flood, they would naturally prefer to use drifts, and rivers were negotiated by means of a human chain. Shortly before the battle of Rorke's Drift in January 1879, British observers posted on Shiyane Hill observed the Zulus crossing the swollen Mzinyathi river at a point where the water was deep and the current sluggish: 'They remained a long time in the river, forming a line across it . . . to assist one another in fording the stream.'[51] In everyday life, each river crossing had a number of specialist *izinyanga*, who lived nearby, knew the river and its peculiarities, and whose duty it was to help travellers across, and no doubt each *impi* would have included a number of such men; indeed, because the warriors came from all parts of the kingdom, it is likely that whenever it was operating on its own soil, there were always men present who knew a particular locale intimately.

All of this walking about on hard, stony ground, incidentally, had one marked effect on the warriors' physical appearance, which excited the curiosity of a number of white travellers. The hunter Baldwin commented that the Zulus 'have no feeling in the soles of their feet, the skin being like the hoof of a cow, and fully half an inch thick.'[52] Henry Harford came across a Zulu corpse lying in the bush a few weeks after the fight at Rorke's Drift, and was fascinated to see that while the flesh had otherwise entirely decomposed, leaving bleached white bones, the leathery soles of the feet were still intact. They were so curious that he took them away with the intention of presenting them to a museum.[53]

Provisioning the army

Another important factor regarding Zulu mobility was the absence of a commissariat. The British army in Zululand had to carry everything with it, from its tents to its food supplies and bottled beer. Although the Zulu army was accompanied in the initial stages of any advance by its mat-carriers, it lived otherwise entirely by forage. At the outset, individual warriors might take with them a skin bag, tied to their waist-belts and containing a cooked calf's liver and a handful of roasted mealies, but these could scarcely sustain them for long. Henry Fynn saw King Shaka's army on the march to attack the Ndwandwe in 1826:

> Every man was ordered to roll up his shield and carry it on his back – a custom observed only when the enemy is known to be at a considerable distance. In the rear of the regiments were the baggage boys, few above the age of 12, and some not more than six. These boys were attached to the chiefs and principal men, carrying their mats, headrests, tobacco, etc., and

driving cattle required for the army's consumption. Some of the chiefs, moreover, were accompanied by girls carrying beer, corn and milk; and when their supply had been exhausted these carriers returned to their homes.

The whole body of men, boys and women amounted, as nearly as we could reckon, to 50,000. All proceeded in close formation, and when looked at a distance nothing could be seen but a cloud of dust.[54]

As Fynn suggests, many of those who accompanied the army at the start returned home after the first few days, although some of the *udibi* boys remained throughout the campaign. Although they were supposed to keep well to the rear when fighting threatened, many could not resist the excitement, and it was not unknown for them to join the fight. When Grosvenor Darke, a white adventurer who served Zibhebhu in the civil wars of the 1880s, fought the royalists at oNdini in 1883, he commented that in the royalist flight one elderly *induna* 'was actually run to earth and stabbed by my little mat-bearers'.[55]

Of course, the longer a campaign lasted, the more likely was the Zulu army to find its food supplies dwindling. In enemy territory, it lived by foraging from civilian homesteads, looting cattle and grain, and since a successful campaign might secure thousands of head of cattle, there was little danger of hardship. When the war took place on Zulu soil, however, as in 1879, this presented obvious problems. Many Zulu families abandoned their homesteads as the war approached them, taking as much of their livestock with them as they could; nevertheless, as the account of one Zulu boy, Muziwento, suggests, the passage of the national army could still be devastating:

In the afternoon [foragers] appeared through the fog. . . . They saw the many sheep belonging to our father and other people . . . and said, 'A bit of food for us, this, master!' They stabbed some of the sheep; they drained our calabashes; they took the (dead) sheep away with them. Suddenly one of the warriors espied an exceedingly fine kid. He seized it. Our father (uncle) seized it. . . . The next moment up came the indunas and scolded the regiment. The men ran off and continued their march.[56]

This system was far from ideal. Not only was it difficult to plunder friendly homesteads, but the British had, in any case, deliberately timed their invasion to take place before the new crops were gathered in. Food was therefore scarce enough, and after Rorke's Drift, British burial parties noted that many of the Zulu corpses were 'quite wizened', suggesting that the days spent undergoing the preparatory ceremonies and on the march had already taken their toll. By the time of the second phase of fighting, in March and April 1879, the mealie crop had been harvested, but after Khambula the British still found a number of Zulu dead, who had overrun part of the camp, with their mouths stuffed full of porridge which they had just then looted from abandoned cooking pots. It was the Zulu custom to eat twice a day, at mid-morning and early evening, and if a battle began at first light, the warriors went into it hungry. In 1828 Isaacs witnessed the return of an unsuccessful expedition, 'in a miserable state, from hunger and fatigue'; the warriors were 'all in a state of exhaustion from want of food'.[57] In the 1880s, the newly appointed British Resident in Zululand commented that many areas had been badly impoverished by the passage of the army in 1879, although whether this was strictly due to the ravages of the Zulu forces, or the deliberate scorched-earth policy practised by the British in the later stages of the war, is uncertain.

Sickness and disease

There is a curious absence of evidence regarding the incidence of disease within the Zulu army. There are suggestions that the army Shaka sent north in 1828 suffered from malaria, but for the most part the Zulu army seems to have remained relatively free of sickness when on campaign. Disease was, of course, a far greater killer than battles among European armies operating in Africa; but the Zulu were accustomed to their environment, and this, coupled with the relatively short duration of active service, and the fact that the army in the field seldom camped in one place long enough to foul its environs, probably meant that the warriors were only marginally more vulnerable on campaign than they were in their daily lives.

Nearing the enemy

The army only marched in a single column whilst on safe territory. Once it reached the vicinity of the enemy, it split into two columns. As Mpatshana explained:

> It is wrong for the army to march in a single column when enemy country has been entered, and an induna guilty of such practice was dismissed. This was said to be bad because, on the enemy appearing and attacking, having the advantage and repelling them, it would follow them up and stab them, there being no other independent support to attack the enemy from another quarter and so relieve the situation.[58]

In the Isandlwana campaign, for example, the army marched for two days in a single column, and on the third split into two, one commanded by the senior *induna*, Ntshingwayo kaMahole, the other by his colleague, Mavumengwana kaNdlela Nutli.

The advance was screened by a sophisticated system of scouts. Far in advance of the army, picked individuals were sent out secretly to observe the enemy, and report his movements. Indeed, according to Isaacs:

Chaka always kept up a system of espionage, by which he knew at all times the condition and strength of every tribe around him, both independent and tributary; and these persons were always directed to make such observations on the passes to and from the country to which they were sent, as might be useful in leading the troops to the scene of action with the surest chance of arriving at their position, without being discovered on the one hand, or surprised on the other.[59]

If possible, scouts even infiltrated the enemy forces; in 1879, the British lived with the permanent suspicion that their Native Contingent and the black civilians they employed as wagon-drivers had been infiltrated by the Zulus. That they probably were is reflected in an apocryphal but highly suggestive story that Zibhebhu kaMapitha, who commanded the scouts in the Isandlwana campaign, had personally entered the British camp there, investigated every part of it, and had even climbed to the top of Isandlwana mountain itself to overlook it.[60] The British realised their error too late: 'All spies taken are shot,' wrote one officer after Isandlwana, 'we have disposed of three or four already. Formerly they were allowed anywhere, and our disaster is to a great extent due to their accurate information of the General's movements.'[61]

Closer to the main Zulu army was another body consisting of men who, although described as scouts, were effectively skirmishers. Two or three men were selected from each company present with the army by their regimental *izinduna*, so as to form a body which might number as many as ten companies. They were pushed out in advance of the main body so as to screen its movements; advancing in open order, they gave the impression 'that they themselves were the main body'. The men were selected for their courage, since they were expected to fall on any enemy scouts or foragers they came across. According to Mpatshana, who was selected as such a scout in the Isandlwana campaign:

The advance guard is thrown out to draw the enemy, but as soon as the guard begin to retreat, it falls back on the main body, which comes up and engages the enemy. When the advance guard perceives they are being followed up by the enemy, they send off runners at once to the main body to advise them of what has been noticed.[62]

These skirmishers were particularly effective in the 1879 campaign. On 21 January, the army moved across the front of Lord Chelmsford's invading

British column near Isandlwana; although the move was masked by hills, the two armies were only then about twelve miles apart. A British patrol discovered local forces moving in the wake of the main army, thereby misleading Lord Chelmsford into thinking that the Zulu threat lay in another direction. In fact, the army was moving even closer to the British camp, into the Ngwebeni valley just five or six miles from Isandlwana. This move, too, was almost detected by British patrols, but Zibhebhu's scouts drove the British back before they understood the significance of what they saw.[63] This effective screening on the part of the Zulus paved the way for their victory at Isandlwana. During the battle itself, it seems to have been skirmishers of either the uKhandempemvu or iNgobamakhosi regiments who overran Major Russell's rocket battery, whilst at Rorke's Drift the garrison noted that the main Zulu attack was preceded by a rush of skirmishers. On 1 June the Prince Imperial of France was killed whilst on patrol, ambushed by just such a party of 'scouts', consisting of members of the iNgobamakhosi, uMbonambi and uNokhenke *amabutho*. During the siege of Eshowe, one of the beleaguered garrison, Captain Pelly Clarke, observed that the British were under constant observation from Zulu scouts posted on the surrounding heights, and left a fascinating description of the speed with which these scouts were supported whenever the occasion demanded:

> A tiny speck would appear on the top of a hill, it would soon after grow bigger in circumference, till it attained that of a huge circle. The 'speck' was the 'lookout' man of a regiment, which, when he had reported 'all correct', would gradually come up the hill and form round him in a circle.... After a short consultation – squatting all the while – the circle would slowly unwind itself, and move till again only the 'speck' would be left; he would wait till joined by the 'lookout' man of the next regiment, when he would hasten to join his own corps.[64]

When the Zulu army at last reached the vicinity of the enemy, one last ritual was necessary. The troops were again formed up into an *umkhumbi*, and sprinkled with a final selection of *intelezi* medicine by the *izinyanga*. Isaacs witnessed such a ceremony in Shaka's time, and described its purposes:

> The Zoolas ... formed in front of the enemy's position, and began to perform the usual superstitious ceremonies of their nation – such as anointing the body with a preparation made by the war-doctors from roots known only to these inyangers, who, with an ox-tail attached to a stick about two feet long, sprinkle the decoction on the warrior, who rubs it over himself, and immediately not only conceives that he is likewise invulnerable, but certain of achieving a victory over his enemies.[65]

This was the last opportunity for the commanders to address their men; to remind them of their military heritage, as Chief Ntshingwayo did to the reserve at Isandlwana, and to urge them, in the manner of commanders the world over, not to disgrace their king, their regiments and their families. Often this had the desired effect, stimulating the adrenalin to such a pitch that the warriors were carried into combat on a wave of excitement. Sometimes, however, it had the opposite effect, for when King Cetshwayo's senior councillor, Mnyamana of the Buthelezi, addressed the great *impi* before the battle of Khambula, he stressed the consequences of defeat to such an extent that the men were unsettled and apprehensive.

In the event, however, it was not always possible to observe such niceties in 1879. When the great *impi* was finally discovered near Isandlwana at noon on 22 January, the battle began regardless of any last minute negotiations the king might have hoped for. Nor was there time for the final *intelezi* ceremonies, and the army went into the maelstrom of modern battle for the first time, unprotected by the time-honoured rituals.

NOTES

1. Account of Mpatshana kaSodondo, Webb and Wright, *JSA* 3.
2. Leslie, *Among the Zulus and Amatongas.*
3. Colonel Harry Sparks, *Chelmsford's Ultimatum to Cetewayo*, Killie Campbell Africana Library, KCM 42329.
4. Account of Mpatshana kaSodondo, Webb and Wright, *JSA* 3.
5. Account of Ndukwana kaMbengwana, Webb and Wright, *JSA* 4.
6. Account of Mpatshana kaSodondo, Webb and Wright, *JSA* 3.
7. Ibid.
8. Filter and Bourquin, *Paulina Dlamini.*
9. Account of Mtshayankomo kaMagolwana, Webb and Wright, *JSA* 4.
10. Account of Mpatshana kaSodondo, Webb and Wright, *JSA* 3.
11. Ibid.
12. Account of Mtshapi kaNoradu in Webb and Wright, *JSA* 4.
13. Account of Ndukwana kaMbengwana, Webb and Wright, *JSA* 4.
14. Account of Mpatshana kaSodondo, Webb and Wright, *JSA* 3.
15. Isaacs, *Travels and Adventure.*
16. Fynn, *Diary.*
17. Isaacs, *Travels And Adventure.*
18. Fynn, *Diary.*
19. Isaacs, *Travels and Adventure.*
20. On this trade see Louis Du Buisson, *The White Man Cometh*, Johannesburg, 1987.
21. Gardiner, *Narrative.*
22. Statement of J.P. Tietsman, 11 December 1846; see Kennedy, *Mpande and the Zulu Kingship, Journal of Natal and Zulu History*, Vol. IV, 1981.
23. Baldwin, *African Hunting and Adventure.*

24. See, for example, account of Mgelija Ngema in Knight (ed.), *Kill Me in the Shadows*, in *Soldiers of the Queen* (hereafter *SOTQ*) 74. Cetshwayo himself confirmed that Dunn was his principal supplier; Cetshwayo's evidence in Webb and Wright, *A Zulu King Speaks*.

25. For a resumé of the gun trade in the 1870s, see Jeff Guy, *A Note on Firearms in the Zulu Kingdom With Special Reference to the Anglo-Zulu War of 1879*, Journal of African History, XII, 1971.

26. Account of Bikwayo kaNoziwana, Webb and Wright, *JSA* 1.

27. Account of Mpatshana kaSodondo, Webb and Wright, *JSA* 3.

28. 'Lower Tugela Correspondent', *Natal Mercury*, 12 February 1879.

29. Return of Firearms Captured at Gingindlovu, Lord Chelmsford Papers, National Army Museum, London.

30. Fynn, *Diary*.

31. Account of Mpatshana kaSodondo, Webb and Wright, *JSA* 3.

32. Ibid.

33. Archibald Forbes, published in *The Illustrated London News*, 12 July 1879.

34. Forbes's dispatch from Landman's Drift, 5 July 1879, reproduced in W.C.F. Moodie, *Moodie's Zulu War*, Pietermaritzburg, 1988. On the subject of the July mutilations, see Ian Knight, *Was Raubenheim Tortured?*, in *SOTQ* 74, September 1993.

35. C.T. Binns, *Dinuzulu*, London 1968, quoting the evidence of one who saw the body.

36. Account of Mpatshana kaSodondo, Webb and Wright, *JSA*, 3.

37. For an assessment of the king's strategic options, see John Laband, *Kingdom in Crisis*.

38. Account of Luke Sofikasho Zungu, Knight (ed.), *Kill Me in the Shadows, SOTQ* 74.

39. Fynn, *Diary*.

40. On regimental cries, see Mpatshana, *JSA* 3, and Samuelson, *Long, Long Ago*. There seems to be some confusion regarding the translation of *'nqaka' amatshe*; as a non-Zulu linguist armed only with a selection of dictionaries, I have preferred Samuelson's version, *catch stones*, which is supported by other contemporary accounts, over Webb and Wright's *smash stones*.

41. See report of Border Agent Fannin in *BPP* CC2242.

42. Hutton's account is quoted in Frank Emery's *The Red Soldier*, London, 1979.

43. See Emery, ibid.

44. Ibid.

45. The trophy does not seem to have survived, but a photograph of it is contained in an album compiled by Lieutenant Freville Cookson of the 91st, and now in the National Army Museum, London. This photograph is reproduced in Ian Castle and Ian Knight's *Fearful Hard Times; The Siege and Relief of Eshowe*, London, 1994.

46. Unpublished notes compiled by Captain Penn Symons, 24th, Royal Regiment of Wales Museum, Brecon.

47. See Gardiner's sketch in *Narrative*, which appears to show warriors in 'war dress wearing kilts, a light cow-tail necklace, headbands, and one or two representative feathers.

48. Account of Mtshapi kaNoradu in Webb and Wright, *JSA* 4.

49. A.C.B. Mynors, *Letters and Diary* (family memoir), Margate, 1879.

50. 1964 feature film *Zulu*.

51. *Defence of Rorke's Drift by an Eyewitness*, published Durban, 1879.

52. Baldwin, *African Hunting and Adventure*.

53. Child, *Zulu War Diary of Henry Harford*.

54. Fynn, *Diary*.

55. Quoted in Guy, *Destruction of the Zulu Kingdom*.

56. G.H. Swinny, *A Zulu Boy's Recollections of the Zulu War and of Cetshwayo's Return*, London, 1884, edited and reprinted by C. de B. Webb in *Natalia*, VIII, December 1978.
57. Isaacs, *Travels and Adventure*.
58. Account of Mpatshana kaSodondo, Webb and Wright, *JSA* 3.
59. Isaacs, *Travels and Adventure*.
60. C.T. Binns, *The Warrior People*, London, 1975.
61. Lieutenant Curling RA, in a letter printed in *The Standard*, 27 March 1879.
62. Account of Mpatshana kaSodondo, Webb and Wright, *JSA* 3.
63. Prince Ndabuko kaMpande – who was with the army – told his story to J.Y. Gibson. See *Story of the Zulus*.
64. One Who Was There (believed to be Captain Pelly Clarke, 103rd Regt), *The Zulu War; With Colonel Pearson at Ekowe, Blackwood's Magazine*, Vol. CXXVI, July 1879.
65. Isaacs, *Travels and Adventure*.

CHAPTER 6

Seeing Nothing but Red

On 26 January 1879, four days after the great battle at Isandlwana, a group of Zulu boys who lived near the battlefield defied the warnings of their parents and visited the devastated field. One of them, Muziwento, left a graphic account of what they found there:

> We arrived early in the morning. We saw the soil that it was red.... We went to see the dead people at Isandlwana. We saw a single warrior dead, staring in our direction, with his war shield in his hand.... We saw countless things dead. Dead was the horse, dead too, the mule, dead was the dog, dead was the monkey, dead were the waggons, dead were the tents, dead were the boxes, dead was everything, even to the very metals....[1]

This is a disturbing image, all the more chilling because it provides a glimpse of the horror that was days old, a nightmare recalled on an otherwise calm day. Even after the passage of more than a century, it was the power to conjure up the apocalyptic destructive forces unleashed by Zulu warfare. The Zulu man fulfilled many functions in his role as a member of the *amabutho*, and by the time a warrior had undergone the preparatory rituals for combat, he was set apart from peaceful society, bound to his fellows by the tightest emotional bonds, and the powerful taboos that surrounded him could only be expiated in the terrible excitement of combat. The Zulu army in the field was like a spring that had been wound to breaking point by days of psychological preparation, and it required only the presence of the enemy for it to snap. And the Zulu experience of battle was raw in a way which shocked even the hardened professional soldiers in the British army who opposed them; it was, quite literally, visceral

As John Laband has pointed out,[2] the Zulu army was committed to the concept of aggressive action from the time of King Shaka, and the reasons for this were only partly practical. Shaka had been a dynamic leader whose wars of conquest had established the framework of the Zulu kingdom; his personal military philosophy, as far as one can tell, was always to attack whenever possible. Although the opportunity to raid outside the kingdom's borders declined during the reigns of subsequent kings, this attitude had, by then, accrued all the weight of tradition. Many commentators have sug-

187

gested that the Zulu might have been more successful if they had waged a defensive or even a guerrilla campaign in 1879, retreating to their natural strongholds, and fighting in areas in which the British were at a greater physical disadvantage. Certainly the British themselves feared this might happen. Coming fresh from the Ninth Cape Frontier War, where the Xhosa pursued just such tactics, the British commander, Lord Chelmsford – and, indeed, most of the men under his command – firmly believed that the Zulu would never engage in a mass attack on a British position in the open. This deeply misleading impression affected British thinking right down to the tactical decisions made by field officers, and only in the final moments of Isandlwana did the penny begin to drop.

In fact, guerrilla or defensive warfare did have a role to play in minor Zulu tactics, but it is difficult to see how a large force living in mountain retreats could have been provisioned for any length of time. More importantly, once the main army was mobilised, its explicit objective was to 'eat up' the enemy, a phrase that embodies the physical and spiritual need of the warriors for a sharp, all-consuming clash. Prolonged campaigning was difficult to sustain; the preparatory rituals needed their cleansing counterparts after combat, whilst supplying an army in the field soon became problematic. Furthermore, the longer a campaign lasted, the more the absence of the warriors from their civilian responsibilities was felt by those at home. In January 1879, for example, the war began at a time when the new harvest was ripening, and the king would soon need to release the men from service if the population at large was to gather in its crops.

Desire for battle

This need for a decisive confrontation expressed itself in an eagerness to attack which was potentially self-destructive. In the Isandlwana campaign, the main Zulu army had not intended to attack the British camp on 22 January because of the impending new moon. As soon as they were discovered, however, the uKhandempemvu *ibutho* advanced, drawing the other regiments after it. If Ntshingwayo and Mavumengwana had conceived a plan to attack the camp, they had no chance to implement it. The best the senior commanders could do was to restrain those regiments on the end of the line, furthest from the British incursion – the uThulwana and its incorporated *amabutho*, all associated with the royal homestead of oNdini – to form them into an *umkhumbi*, then lead them away as a reserve. Even then, some elements under an impetuous regimental officer of the uThulwana, Qethuka kaManqondo, broke away and joined the attack.

This lack of discipline in the face of provocation cost the Zulu dear. Even after Isandlwana, some Zulus, considering the appalling losses they had suffered in winning the victory, attributed them to the fact that the final administration of *intelezi* medicine had not taken place. Yet there were potentially worse consequences; on the very morning that Isandlwana was fought in the middle reaches of the kingdom, the local forces deputised by Cetshwayo to hinder the advance of Colonel Pearson's coastal column were also drawn into battle unexpectedly. They had been lying behind the spurs of a hill known as Wombane, above the Nyezane river, and were also discovered by British patrols pursuing their scouts; in the ensuing battle, the commander, Godide kaNdlela – Mavumengwana's brother – was unable to impose even that level of control which finally emerged during the attack on Isandlwana. At Nyezane the Zulu attacks were badly coordinated, and only one wing of the army was fully deployed; it was insufficient to overcome Pearson's firepower, and the Zulus were driven off. Later, during the second phase of the war, the British were able deliberately to exploit this tendency with decisive results at the battle of Khambula Hill. Here the Zulus surrounded the British camp on three sides, but the British commander, Colonel Wood, noticed that the Zulu right – the iNgobamakhosi – were in position before the rest of the army. He sent out a foray to goad it to attack and, despite the fact that the Zulu commanders had carefully planned their tactics on this occasion, the battle once again developed against their wishes. The Zulu assaults were made piecemeal against the British fortifications, allowing Wood to shift his guns to meet each new attack. Afterwards, the Zulus realised their fatal error, as a warrior of the uThulwana explained:

The iNgobamakhosi rushed after [the British].... Then the uKhandem-pemvu on the other side rushed on, too – there was a rivalry between the uKhandempemvu and the iNgobamakhosi as to whom should be the first in the camp, so they both got on ahead, and by the time we came up to attack the front they were exhausted and almost beaten.... The two regiments forming the [flanks] were quite exhausted and useless, and we could not properly surround the position.[3]

Nor was this problem confined to the 1879 campaign. In 1838, during King Dingane's war against the Voortrekkers, the Zulus were confronted by a Boer force which had carefully constructed a defensive wagon-laager in a strong natural position on the Ncome river. Although the Zulu force, perhaps 10,000 men commanded by Chief Ndlela kaSompisi, greatly outnumbered the Boers, the Zulu deployment was hampered by the terrain. The Zulus attempted to surround the position in the dark, but their line of advance entailed crossing the river before they could do so. Dawn on 16 December found Ndlela's force split in two, with only about half his men on the Boer bank. Despite this, those *amabutho* who had managed to get across began their attack at dawn, with the result, as at Khambula, that the rest of the army could not deploy fully, and the Boers were able to deal in turn with a series of badly coordinated attacks. By the end of the day the Zulu had been broken, and the Ncome ran red with their blood. Although King Cetshwayo and his councillors were well aware of the lessons to be learned from 'Blood River', their caution made no impression on the overconfident young men who made up the ranks of the *amabutho*.

Another consequence of the unexpected encounter at Isandlwana was that the Zulu attack developed later in the day than was usually preferred. Generally, if circumstances allowed, the Zulu approached their enemy late in the evening, bivouacked over night, then launched their attack at dawn; this was a time of day known as 'the horns of the morning', when the horns of cattle could first be discerned against the lightening sky. In theory, such an attack gave the Zulus sufficient light to make their dispositions as the attack developed, while catching their enemy both off-guard and at a psychologically low ebb. The battle of Ntombe, on 12 March 1879, was an almost perfect example of a classic Zulu attack. A British supply convoy, escorted by a company of the 80th regiment, had been stranded for several days either side of the swollen Ntombe River. Despite the fact that Zulu spies were reportedly seen in the British laager, no attempt was made properly to fortify the position. A shot was heard in the early hours of the morning − presumably a careless warrior had accidentally discharged his firearm as the *impi* took up its position − but the British ignored this warning. It was not until sunrise that the sentries spotted a large Zulu force which had advanced to within a few hundred yards of the position, and was already charging down on them. The British had no time to form up, and were overrun with heavy casualties.

In 1838, the Zulu attack on the Boer encampments along the Drakensberg foothills went in just before dawn, as indeed did the assault on the Blood River position. Similarly, at Gingindlovu, in April 1879, British troops marching to the relief of the beleaguered garrison at Eshowe noted Zulu campfires gathering in the hills ahead of them on the evening of the 1st. The attack began at dawn the next morning, with the initial Zulu deployment masked by a dense mist hanging in the river valley. When the mist burnt off to reveal the army advancing rapidly to the attack, the spectacle was unnerving, but on this occasion the British were prepared and the attack was repulsed. Although the British remained convinced throughout the war that the Zulus would try to attack them at night − and false alarms were frequent in their camps as a result − this was not Zulu practice. Darkness was not only impractical, it was also a time of *umnyama*, when the Zulus were vulnerable to evil influences. Only one of the Zulu War battles included night-fighting, and that was

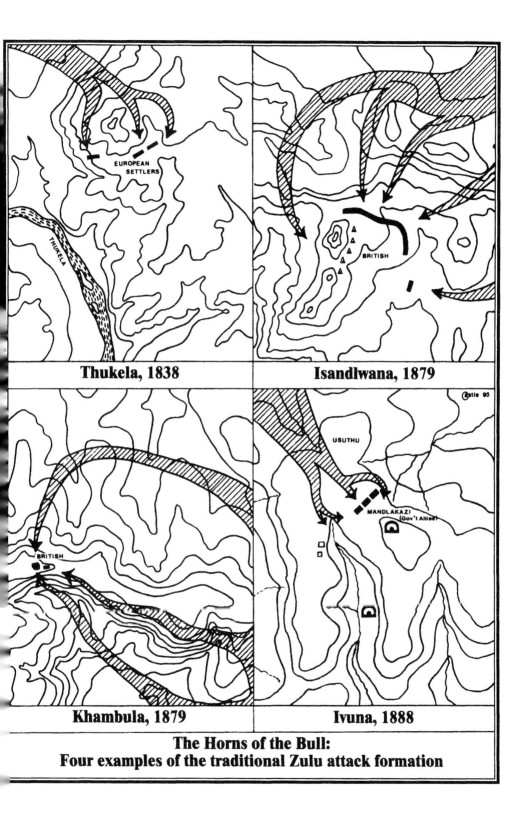

Thukela, 1838

Isandlwana, 1879

Khambula, 1879

Ivuna, 1888

The Horns of the Bull:
Four examples of the traditional Zulu attack formation

Rorke's Drift, a far from typical engagement. Even then, the attack had begun earlier in the afternoon, and the Zulus were deeply committed when dusk fell; their apparent success in overrunning part of the British position no doubt encouraged them to continue the attack longer than might otherwise have been the case.

Battle tactics

The favourite Zulu attack formation was an encircling movement known as the *impondo zankomo* — literally 'the beast's horns', after a symbolic resemblance to a charging bull. This formation employed four basic tactical units; the *isifuba*, or chest, which advanced directly towards the enemy's front, and two flanking parties, called *izimpondo*, or horns, which rushed out to surround him on either side. A further body, *umuva*, the loins, was kept to the rear, and served as a reserve, plugging any gaps that developed in the attack. It is said that the loins were often seated with their backs to the enemy, so as to prevent them becoming unduly excited; it is difficult to find examples of this in practice, but reserves were certainly kept out of sight on occasion. If the force was accompanied by a particularly young *ibutho*, which had just *kleza*'d, this, too, was sometimes held back; known as the *isibiba* — 'those that remain behind' — it was only sent into action to join the pursuit or to round up the enemy's cattle and other booty after victory was assured.

The *impondo zankomo* was supposedly invented by King Shaka himself, although there is very little direct evidence from either white or Zulu sources regarding his tactics. Both Fynn and Isaacs left accounts of battles in which they participated, but their descriptions are typical of the limited perspective of the combatant: full of personal incident, but revealing no very clear understanding of wider events on the battlefield. Although Zulu traditions collected by Stuart and others at the end of the nineteenth century constantly refer to the 'beasts' horns' formation, the concept was by then so rooted in Zulu military thinking that the references may be anachronistic. It is also interesting to note that other southern African groups, such as the Xhosa, likewise used encircling tactics, quite independently of Zulu influence.[4] The best that can be said with certainty is that the *impondo zankomo* emerged early in the kingdom's history, and quite possibly under Shaka. It was undoubtedly in vogue in the 1830s, since in 1838 it was used to devastating effect against an army of Port Natal settlers and their retainers, the so-called 'Grand Army of Natal', who had taken to the field to support the Voortrekkers in their war against King Dingane. Just across the Thukela near the Lower Drift — not far from the spot where Colonel Pearson crossed in 1879 — the settlers had blundered into the advance guard of a Zulu army sent to check them. The settlers deployed in three bodies to prevent the Zulu encircling movement, but the Zulus pressed home their

A warrior in war-dress, a much reduced version of the full ceremonial regalia. By 1879 the practice of wearing even this had largely died away. The shield is the *umbumbuluzo* type. (Royal Archives)

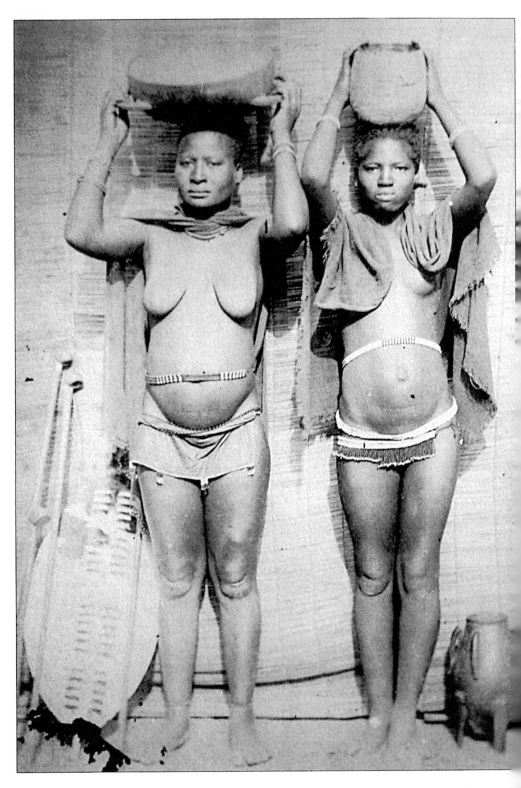

The commissariat; girls like these carried food for the first few days of campaigning, but beyond that the Zulu army wa[s] dependent on foraging.

Above: The uniformity of ceremonial costume within a particular *ibutho* is demonstrated by this photograph, which pre-dates the 1879 war. The white cow-tail head-dress was a typical element in the uniform of a young, unmarried *ibutho*. (Royal Archives)
Below: A Zulu blacksmith at work; he is heating the fire by means of goat-skin bellows. (Natal Museum)

Above: Alan Gardiner's sketch of King Dingane's *komkhulu* eMgungundlovu, in the 1830s.
The complex was typical of the design of the great *amakhanda*, though few attained such magnificent proportions.
Below: A typical *ikhanda:* King Dingane's uKhangela homestead.

Above: Life in the *amakhanda*; cooks preparing food for the *isigodlo* at King Cetshwayo's oNdini. This engraving is a composite based on a number of photographs apparently taken at Cetshwayo's 'coronation'. **Right:** An *unyango*, one of the shield-stores within the *amakhanda* which housed the regimental war-shields, and kept them safe from rodents and damp.

Above: The *isigodlo*; a model of King Cetshwayo's personal quarters at the oNdini homestead. (Zululand Historical Museum, oNdini)

Right: Although this engraving dates from 1883, it shows a familiar sight from the great days of the Zulu kingdom: girls carrying foodstuffs to the occupants of an *ikhanda*, in this case King Cetshwayo's rebuilt oNdini. (Rai England Collection)

Opposite page, top: The *amabutho* as labour force: Swazi 'warriors' hoeing the king's fields. The sight would have been much the same among the Zulu.

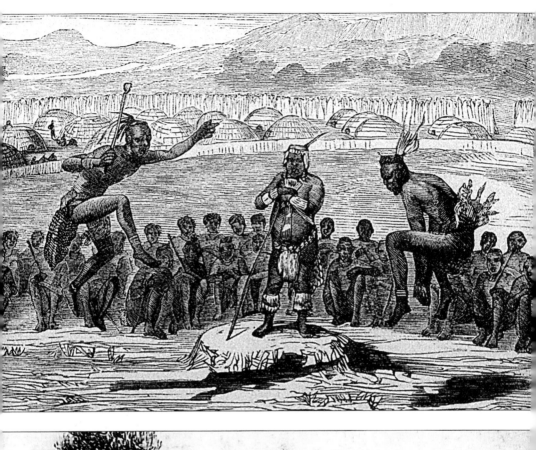

Opposite page, top: Begging for shields, from a description by Gardiner: the *izinduna* 'Georgo' and Dambuza in spirited dispute before King Dingane. (S. B. Bourquin)

Opposite page, bottom: Warriors parading before Prince Hamu kaNzibe, one of the most powerful regional *izikhulu*; a sketch from about the time of Cetshwayo's coronation, by Thomas Baines. (S. B. Bourquin)

Above: King Mpande reviewing one of his regiments in the kwaNodwengu *ikhanda*, 1850s

Below: Individuals step out from an *ibutho* to *giya*, to proclaim their achievements in battle and fight a solitary mock-duel; an important part of the ceremonial of the *amabutho*.

Opposite page: King Cetshwayo kaMpande, who ruled the Zulu kingdom from 1873 to 1879: it was Cetshwayo's attempt to use the *amabutho* as a means of restoring central authority which antagonised the British.
Above: Men of power. This is thought to be a portrait of Chief Ntshingwayo kaMahole, one of King Cetshwayo's most trusted advisors, and the senior general in 1879. (Royal Commonwealth Library)

Zibhebhu kaMapitha, chief of the Mandlakazi, a powerful *isikhulu* despite his youth; he was
one of the most dynamic commanders in the 1879 war, but a bitter opponent of the royalist faction
in the internecine strife which followed. (Natal Archives Depot)

Right: Sigcwelegcwele kaMhlekehleke, a junior chief but an *isilomo* – one of the king's favourites – who commanded the iNgobamakhosi throughout the 1879 war. (S. B. Bourquin)

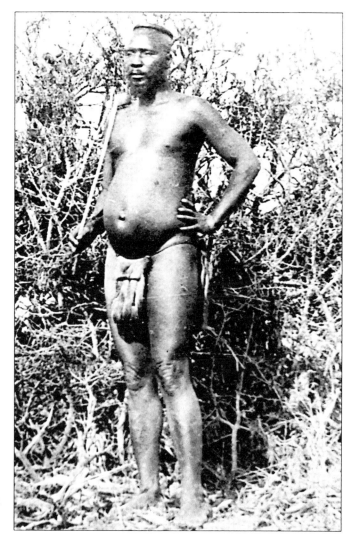

Below: Prince Dabulamanzi kaMpande, who held no official command in 1879, but none the less led the oNdini *amabutho* in the attack on Rorke's Drift. He is photographed here in 1873 with the white trader, John Dunn. (S. B. Bourquin)

Above: According to tradition, battles in the pre-Shakan era consisted of an exchange of throwing spears and were not likely to involve heavy casualties. (S. B. Bourquin)

Below: An *ibutho* on the march slakes its thirst as it crosses a river. (S. B. Bourquin)

Opposite page: Despite its over-dramatic style – it was published at the time of the 1906 Bambatha Rebellion – this picture does at least show an important aspect of the pre-combat rituals; an *inyanga* sprinkles a regiment with *intelezi* medicine.

Warriors advancing to the attack, 1879. Although the warriors are shown in a little too much regalia and are bunched too closely together, this engraving none the less gives a good impression of their general appearance in the field. Note the number of firearms.

attacks despite heavy casualties, and one body collapsed under the pressure. In the first major clash of its type, the Natal army was pushed back to the river, surrounded and slaughtered.

All of the major set-piece battles of the Anglo-Zulu War were characterised by the Zulu use of the 'beasts' horns' formation. The British knew that it was a favourite ploy – Lord Chelmsford had prepared an intelligence pamphlet, issued to each of his officers, which included a sketch of it[5] – but, in the early battles at least, failed to appreciate the efficiency and dispatch with which it was executed. At Nyezane Colonel Pearson's column was caught on the march, and his subsequent victory was only due to the fact that the Zulus failed to deploy properly. By contrast, the main army manoeuvred with great skill at Isandlwana. It emerged from the Ngwebeni valley in some confusion, but by the time it had covered the three or four miles to the Nyoni ridge, which overlooked the British camp, the chest and horns had been properly formed.[6] Furthermore, one horn was often thrown out secretively, making good use of natural cover, so as to surprise the enemy when they were driven back by the more obvious chest and remaining horn; and so it was at Isandlwana. The right horn – the uNokhenke, uDududu, iMbube and iSangqu *amabutho* – slipped into the valley behind Isandlwana hill largely undetected by the British. 'We worked round ... under cover of the long grass and dongas,' recalled one of the uNokhenke, '... the ground is high and full of dongas and stones, and the soldiers did not see us until we were right upon them.'[7] A British survivor, Captain Essex, witnessed it moving across his front early in the battle:

> Their line was about 1,000 yards in extent, but arranged like a horn – that is, very thin and extended on their right, but gradually thickening towards ours. They did not advance, but moved steadily towards our left, each man running from rock to rock, for the ground was covered with large boulders, with the evident intention of outflanking us.[8]

Ideally, the points of the horns were supposed to meet behind the enemy position, so as to pin him in place to be crushed by the chest. At Isandlwana the points of the horns almost met on the neck below Isandlwana; only the determined resistance of the British infantry kept them back long enough to allow a few survivors to slip through the net.

Skirmishing tactics

The 'chest and horns' tactic worked equally well in minor clashes as in set-piece battles; indeed, it was often more effective then, since it was seldom employed against defended positions. Small parties of the enemy were always in danger, whether they were armed with firearms or not, when fighting in unfamiliar country, as they seldom had the firepower to keep the Zulus at bay. Throughout 1879, a low-intensity war raged in the north-western marches of the kingdom, punctuated by the two great clashes at Hlobane and Khambula in March. This area was sparsely populated, and was the territory of the abaQulusi, the descendants of an *ikhanda*, eba-Qulusini, established in the region by King Shaka. It was also the home of Mbilini waMswati, a renegade Swazi prince giving allegiance to Cetshwayo, who had strong links with the abaQulusi, and who proved to be one of the most daring Zulu commanders of the war. Mbilini and the abaQulusi constantly harassed the operations of the local British commander, Colonel Wood, raiding local settlements and ambushing patrols.[9] Although this type of fighting was particularly suited to the region's broken terrain, it was not notably different in form from similar incidents elsewhere in the country. Around Eshowe, in the coastal sector, for example, there were frequent skirmishes between the British garrison and the Zulu forces deployed to keep them under surveillance. When, on 1 March, the garrison made a foray to destroy eSiqwakeni, an *ikhanda* nearby which had served as a Zulu base, the Zulus rallied and harassed the British as they withdrew. The Zulus made fine use of the cover, moving rapidly from one vantage point to another, firing from the bush, and constantly trying to outflank and surround any British parties who lagged behind. 'It was really a pleasure to watch the way these Zulus skirmished,' wrote one of the British party: 'No crowding, no delay, as soon as they were driven from one cover they would hasten rapidly to the next awkward bit of country through which our column would have to pass. Luckily for us their shooting was inferior or we should have suffered severely.'[10]

Such skirmishes became more frequent as the war progressed. After each pitched battle the king allowed the army to disperse and rest at their homes. As the British advanced deeper into Zulu territory, more and more indi-vidual warriors stayed in the countryside to fight in defence of their homes. The 1879 war had a particularly damaging effect on the civilian population. When their menfolk were away, women were required to observe various important rituals, but in 1879 there were the additional hardships brought about because the fighting took place in Zululand itself. Most of the pre-Shakan chiefdoms had strongholds to which they retired in times of trouble – hidden caves or inaccessible mountains – and they were used again in 1879 whenever fighting drew near, to shelter women, children and cattle. Some property was carried away to safety, but homesteads and crops were largely abandoned, to be looted either by passing Zulu forces, or to be burnt as part of a deliberate British attempt to starve the nation into submission. As early as 12 January, just one day after the war began, the followers of Chief Sihayo kaXongo resisted British attempts to destroy his homesteads in the Batshe valley. Sihayo's retainers took up secure positions among boulders and shallow caves at the foot of the Ngedla mountain and, despite being heavily outnumbered, could only be extricated with difficulty.

The action at Sihayo's stronghold was typical of Zulu defensive actions, and suggests something of what the army might have achieved had it abandoned the more cumbersome and ultimately outdated mass-attack techniques. Similarly, on 1 June, British cavalry advancing ahead of the main columns encountered Zulu forces in position at the foot of the eZungeni mountain, overlooking the uPhoko stream. The ground was broken, and the Zulus opened a heavy fire from the foot of the hills. The British formed a skirmish line of dismounted irregular cavalrymen, and pushed forward to destroy several *imizi*, but realising that the Zulus were making good use of the cover to slip around their flanks, decided to withdraw. A party of regular cavalry – the 17th Lancers – arrived and were keen to try their luck, but found themselves in an equally vulnerable position. They retired, having lost their adjutant to Zulu sniper fire, and were followed for several miles by the Zulus, whose skirmishing had once again proved most effective.[11]

Tactics against cavalry

Under normal circumstances, the Zulus held cavalry in no great dread. The horse was hardly known in the kingdom until the arrival of the Voortrekkers, but as early as the battle of eTaleni in April 1838 the Zulu had adapted tactics to counter mounted troops. On that occasion, part of the Zulu force was concealed in long grass, and a herd of cattle was left on a conspicuous slope to tempt a Boer advance. The tactic was largely successful, since the Boers were lured into the trap and badly mauled. The Zulus tried similar tactics a few months later on the Mahlabathini plain, again with some success. Clearly it was an effective counter against cavalry, as it very nearly worked again in 1879; at Hlobane, one Boer volunteer recalled that the local abaQulusi forces had attempted to use cattle to mask their advance.[12] On 3 July, a British patrol scouting the Mahlabathini plain, opposite oNdini, narrowly avoided the most sophisticated trap laid by the Zulus during the entire war. The patrol encountered small groups of Zulus scattered across the plain and gave chase. Only the alertness of the British commander, Lieutenant-Colonel Buller, caused him to restrain his men, and just in time: the Zulus had been leading them towards a carefully prepared patch of ground, where grass had been plaited to trap the horses, and several thousand Zulus – chiefly of the uMxapho *ibutho* – were concealed on either side. In the event the British reined in short, and the uMxapho had little option but to rise to the attack prematurely; even so, the British were only just able to extricate themselves. Chief Zibhebhu kaMapitha of the Mandlakazi, who was arguably the most innovative and determined of the mainstream Zulu commanders in 1879, is credited with having planned the attack.

The attack

When advancing to the attack, the Zulus moved with a speed and precision that surprised the British. They attacked not in dense masses at a run, but rather in open order lines, in formations perhaps 200 yards deep, and screened by skirmishers. Their pace was described as 'a very fast half-walk and half-run'[13] – probably something like a modern jogging pace. James Brickhill, a civilian interpreter who survived Isandlwana, commented that the main Zulu attack 'came on in lines, but very evenly distributed. Nowhere could you catch three men walking together, and rarely two, so that in some places their front was three-quarters of a mile in advance of their rear.'[14]

The careful use by the Zulus of cover during their advance was observed time and again by the British. Another anonymous survivor of Isandlwana noted that as the Zulus crested the Nyoni ridge and came within sight of the camp, they 'appeared almost to grow out of the earth. From rock and bush on the heights above started scores of men; some with rifles, others with shields and assegais.'[15] Lieutenant Edward Hutton of the 60th left a rather more complete description of the Zulu army deploying for the attack at Gingindlovu:

> The dark masses of men, in open order and under admirable discipline, followed each other in quick succession, running at a steady pace through the long grass. Having moved steadily round so as exactly to face our front, the larger portion of the Zulus broke into three lines, in knots and groups of from five to ten men, and advanced towards us ... [they] continued to advance, still at a run, until they were about 800 yards from us, when they began to open fire. In spite of the excitement of the moment we could not but admire the perfect manner in which these Zulus skirmished. A knot of five or six would rise and dart through the long grass, dodging from side to side with heads down, rifles and shields kept low and out of sight. They would then suddenly sink into the long grass, and nothing but puffs of curling smoke would show their whereabouts. Then they advanced again....[16]

There are echoes, in this account, of the most modern infantry tactics – fire and movement, the short rush supported by rifle-fire. Although Zulu tactics remained largely unchanged from King Shaka's time to 1879, it seems likely that these rushes from cover to cover had only developed since the introduction of firearms. Even so, battles were decided in 1879 much as

they had been under Shaka; once the *amabutho* had advanced close enough
to the enemy to chance a charge, their formations closed up, and they
rushed in to use their stabbing spears. Bertram Mitford, that ever curious
traveller, asked a group of veterans in 1882 how they would rush upon the
enemy:

> They ... went through various manoeuvres for my entertainment, showing
> me how they made the charges which proved so fatal to our troops. They
> would rush forward about fifty yards, and imitating the sound of a volley,
> drop flat amidst the grass; then when firing was supposed to have slackened,
> up they sprung, and assegai and shield in hand charged like lightning upon
> the imaginary foe, shouting 'Usutu'.[17]

The speed of this final advance was terrifying. When the British gave the
order to cease firing and fall back at Isandlwana, the Zulus were pinned
down some two or three hundred yards from the British position. Lieutenant Curling of the Artillery noted that in the time it took for his experienced men to limber his guns, the Zulus had rushed in so quickly that one
gunner had actually been stabbed as he mounted the axle-tree seat.[18] A
Zulu veteran of the battle, uMhoti of the uKhandempemvu, thought the
final charge so swift that 'like a flame the whole Zulu force sprang to its feet
and darted upon them'.[19]

The final impact was preceded, at perhaps thirty yards' range, by a shower
of throwing spears. Since these struck the enemy only a few moments before
the warriors closed hand-to-hand, they had the effect of breaking up the
enemy formations and demoralising them. Against African troops carrying
shields, they probably caused few enough casualties, but European troops
had no means of protecting themselves, and thrown spears were particularly
effective when falling among mounted troops, whose horses reacted with
terror when struck. Walter Stafford, a captain in the Natal Native Continent, recalled that as the Zulus charged home at Isandlwana, 'the assegais
came down like hailstones'.[20] As Mangwanana Mcunu of the uVe recalled, in
1879 it was also Zulu practice to fire a volley before the final charge: 'I fired
one shot with [my] gun at Isandlwana and then held it with my shield and
took hold of my assegais, it was our custom always to fire one shot and then
charge as it was a long job to load the gun again.'[21]

This is a particularly revealing passage, not only because it suggests the
inadequacies of the firearms carried by the Zulus, but also because it
indicates the extent to which they had failed to adapt their military thinking
to take advantage of them. If the Zulu began the war believing that the
large quantities of guns in their possession made them the equal of the
British, they merely assumed that it would be sufficient to use those arms in

support of their existing tactics. For the greater part of the war, they made no attempt, unlike the Xhosa on the Cape frontier, to evolve new methods of fighting which maximised the potential of their guns. The Xhosa tactics of fighting in the bush, for example, of ambushing parties of British soldiers, firing on them at close range, and then attacking, were not copied by the Zulu. Nor were the tactics adopted by the BaSotho in the wars of the 1850s and 1860s, of riding down on their enemy on horseback, and firing a volley at close range. The Zulus merely used their firearms as if they were an improved version of the throwing spear. Even then, the poor quality of those arms soon became apparent in 1879. Most of the guns were obsolete patterns, and their condition had not been improved by the Zulu reluctance to clean and test them. Some were so badly rusted that they presented more of a danger to the marksman than the target. Many, indeed, had never been accurate when new; the old 'Tower' or Brown Bess muskets, which were probably the single most common type in Zulu possession, had originally been designed to be effective when aimed at mass targets at ranges of no more than 100 yards range and even lacked rear sights to facilitate aiming. Few guns supplied by gun-runners came complete with cleaning tools and spare parts, and many warriors had only the haziest idea of how to get the best out of their weapons. King Cetshwayo had realised this, and had made some attempt to give some of his warriors elementary training before the war began, but the majority were still under the impression that the higher the sights were set on the firearm, the further it would shoot. Lieutenant Knight of 'The Buffs', who was on the receiving end of Zulu musketry at Nyezane, explained the problem:

> ... their want of skill (in firing) may be attributed in great measure to a misapprehension as to the use of the sights of their rifles. Knowing that when a white man wants to hit an object a long way off he puts up his back sight, they concluded that the effect of so doing is to cause the rifle to shoot harder, and wishing to develop the full powers of their arms at all times, they invariably used their rifles with the back-sight up, a misconception to which many a British soldier owes his life.[22]

This could of course be a disconcerting experience for anyone on the receiving end – British accounts are full of references to the disturbing effect of shot whizzing past just above head height – and often had unpleasant consequences for those in an elevated position. The use of irregular missiles, which roared past with a variety of howls or whines, could be similarly unsettling. Nevertheless, Zulu marksmanship proved disappointing throughout the war, and the case of Rorke's Drift aptly demonstrates the point. Early in the battle, the Zulus occupied a line of boulders and shallow caves which ran round the base of Shiyane hill, above the British post. In many ways an ideal sniper's nest, this position looked right down into the British perimeter at a range of three to four hundred yards. However, although the Zulu marksmen inflicted several casualties on the British force, ultimately forcing the British to abandon part of their line, their ratio of hits to shots fired was very poor. For the most part they were firing at ranges that were two or even three times beyond the effective range of their firearms, so that although a large quantity of shot struck down into the British position, it did so largely at random. Furthermore, the Zulus were firing with the evening sun in their eyes, which can hardly have improved their accuracy; and they, in turn, were being fired back at by British soldiers whose own rifles were particularly effective at just such ranges.

The superior range and performance of the British guns was undoubtedly a shock to the Zulus who first encountered it. 'We were still far away from them,' recalled Chief Zimema of the uMxapho *ibutho*, who fought at Nyezane, 'when the white men began to throw their bullets at us, but we could not shoot at them because our rifles would not shoot so far'.[23] It is true that Zulu marksmanship improved marginally throughout the war; there were a number of good shots in Zululand, many of whom had learned their craft from the professional hunting parties which flooded into the country in Mpande's reign, and they came into their own as the number of skirmishes increased. After Isandlwana the Zulus captured over 1000 Martini-Henry rifles, and 500,000 rounds of .450 Boxer ammunition. Some of these guns were used to good effect later, notably at Khambula, where fire from a group of sharp-shooters posted in the long grass sprouting from the dung-heap caused significant casualties whenever British troops forayed into the open, and even made part of their defences untenable for a time. It is interesting to note, however, that when the camp at Isandlwana was looted, many Zulus – who had presumably not been lucky enough to acquire a breech-loader – simply broke open ammunition boxes, tore the bullets out of cartridges with their teeth, and added the powder to the supply they carried for their old muzzle-loaders.[24] No doubt Mangwanana's comment that 'a gun is a coward's weapon, and a man has to be a man to fight with assegais. If a man is a man he will fight at close quarters',[25] reflected the disillusion felt by many warriors with the European weapons they possessed, and reinforced the essentially conservative desire to rely on the proven fighting techniques of the past.

Command in battle

It was the usual practice of senior Zulu commanders to direct the battle from a safe position in the rear, usually from an eminence which gave them a commanding view of the battle as it unfolded. Fynn observed Shaka watching the fight at Ndolowane in 1826 from just such a position,[26] whilst Cetshwayo directed the uSuthu from a ridge overlooking the battlefield at 'Ndondakusuka.[27] Ntshingwayo and Mavumengwana took up a position above a slight cliff on the iNyoni heights at Isandlwana, while Mnyamana kaNgqengelele Buthelezi was spotted by the British at Khambula issuing commands from a knoll overlooking the line of the Zulu approach. Zulu commanders were expected not to expose themselves unnecessarily to the enemy, and from their elevated position directed the battle by means of runners. Regimental *izinduna*, however, frequently led their men into battle themselves. A number of important individuals held commands in the *impi* at Isandlwana, for example, and took their share of the fighting; both Zibhebhu kaMapitha and the king's own brother, Prince Ndabuko ka-Mpande, pursued the British fugitives right down to the Mzinyathi river. Prince Dabulamanzi kaMpande led the attack on Rorke's Drift himself; he was later slightly wounded commanding the right horn at Gingindlovu, as Zibhebhu had been at Isandlwana. The chiefs and other men of status who held the position of *izinduna* within the *amabutho* were no less expected to lead from the front. Colonel Wood recalled that the Zulu officers were most conspicuous at Khambula, exhorting their men from the front,[28] and Cetshwayo himself later admitted that many *izinduna* had been killed there, as they had 'exposed themselves a great deal, as they attempted to lead on their men'.[29]

In urging the *amabutho* forward, often in the face of terrible fire, the *izinduna* consciously called upon the rivalry between them. The men of the various units could often be drawn to the attack by the shouting of their individual war-cries. These were potent sources of regimental pride, and, although a Zulu national war-cry was almost always used in the final assault –in 1879 it was the name of Cetshwayo's faction in the war of 1856, '*uSuthu!*' – each regiment had its own distinctive cry. For the uKhandem-pemvu, for example, it was '*Izulu!*', and British survivors of Isandlwana recalled hearing the cry as the regiment rallied to the last attack. The same regiment also used the cry '*Nqaka amatshe!*' – 'catch stones' – a phrase from their regimental chant, a boast that it would treat the enemy's bullets as contemptuously as if they were stones flung at them by a child.[30] Indeed, shouts of encouragement were a common feature of Zulu warfare, and often consisted of phrases that recalled the past glories of either the king or the particular regiment. So were taunts intended to unnerve the enemy; at Khambula, some within the Zulu army were heard to shout as they advanced, 'We are the boys from Isandlwana!'

Isandlwana, again, provides a telling example of how effective such exhortation could be. At the height of the battle, the advance of the Zulu chest and left horn had faltered under British fire, and the warriors had gone to ground in dongas and long grass. The uKhandempemvu lay directly below the Zulu commanders on the iNyoni ridge, who sent down one of its officers, Ndlaka, to urge it on. Ndlaka rushed among his men shouting, 'The Little Branch of Leaves that Extinguished the Great Fire [a well-known praise-name for Cetshwayo] gave no such order as this!'[31] With the *izinduna* urging them to 'go! and toss them into 'Maritzburg!', the uKhandempemvu rose up, braved the British fire, and rushed forward. Ndlaka himself was killed, shot through the head, but all along the line, *izinduna* of the other *amabutho* challenged their men to follow the uKhandempemvu's example. Their great rivals, the iNgobamakhosi, were particularly stung; 'Why are you lying down?' cried one of their officers, Sikizane kaNomageje. 'What was it you said to the uKhandempemvu? There are the uKhandempemvu going into the tents.'[32] In the face of this last great forward movement, the British line at Isandlwana collapsed. Later, at Khambula and oNdini, the same regiments who had challenged one another before the king again played a conspicuous part in the attacks.

Running the gauntlet

Of course, in 1879, making that final rush could be a terrible experience. In Shaka's wars, and even when fighting the Boers, the types of weapon used ensured that the Zulus suffered few casualties until they reached the immediate vicinity of the enemy. The British, however, were one of the leading industrial nations of the world, and their army possessed the best weapons the technology of the time allowed. At ranges of over 3000 yards, the attacking Zulu were subjected to artillery fire; rockets, although inaccurate, unstable and unreliable, nonetheless had a considerable destructive reach. Rifle fire was commonly opened at 800 yards, and was particularly destructive at less than 400 yards. The Gatling gun, a crude hand-cranked machine-gun which – when it did not jam – spewed out bullets at the rate of 300 a minute, was first used in action by British troops at the battle of Nyezane, and later at oNdini. In attacking a British position, the Zulus could expect to be subjected to fire from these weapons in a variety of combinations. Many Zulus in the younger *amabutho* had not seen action before, and certainly had no experience of the terrible effects of British firepower. Since it characterised the Zulu experience of battle in 1879, it is worth describing at some length.

Although the Zulu knew of artillery, they had no understanding of its principles. It was universally known to them by the term *imbayimbayi*, apparently a corruption of the English phrase 'by and bye', which was first recorded by Alan Gardiner in 1836. According to Gardiner, the term had originated in a habit of the first British adventurers to arrive in Natal, who told Zulus who enquired the purpose of their cannon that they would find out, 'by and bye'.[33] Nevertheless, the Zulu had little practical experience of artillery; small ships' guns mounted on improvised carriages were used by the Boers in 1838, but it was not until 1879 that the Zulu were exposed to its full effect. The Zulu tended to regard heavy guns as rifles writ large: 'I looked inside it afterwards,' recalled Sofikasho Zungo of iNgobamakhosi, referring to one of the British 7-pounders captured at Isandlwana, 'and could not see how the shell went in, I could see [only] the hole where it came out'.[34] When the guns were recovered at the end of the war, the British found that the Zulus had attempted to fire them by screwing rifle percussion-caps into the vents. Artillery fire could, therefore, be particularly disheartening, because its destructive effect was largely incomprehensible. 'I observed them several times,' said Gunner Carroll of the RMA, of a skirmish near Eshowe,

> looking round wondering where the [shrapnel] bullets came from, which they could not understand, the shrapnel bursting fifty yards from them and the bullets flying about their ears, it is no wonder they were startled, for to see a volley sent into their very midst and not knowing where it came from was enough to startle the bravest of them.[35]

At Isandlwana, the Zulus apparently soon noticed that before a shell fell among them, the British gunners stood back from their piece; the warriors gave a warning shout 'Moya!' – 'Air!' – and then threw themselves down to avoid the blast. Although one or two shots at Isandlwana were particularly destructive,[36] both British survivors and some Zulu veterans suggested that artillery fire at the battle was largely ineffectual. This was perhaps true – the British had only two field guns at Isandlwana, and those were 7-pounders whose muzzle velocity was notoriously low, and seems to have caused fewer casualties among the widely spaced Zulus than might have been expected. Nevertheless, this impression was essentially misleading, for after the battle it was admitted that the uKhandempemvu ibutho – whose attack had taken them into the face of the guns – had suffered noticeably from shellfire, and in the later battles the British were able to mass their guns to good effect. 'Ubain-bai?' commented Mitford, on the reaction of a group of veterans to the effect of shellfire:

> Haow! Didn't like them at all. First the warriors tried to dodge them, and scattered when they saw them coming, till at last on one occasion when a lot had dispersed from where the missile was expected to fall, it astonished them by dropping right in the thick of the group that had just dodged it. Arms, and legs, and heads flew in every direction.[37]

These casualties were no doubt exaggerated by the Zulu persistence in launching attacks in the open, and by the ineffectiveness of natural cover as a protection against shellfire. 'There were many "bye and byes",' recalled Sofikasho Zungu of Khambula, 'and they fired pot-legs [shrapnel or canister] at us and we died in hundreds.'[38] After Khambula, the British burial parties noted that here and there clumps of Zulus were found together, horribly mangled by shellfire. Sofikasho Zulu has left a graphic account of what it was like to be on the receiving end: 'I saw one [Zulu],' he said, 'whose head was struck off right next to me, and his body stood up shivering with arms clenched until it fell.'[39]

The British placed great faith in rockets which, despite their inadequacies, were thought to strike terror into unsophisticated enemies because of the noise, smoke and sparks they emitted in flight. The Zulus regarded them with some curiosity, but it was not so much their psychological effect that they dreaded as their destructive power. At Nyezane Chief Zimema recalled that they thought the British were firing 'a long pipe' at them.[40] Some referred to rockets as 'paraffin', from the combustible liquid that white traders had introduced among them. Others, more romantically, and with perhaps a touch more horror, called rockets *imbane weZulu* – 'lightning from heaven'.[41] Although the number of men killed by rocket fire in 1879 was few, the burn injuries caused by the rocket's propellant were horrific. At Nyezane, where the British themselves were generally disappointed in the effectiveness of their rockets, one observer nonetheless noted that they 'scorch whoever they go hear – we saw several bodies with burn marks upon them',[42] and another noted that several Zulu corpses 'were terribly burned'. Sofikasho claimed that 'the paraffin that was shot at us made a great noise and burnt natives so badly they couldn't recognise who they were.'[43] After the war, British travellers noted a number of men bearing curious scars from rocket-fire; one, apparently wounded at Isandlwana, was 'marked about the chest and shoulders as if he had been tattooed with Chinese white',[44] whilst another had been struck on the chest by a rocket which 'had literally melted the flesh off his chest, then taking a course down his side and leg, had cut a deep furrow down his thigh and calf, making the leg four inches shorter than the other one'.[45]

It was musketry fire, however, that was the most destructive, as Sihlala of the uMxapho found at Nyezane: 'The whites shot us down in numbers, in some places our dead and wounded covered the ground, we lost heavily, especially from the small guns. . . . The [rocket] killed people but the small guns are the worst.'[46]

At Isandlwana, the destructiveness of British rifle fire was noted by a number of observers. Driver Elias Tucker, RA, thought the cool and disciplined fire of the British infantry was 'cutting roads through them',[47] whilst Lieutenant Higginson of the NCC thought it 'simply swept them away'.[48] This was only to be expected, since the Martini-Henry rifle, with which the British regulars were armed, was a highly effective weapon at close range, provided a natural tendency to blaze away at random was kept under control by the officers. At Rorke's Drift, Harry Lugg of the Natal Mounted Police recalled with awe that at close range the British fire 'knocked them down as fast as they came'.[49] After the battle, Lieutenant Chard commented on the appalling injuries this fire had caused – heads split open or blown apart by the heavy calibre bullets.[50] Yet at the same battle, another member of the British garrison, Private Hitch of the 24th, noted the curious disregard with which the Zulus reacted to gunfire. 'It was not until the bayonet was freely used that they flinched in the least bit,' he said. 'Had the Zulus taken the bayonet as freely as they took the bullets, we could not have stood more than fifteen minutes.'[51] Although one warrior's observation that at Isandlwana the Zulus merely tossed their heads from side to side to let the bullets pass smacks of bravado, there is no doubt that, early in the war at least, the Zulu belief in their *intelezi* medicine, and their stoic disregard for a menace that could not in any case be seen, led to them exposing themselves to an extraordinary degree to rifle fire.

It says much for the reserve of raw courage summoned by individual Zulu that they were prepared to sustain attacks in the face of such fire until it became clear that there was no hope of victory. Sofikasho Zungu, talking of oNdini, described the shock and confusion of those who experienced it: 'There was one great roar of big guns and smoke from them, and also the flames of paraffin that I saw at Kamboola. We soon broke and ran, there was such a roar of guns we were utterly bewildered. One shot went close to my head and I fell down and thought I was dead.'[52]

Perhaps the most graphic account of what it was like to be on the receiving end of British fire was left by Chief Zimema, who fought at Nyezane:

> ... we heard one of our men shout with pain as he was shot, and saw him fall. We rushed into battle ... they brought out their 'by and by' and we heard what we thought was a long pipe coming through the air towards us. ... We never got nearer than 50 paces to the English, and although we tried to climb over our fallen brothers we could not get very far ahead because the white men were firing heavily close to the ground into our front ranks, while the 'by and by' was firing over our heads into the regiments behind us. ... Some of our men had their arms torn right off by [shells]. The battle was so fierce that we had to wipe the blood and the brains of the killed and wounded from our heads, faces, arms, legs and shields after the fighting.[53]

Inevitably, as the war progressed, and the chances of victory became slimmer in each successive battle, the Zulus became more and more reluctant to endure such horrors to no good end.

'Seeing nothing but red'

It should be noted, too, that the Zulus had to pass through this ordeal even in a successful battle, and it can have only increased the ferocity of their final attack. On those occasions where they were able to penetrate the British fire zone and come to grips with the enemy, the emotional and physical strain of the suffering they had endured was released in a ferocious outburst of unrestrained violence. The warriors were, in any case, in an intensely heightened emotional state, buoyed up by the psychological effects of their preparatory rituals, a mood they most frequently characterised as collective rage. Speaking of Khambula, Mehlokazulu kaSihayo – whose regiment, the iNgobamakhosi, had, significantly, begun the attack too soon – said 'we went there cross, our hearts were full, and we intended to do the same as at Isandlwana'.[54] Mgelija Ngema of the uVe recalled that 'my feeling towards the soldiers was very angry for them coming with their guns to kill us'.[55] By the time the Zulu warrior was therefore physically able to engage in hand-to-hand combat, the adrenalin rush of combat had narrowed his view to the stark universe of battle; he was in an emotional condition that shocked European commentators described simply as 'blood-lust'. A warrior named uNzuzi Mandla of the uVe has left the most vivid description of his state of mind during the height of the battle of Isandlwana: 'During the first phases of the battle,' he recalled, 'our eyes were dark and we stabbed everything we came across. But when we got light into our eyes again we spared what stock was left....'[56] According to Mitford, the Zulus recognised this condition as 'seeing nothing but blood!'[57]

It is possible, incidentally, that this state was further exaggerated by the use of narcotics. Tobacco was popular among the Zulus, who did not smoke it, but ground the dried leaves and took it as snuff. It was carried in vegetable gourds, nut-shells and containers of bone or horn, which were attached to a thong around the neck, or slipped through the pierced lobe of the ear. It was sometimes mixed with powdered aloe, to make it more pungent, and there are suggestions that men embarking on a campaign would further mix it with ground cannabis. If so, this would have dulled the physical effect of exhaustion and pain, and further stimulated the excitement of battle. There are frequent contemporary mentions of Zulus taking snuff during lulls in battle, and, in fact, the uNdi *amabutho* were seen to do so just before attacking Rorke's Drift. If the snuff did indeed include drugs, these references become particularly significant.

Such emotional intensity – by no means an unusual feature of any battle

– adds a hallucinogenic, nightmare quality to Zulu accounts of the fighting. At Isandlwana, many young warriors who had never seen a white man before, and who had been told to kill everything wearing clothes, stabbed repeatedly into the sacks of supplies piled up on the British wagons.[58] After Khambula, the trader Vijn was asked

> what it meant that at the beginning of the battle so many white birds, such as they had never seen before, came flying over them from the side of the Whites? And why were they attacked also by dogs and apes, clothed and carrying firearms on their shoulders? One of them even told me that he had seen four lions in the laager.[59]

At oNdini many Zulu who had been present believed that the British square had been protected by fences of corrugated iron, although no such defences existed.

As uNzuzi's account suggests, hand-to-hand fighting that involved the Zulu was extremely destructive. Since the widespread adoption of firearms by armies in Europe and North America, hand-to-hand fighting had become increasingly rare in western forms of combat. Most exchanges were decided by short-range fire-fights, one side or other usually giving away at the last minute to avoid mêlée. Hand-to-hand fighting is notoriously the most psychologically damaging form of combat, and usually shied away from as a result; it is a naked confrontation that exposes the participants to the full horror of their actions. Yet among the Zulu, because of their reliance on stabbing weapons, this was exactly the sort of fighting upon which they were dependent; indeed the word 'stabbing' was often used as a euphemism for fighting itself For the Zulu, therefore, fighting intentionally embraced those aspects from which European armies flinched; the raw primeval act of killing, at a distance close enough to see the look in the victim's eye, to smell his blood and be splashed by it. Fighting was a physical, grisly business, and part of the purpose of the preparatory rituals was undoubtedly to shelter the warrior from the terrible nature of his experience; and he was further protected by a culture that defined courage in such terms. As Mangwanana put it, 'If a man is a man he will fight at close quarters.'[60]

In the battles of Shaka's wars, combat involved a short, sharp tussle, a clatter of shields, strikes and parries, until one contestant succeeded in delivering a stab to the abdomen or rib-cage. Such fights must have been chaotic enough at the best of times, but when fighting against whites, the huge quantities of smoke produced by black-powder firearms added another element to the confusion. Mehlokazulu, whose account of Isandl-wana is one of the most complete from a Zulu source, conjures up the mayhem of the final hand-to-hand phase:

... what with the smoke, dust and intermingling of mounted men, footmen, Zulus and natives, it was difficult to tell who was mounted and who was not.... Some Zulus threw assegais at [British soldiers], others shot at them; but they did not get close – they avoided the bayonet; for any man who went up to stab a soldier was fixed through the throat or stomach, and at once fell.[61]

It is interesting that the Zulus, who showed such disregard for the bullets which so cut them down, should have 'flinched' in front of the bayonet. No doubt part of the reason was psychological – the bayonet was all too visible and tangible a threat, unlike the bullet, and the Zulus understood the full import of stabbing weapons – but the weapon itself possibly outclassed the stabbing spear. Attached to the end of a rifle, it gave the soldier a reach of six feet, perhaps twice that of the Zulu stabbing spear, and a trained and cool man had a better than average chance of transfixing his opponent before the Zulu could strike back. Nevertheless, ultimately it was only an effective weapon so long as the soldiers were able to retain some formation; when fighting individually they were vulnerable from attack in all directions, since, as Mehlokazulu explained, 'occasionally when a soldier was engaged with a soldier in front with an assegai, another Zulu killed him from behind'.[62] A warrior named uMhoti of the uKhandempemvu described the typically brutal nature – and outcome – of many of these individual struggles:

> I then attacked a soldier whose bayonet pierced my shield and while he was trying to extract it, I stabbed him in the shoulder. He dropped his rifle and seized me round the neck and threw me on the ground under him. My eyes felt as if they were bursting, and I was almost choked when I succeeded in grasping the spear which was still sticking in his shoulder and forced it into his vitals and he rolled over, lifeless. My body was covered with sweat and quivering terribly with the choking I had received from this brave man.[63]

As the 'chest and horns' finally drew together, the last stages of a successful Zulu battle were inevitably played out among a struggling mass of men which hampered further tactical movement and even individual actions. Sofikasho Zungu's lasting impression of Isandlwana was of a 'twisting mass of men'. At one point he 'suddenly noticed I was fired at from behind by some soldiers.... I would have liked to have attacked them but could not get to them.'[64] At the end, the killing achieved levels of stark primeval savagery. 'In the last struggle,' said uMhoti, 'the butts of rifles and stones were used, the soldiers having no cartridges.'[65] Each time a Zulu stabbed an enemy, he shouted the war-cry, 'uSuthu!', or 'Ngadla' – 'I have eaten!'[66]

'Dead was everything...'

Under such circumstances, the Zulus inevitably killed every living thing they came across. Partly this was the result of the urgings of their commanders to 'eat up' the enemy, a phrase that implied total destruction of not only his fighting personnel but also his dependants and livestock, so that no trace of him might survive. More significantly, however, it was the result of the destructive fury unleashed by the final onslaught. Fynn had noted with horror the Zulu slaughter of Ndwandwe non-combatants at Ndolowane in 1826, and the hunter Baldwin left a horrific description of the aftermath of the battle of 'Ndondakusuka in 1856:

> The whole air was tainted with dead bodies for the last twelve miles, which I walked against a head wind. They were lying in every possible attitude along the road, men, women, and children of all possible sizes and ages; the warriors untouched, with their war-dresses on, but all in a dreadful state of decomposition. I was never so glad of anything in my life as of getting the Tugela between me and the dead, as, what with the strong head wind and the horrible effluvia, it was quite overpowering, and proved eventually too much for the stomachs of even my [retainers]. For a long time they endeavoured, by taking widish circles, to avoid treading on, or coming very near, the dead, being very superstitious; but as we neared the Tugela, the bodies lay so thick in the road on each side that it was impossible to avoid them any longer.... I saw many instances of mothers with babies on their backs, with assegais through both, and children of all ages assegaid between the shoulder blades.[67]

This scene is not markedly different from British accounts of the devastated field of Isandlwana, or of Major Tucker's description of the Ntombe river battlefield a few hours after the Zulus retired:

> ... a fearful and horrible sight presented itself, the stillness of the spot was awful; there were our men lying about the place, some naked and some only half clad ... all the bodies were full of assegai wounds and nearly all were disembowelled ... I saw but one body that I could call unmutilated....
>
> Nearly everything had been broken or torn to pieces, the tents being in shreds and the ammunition boxes broken to atoms, the mealies and flour thrown about all over the place. They had killed all the dogs save one....[68]

'We spared no lives,' admitted Gumpega Kwabe fifty years later, 'and did not ask for mercy ourselves. We killed every white man left in the camp and the horses and cattle too.'[69] Indeed, the king repeatedly urged his *izinduna* to secure him some British prisoners, preferably officers, in order to obtain intelligence of British intentions, and as a useful bargaining counter.

'Don't you see how useful it would have been to me to have had some officer prisoners?' he asked them,[70] but their rather shame-faced reply, that they could not tell the officers from the ordinary soldiers, concealed a deeper truth, that in the heat of battle it was impossible to restrain their men from killing every enemy they came across. It is significant that the only white prisoner taken by the Zulus during the 1879 war – Trooper Grandier of Weatherley's Border Horse, captured at Hlobane – was found on the field when the fighting was over, and passions had cooled. At Isandlwana, those who cried out in Zulu for mercy were given a forceful reminder of the reality of their position: 'How can we give you mercy when you have come to us and want to take away our country and eat us up?'[71] – and slaughtered with the rest.

In the aftermath of battle, the British were shocked to witness the condition of the corpses of those killed by the Zulu. Their horror at finding men apparently 'cut to pieces' is understandable, but this was an inevitable consequence of the nature of the fighting, and of Zulu belief. Many men were repeatedly stabbed in the frenzy of combat: it was not always possible to deliver a single deadly thrust with a spear, and there was a natural tendency to keep striking at an opponent until he fell, and was therefore no longer a threat. In addition, many of those who were killed were stabbed again by Zulus coming up behind. This was in accordance with a belief known as *hlomula*, which suggested that part of the glory of overcoming a particularly dangerous foe accrued not only to the slayer, but also to others who took part in the fight and demonstrated their claim by stabbing the corpse. As Mpatshana kaSodondo put it:

> ... those hlomula'ing became more numerous by reason of the fact that they had been fighting such formidable opponents, who were like lions – for it is the custom among us in lion-hunting that the one who hiomula's first, i.e. after the first to stab, gets a leg, the second gets a foreleg, whilst the last gets the head. This custom was observed with regard to Isandlwana because it was recognised that fighting against such a foe and killing some of them was of the same high grade as lion-hunting ... anyone hlomula'ing first, second or third ... was looked on as responsible in some way for its death.[72]

Although this custom, therefore, was to some extent a mark of respect, the British were appalled, and the sight of their dead in the early battles of the war undoubtedly contributed to their thirst for revenge later in the war. Perhaps the most explicit description of the effects of the *hlomula* custom – and of the physical damage caused by Zulu weapons – can be found in the perceptive report on the body of the exiled Prince Imperial, killed on 1 June 1879:

There was one longish wound on the right breast which was evidently
mortal, for the assegai passed through the body, and the point had pene-
trated the skin of the back. There were two hurts also in the left side which
might well be mortal, and less serious wounds all over the upper part of the
chest, and one in the right thigh. The eye was out, but whether by the thrust
of an assegai or by the impact of a bullet of some kind it was impossible to
say. There was a large gash in the abdomen exposing the intestines. . . . Many
of the wounds were so slight that I think they too must have been inflicted
after death, all members of the party probably 'washing their spears', in
pursuance of some ceremonious regulation on the subject of the enemy
dead.[73]

The gash on the abdomen, noted here, was particularly significant, since
it was another important part of Zulu ritual that they *qaqa* their enemy —
that is, slash open his stomach. This, together with removing part of his
clothing, which was then worn by the man who killed him, was another
expression of the pervading dread of *umnyama*. Every Zulu who had been
contaminated by blood shed under violent circumstances was obliged to
zila, to abstain from the normal activities of daily life until he had undergone the necessary cleansing rituals. A body lying out in the African sun
very quickly begins to swell as the gases expand, and the Zulus believed that
this was the spirit of the dead warrior trying to escape. His death placed an
obligation on the killer to open the corpse's stomach, to allow the spirit to
escape: if he did not, the slayer would be haunted by the troubled spirit,
who would expose him to the full horror of *umnyama*. He would be spiritually unclean, and his own body would bloat, until madness obscured his
suffering. At Isandlwana, recalled Mehlokazulu, 'all the dead bodies were
cut open, because if that had not been done the Zulus would have become
swollen like the dead bodies'.[74] For the most part, the Zulus removed the
tunics and shirts of British dead, but left them with their trousers on. As
Mpatshana explained:

> It is our custom for one killing another to take off the deceased's things and
> put them on, even the penis-cover. He *zila's* with them by so doing. . . . If he
> has killed two or more he will take articles from each and put them on. He
> will not put on his own things until the doctor has treated him and given him
> medicines to suck from the finger-tips. . . . We took off the European's things
> at Isandlwana; they were all stripped. This was done to zila with. The things
> of the deceased are put on, for the warrior does not want his things smeared
> with blood and things of harmful influence.[75]

In the aftermath of such carnage, a battle where a Zulu army had been
successful was little more than an abattoir. The memory of the fresh

slaughter was still vivid to uNsuzi Mandla fifty years later, and betrays the utter lack of dignity of death in combat. 'The green grass was red with running blood,' he said, 'and the veld was slippery, for it was covered with the brains and entrails of the slain. The bodies of black and white were mixed up together with the carcasses of horses, oxen and mules.'[76] It was a sight that left few who saw it with any illusions that death in battle carried with it even the smallest trace of glory.

NOTES

1. Webb (ed.), *Zulu Boy's Recollections*.
2. John Laband, *Kingdom in Crisis*.
3. Mitford, *Through the Zulu Country*.
4. See Pieres, *House of Phalo*.
5. Fynney, *TZA*.
6. For the Zulu movements at Isandlwana, see Knight, *Zulu*, and Laband, *Kingdom in Crisis*.
7. Mitford, *Through the Zulu Country*.
8. Essex's evidence, WO 33/34.
9. Huw M. Jones in *Why Khambula?*, SOTQ 74, September 1993 argues that the Zulu tactics in the northern reaches were heavily influenced by Swazi practices; without necessarily denying a Swazi influence, the present author sees little to distinguish them from tactics employed by the Zulus around Eshowe, and in the face of the final British advance on oNdini.
10. Lieutenant W.N. Lloyd, *The Defence of Ekowe*, Woolwich, 1881 (reprinted in *Natalia* V, December 1975). For full account of the skirmishing around Eshowe, see Castle and Knight, *Fearful Hard Times*.
11. The most detailed account of this incident is John Laband's *Chopping Wood with a Razor; the Skirmish at eZungeni Mountain and the Unnecessary Death of Lieutenant Frith* in SOTQ 74.
12. Account of Daniel Kritzinger in Knight (ed.), *Kill Me in the Shadows*, ibid.
13. Letter from Lieutenant H. Smith-Dorrien to his father after Isandlwana, reproduced in Frank Emery's *The Red Soldier*.
14. James Brickhill's account, *The Natal Magazine*, September 1879.
15. Letter from an unidentified officer 'attached to Colonel Glyn's Column', *The Times*, 10 April 1879.
16. Hutton's account, in Frank Emery, *The Red Soldier*.
17. Mitford, *Through the Zulu Country*.
18. Curling, letter in *The Standard*, 27 March 1879, and evidence at Court of Inquiry reported in *The Times*, 17 March 1879.
19. Papers of Trooper F. Symons, Natal Carbineers, in Killie Campbell Africana Library collections.
20. Watler Stafford, account dated 1939 in Talana Museum, Dundee, Natal.
21. Account of Mangwanana Mcunu in Knight (ed.) *Kill Me in the Shadows*, SOTQ 74.
22. Captain H.R. Knight, *Reminiscences of Etshowe, United Services Magazine*, Vol. VIII, London, 1894. Quoted in Castle and Knight, *Fearful Hard Times*.
23. Account of Chief Zimema, *Natal Mercury* supplement, 22 January 1929.

24. Mitford, visiting the site in 1882, found empty cartridges bearing teeth-marks; *Through the Zulu Country.*

25. Account of Mangwanana Mcunu in Knight (ed.) *Kill Me in the Shadows, SOTQ* 74.

26. Fynn, *Diary.*

27. For an account of the 'Ndondakusuka battle, see Gilbert Torlage's *The War of the Children* in *SOTQ* 74, September 1993.

28. Wood, *Midshipman to Field Marshal.*

29. Cetshwayo's Story, in Webb and Wright, *A Zulu King Speaks.*

30. Wally Erskine, who survived Isandlwana, heard the shout there; see his letters in the *Times of Natal*, 26 February 1879.

31. This well-known incident is referred to in many Zulu accounts of the battle; see, for example, the warrior of the uMbonambi in Mitford, *Through the Zulu Country.* Ndlaka's words are recorded by H.C. Lugg in *Historic Natal and Zululand*, Pietermaritzburg, 1979.

32. Account of Mpatshana kaSodondo, Webb and Wright, *JSA* 3.

33. Gardiner, *Narrative.*

34. Account of Sofikasho Zungu in Knight (ed.), *Kill Me in the Shadows, SOTQ* 74.

35. Unpublished diary in family possession; author's copy.

36. 'The artillery threw about twenty-five shots from different parts of the field during the battle. Four of these were very effective, each tearing up what appeared to be an acre of ground in the enemy's masses. . . .' Brickhill, *Natal Magazine.*

37. Mitford, *Through the Zulu Country.*

38. Account of Sofikasho Zungu in Knight (ed.) *Kill Me in the Shadows, SOTQ* 74.

39. Ibid.

40. Chief Zimema's account, *Natal Mercury* supplement, 1929.

41. See Colonel Harry Sparks, *Chelmsford's Ultimatum*, Killie Campbell Library. There are references, too, to the iNgobamakhosi striking up with an improvised chant about the 'lightning of heaven' around the time they encountered rockets at Isandlwana. See Knight, *Zulu.*

42. Lieutenant Robarts, Durban Mounted Rifles, letters in family possession, quoted in Castle and Knight, *Fearful Hard Times.*

43. Account of Sofikasho Zungu, Knight (ed.), *Kill Me in the Shadows, SOTQ* 74.

44. Mitford, *Zulu Country.*

45. Captain W.R. Ludlow, *Zululand and Cetewayo*, London, 1882.

46. 'Statement of Sihlahla taken by J.W. Shepstone, 3 June 1879', *BBP* C2454.

47. See Frank Emery, *Isandlwana: a Survivor's Story in Soldiers of the Queen*, Issue 18, September 1979.

48. Higginson's report of 18 February 1879 in WO 32/7726.

49. Harry Lugg's account, *North Devon Herald*, 24 April 1879.

50. Chard's letter written at Queen Victoria's request, February 1880, included in Norman Holme's *The Silver Wreath*, London, 1979.

51. Hitch's account reproduced in Holme, *The Silver Wreath.*

52. Account of Sofikasho Zungu in Knight (ed.), *Kill Me in the Shadows, SOTQ* 74.

53. Account of Chief Zimema, *Natal Mercury* supplement, 1929.

54. Account of Mehlokazulu kaSihayo, included in Charles Norris-Newman, *In Zululand with the British*, London, 1880.

55. Account of Mgelija Ngema in Knight (ed.) *Kill Me in the Shadows, SOTQ* 74.

56. Account of Nzuzi Mandla, *Natal Mercury* supplement, 22 January 1929.

57. Mitford, *Through the Zulu Country.*

58. Laband, *Kingdom in Crisis*.

59. Vijn, *Cetshwayo's Dutchman*.

60. Account of Mangwanana Mcunu, Knight (ed.), *Kill Me in the Shadows, SOTQ* 74.

61. Account of Mehlokazulu kaSihayo, in Norris-Newman, *In Zululand*.

62. Ibid.

63. Account of uMhoti, Symons papers, KCL.

64. Account of Sofikasho Zungu, Knight (ed.) *Kill Me in the Shadows, SOTQ* 74.

65. Account of uMhoti, Symons Papers, KCL.

66. See Mtshayankomo kaMagolwane, Webb and Wright, *JSA* 4.

67. Baldwin, *African Hunting and Adventure*.

68. Tucker's letter to his father, March 1879, reproduced in Frank Emery's *The Red Soldier*.

69. Account of Kumbeka Kwabe, *Natal Mercury* supplement, 22 January 1879.

70. Cetshwayo's Story, in Webb and Wright, *A Zulu King Speaks*.

71. Account of uNzuzi Mandla, *Natal Mercury* supplement, 22 January 1929.

72. Account of Mpatshana kaSodondo, Webb and Wright, *JSA* 3.

73. Report in *The Times of Natal*, quoted in *Moodie's Zulu War*.

74. Account of Mehlokazulu kaSihayo in Norris-Newman, *In Zululand with the British*.

75. Account of Mpatshana kaSodondo, Webb and Wright, *JSA* 3.

76. Account of uNzuzi Mandla in *Natal Mercury* supplement, 22 January 1929.

CHAPTER 7

Wet with Yesterday's Blood

After the battle of oNdini in July 1879, when Zulu resistance to the British military presence had largely ceased, a British officer, Captain William Molyneux, travelling about the country, made a perceptive observation on the price ordinary Zulus had made in defending their kingdom:

> One large kraal I visited . . . was full of wounded men, who were as friendly as possible . . . and as merry as could be. One had lost two brothers at Isandlwana, and had been wounded at Ulundi himself; his regiment was the Nkobamakosi . . . commanded by Usicwelecwele. How he had got home in a fortnight he scarcely knew; it was very hard work, for he had been wounded in the thigh, but the other boys helped him. . . . An old man, who had lost half his right arm . . . had fought . . . at Inyezane and Ginghilovo, and at the latter place the bone of his arm had been smashed by a bullet below the elbow; but he had cut the loose part off, and the wound had healed now. The many little mounds outside, covered with stones, told how many of the poor fellows had crawled home simply to die.[1]

Molyneux's observation reflected a grim truth witnessed by Henry Fynn fifty years earlier; that whether in victory of defeat, the Zulus had no organised system to remove their wounded from the battlefield, or supply them with first aid. 'Many of Shaka's wounded managed to crawl on hands and knees in the hope of getting assistance,' Fynn noted after the battle of Ndolowane, 'but for the enemy's wounded there was no hope.'[2] The duty of succouring the wounded simply fell to the friends and relatives of the injured, who had to pick over the battlefield once the fighting was over to search them out. Such were the ties of kin and friendship that this method was often surprisingly effective; in 1882 the traveller Bertram Mitford met a young Zulu who had suffered a bad leg wound 'at Isandhlwana soon after the fight commenced, and had lain upon the ground until two of his brothers carried him out of harm's way.'[3] Indeed, so many were the wounded after Isandlwana that as King Cetshwayo himself later admitted, the army 'remained encamped close to the battlefield for three days, chiefly owing to the large number of wounded, including two sons of Ntshing-wayo, whom they could not move; many of the wounded were in a dying state'.[4]

After the British victory at Khambula in March 1879, British patrols noted that in some sections of the retreating Zulu army, every two able men carried a third, wounded, between them. Yet this care was essentially haphazard, and the prospects for an injured warrior in the immediate aftermath of even a successful battle were not good. Some men simply had no kinsmen to think of them, while others inevitably became separated in the confusion of combat, and it was easy to miss individual wounded lying in areas where fighting had been fierce, among long grass, or in difficult terrain. Countless Zulu must have bled to death simply because they were not found in time and given even elementary treatment. Furthermore, no matter how dedicated or compassionate their colleagues, there was a limit to how long the wounded could be carried, especially in the face of physical obstacles. After Rorke's Drift the British noticed piles of bloodied Zulu shields on the banks of the Mzinyathi river, suggesting that the wounded had been dragged at least that far. But the river was chest-high, and crossing it was a difficult enough task for an uninjured man, and the likelihood that many of the wounded were safely got across had to be slim. Similarly, after Nyezane, Zulu dead were found in large numbers on the banks of the Nyezane river, where those carrying wounded away had been forced to abandon them in the face of the British pursuit. Even those who were evacuated successfully faced the prospect of a long and agonising journey to their homestead. Although a life in the bush had taught most Zulu men how to staunch bleeding by thrusting a handful of grass into the open wound, or to strap up broken limbs with improvised splints, there was no likelihood of specialist medical care until the wounded returned home. Those whose friends did not find them, and who were therefore abandoned on the field, had simply to make their escape as best they could, and the British were often both appalled and astonished by their endurance. Lieutenant Robarts of the Victoria Mounted Rifles described the stoicism displayed by the Zulu wounded after Nyezane:

> ... very pitiful It was to see the poor fellows lying with fearful wounds. They were very quiet, and seemed to bear pain well, no groaning or crying out. We could not do anything for them except give them water to drink ... one of them had crawled at least a quarter of a mile with a broken leg. One poor fellow was in an antbear hole about 70 yards from the vedettes in front of them, and they did not see him for a long time until he called out – asking them to find him.[5]

Each battle no doubt produced a crop of similar stories, and wounded men haunted the vicinity of the battlefield for days or even weeks afterwards. Several days after the battle of Gingindlovu, another British observer found a wounded warrior who had been hit in the heel and ankle, and who had crawled 'miles on his hands and knees, till the latter were swollen in the most horrible way and all the flesh worn off'.[6] One Zulu had managed to crawl back to the previous night's bivouac, some miles from the engagement, before succumbing to a terrible gunshot wound to the stomach. Mgelija Ngema of the uVe was wounded three times at Khambula – 'here in my leg and thigh and also here in the face ... I suffered great pain as my leg bone was shattered and many pieces of bone have come out.' 'I crawled away,' he admitted, 'and it took me over a month to get back [home].' Yet Mgelija lived to tell his story as late as 1936.[7]

Medical facilities

In truth, the Zulu warrior had little option but to bear his suffering as best he could. Inured to a degree of hardship in his daily life, he had no hope of immediate and sophisticated medical attention, and was dependent on his own resources of strength and courage for survival. Evidence of his capacity to survive often amazed Europeans who witnessed it, and it is worth dwelling for a moment on their descriptions, since they suggest not only something of the truly horrific range of wounds that warriors could expect to suffer in combat, but also a capacity to endure which is indicative of their general level of fitness, and the extent to which the *izinyanga* were able to administer successful treatment. In the 1850s, the trader Leslie met a man who

> was covered with scars gained in battle. He had a shot in his thigh; it came out at his groin, struck his knee, and fell to the ground; he had a scar across his head from the butt-end of a gun; these he got from the Boers. His shoulder was all scarred from an encounter with a lion. His thigh was pierced by a buffalo. His knee was laid open by an assegai in the battle between Panda and Dingaan. He had a gash down his back, and another through his arm, and last of all, he had his arm broken by a shot at Endona Gosuku ['Ndondakusuka].[8]

Lieutenant Henry Harford, who had been through the Isandlwana campaign, had a similar experience, later discussing the battle with a Zulu who had received a full measure of British firepower, all, apparently, on the same occasion:

> One bullet had gone through his hand, three had gone through his shoulder and smashed his shoulder blade, two had cut the skin and slightly into the flesh right down the chest and stomach, and one had gone clean through the fleshy part of the thigh. The others were mere scratches in comparison with

these, but there he was, after about eight months, as well as ever and ready for another set-to.[9]

In 1902, Harry Lugg, who, as a trooper in the Natal Mounted Police, had fought at Rorke's Drift, also met one of those who had been on the other side of the barricade. This warrior, too, had suffered a remarkable number of injuries, all in the same battle – one bullet had creased his scalp, another had hit his left shoulder, and two had passed through the calf of his leg.[10] Similar incidents were remembered by the Zulus; a warrior named Ndube kaManqondo of the uMxapho *ibutho* was shot at oNdini: the bullet struck him under the left arm and exited through the top of his back, breaking 'one or two ribs'. He survived, and the incident earned him the praise-name 'The one who is hampered when lying down; his side is red'.[11] Mkehlengana recalled that his father, Zulu kaNogandaya, a ferocious warrior of Shaka's day, suffered five serious wounds during his career:

1, just above knee-cap, left leg, assegai, flesh wound, entered on one side and out the other; 2, about eight inches further up on the same leg, flesh wound, assegai, in one side, out other; 3, high up outer part of left arm, causing him for time being to lose the use of it; 4, in the small of the back, left side; 5, slight one on the chest. He used to boast that no wound could ever enter his body.[12]

This last comment is particularly revealing, since it must be noted that all of these injuries were of a similar nature; they were essentially flesh wounds, or at least did not involve damage to major internal organs or the head. The Zulu *izinyanga* were quite capable of dealing with cuts, fractures and piercing injuries, so long as the wounds were clean and no infection followed. Zulu medicine, indeed, consisted largely of measures to counter infection, and sew up open wounds. A description of the injuries sustained by Diyikana kaHlakanyana of the iMpohlo *ibutho*, wounded in one of King Dingane's campaigns in the 1830s, suggests the sort of treatment which was administered:

He had three large wounds on the body. One was on the head, extending from above the right eye to the ear; another was on the chest, from above the nipple to the right shoulder; another on the stomach, to the side and round to the back where the ribs end. That one had to be stitched up with a sinew; his intestines were thoroughly washed and pushed back inside.[13]

Certainly, great warriors who ranked as *izilomo*, the king's favourites, were assured of the best attention. The king, on hearing that they were wounded, often sent his personal *izinyanga* to attend them. Isaacs recalls that when, on one occasion, he suffered so badly from a boil on his foot that he could not walk, Shaka sent a doctor to attend him,[14] and references to the king's *izinyanga* being sent to help men wounded in battle continue up to the end of the 1879 war.

The *izinyanga*, in their capacity as herbalists, had a limited range of natural medicines, mostly leaves and moss, which they applied to wounds. These were a crude but nonetheless valid counter to infection, and British observers were often surprised at how well individual Zulu recovered. Dr Blair Browne, a conscientious and inquisitive Scottish surgeon who accompanied the British forces, examined a number of Zulus at the end of hostilities, and observed:

> The number of simple penetrations of muscles was remarkable. I found one with the most distinct marks of a gunshot wound of the knee, which anyone would have said, from the line of flight the bullet must have taken, and from the situation of wounds of entrance and exit, must have penetrated the joint. The bullet hit the inner border of the patella grooving it distinctly, and made its exit posterially half an inch internally to the tendons forming the outer upper margin of the popliteal space. A month after the injury it was completely healed, the joint being perfectly mobile, without aid of surgery. Through an interpreter he told me all about the progress of healing and the means adopted to get it well. There is a small flat-leafed orchid which grows plentifully on the Veldt. A leaf of this was secured on both wounds and changed occasionally; this was all that was done.[15]

John Gill, a colleague of Browne's, added details observed from wounded Zulus captured at Khambula:

> They somehow crawl out of doors every day and nurse their fractured limbs with both hands, squeezing the wounds a good deal, and constantly washing them with a small stream of water, which they cleverly manage to eject from their own mouths on to the wounds, though held at a distance of two feet or more. One man, shot through the head of the tibia – a fearful smash, knee-joint opened in all directions – has got quite fat under the above treatment and ordinary soldier's rations; the joint is of course in a very bad position, but I suppose he will eventually recover.[16]

Yet the impression given by all of these optimistic accounts is essentially misleading. The nature of the injuries which *izinyanga* could treat successfully was limited, and their skill was certainly insufficient to deal with the full horror of the war of 1879. Because of its relatively high velocity, bullets fired by British Martini-Henry's tended to clip cleanly through muscle and flesh, causing wounds that were not fundamentally different from common stab wounds, and could easily be stitched up. Their effect on striking bone, however, was quite literally shattering, since the force of the blow often splintered long bones lengthways. Even British surgeons, whose medical knowledge had improved dramatically over the previous century, had no treatment for such injuries beyond amputation; as Molyneux's account suggests, the Zulu had also to rely on the same treatment, but without the benefit of European anaesthetics and medicines. Such injuries, along with wounds to the chest or head, were usually fatal, 'not so much ... by the deadliness of the wound', as Lieutenant Hutton of the 60th noted after Gingindlovu, 'as by the ... shock to the system of impact'.[17] Indeed, despite the incidents quoted above, it seems that a greater proportion of those wounded in the battles of 1879, even those who lived long enough to reach their homes, eventually died of their injuries. As Bertram Mitford observed in 1882:

> I was surprised at the fewness of wounded men I fell in with during my progress through the country. Whether, owing to rude surgery, numbers died whom the most ordinary skill could easily have saved, I cannot say, but considering that every man with whom I conversed had taken part in one or more of the battles, the fewness of those who had wounds to show *was* rather remarkable.[18]

It is possible to do no more than speculate whether such a proportion of fatalities differed greatly from the earlier battles against African enemies, but the sheer destructive power of the British weapons would suggest logically that it did.

The dead

And those who died on the battlefield? The last rites due to them, such as they were, were also in the care of their friends and relatives. As Mpatshana of the uVe explained of Isandlwana: 'The bodies were not buried. But those of our *impi* were here and there covered over with their shields - it is put over by a relative or friend. Many were not covered because their friends etc. did not look about sufficiently and find the corpses.'[19]

In Zulu culture, it was not the body of the fallen which was important, but his spirit. In peacetime, it was necessary to perform a number of important mourning rituals to ensure the spirit's safe passage to the realm of the ancestors, but Mgelija's blunt comment that 'when a soldier's killed by an assegai he is down and finished with'[20] probably reflects the fact that warriors were already prepared for the possibility of death in battle by the rituals they undertook before the campaign started. Their friends were

required only to perform a token burial as a mark of respect, either to cover
them over with a shield, or place the body in some convenient hole. After
Isandlwana many Zulu dead were tumbled into a donga at the foot of the
iNyoni heights, which cut across the army's line of withdrawal. Others were
buried in grain-pits in nearby abandoned homesteads, or even in ant-bear
holes. The phrase used to describe the death of a warrior in battle was that he
'was left behind'[21] on the battlefield, and indeed he was, both figuratively
and literally. The enemy dead, of course, were left where they fell, and no
attempt was made to bury them; indeed, once the passion of conflict had
passed and the dead grew stiff, they became a potent source of *umnyama*, to
be avoided at all cost. The British noted many times after a victory that their
African allies – whom they tried to employ on burial details – showed a
reluctance to touch a cold corpse which bordered on superstitious dread.

Because of this, human remains littered Zulu battlefields for years after.
When British burial parties first visited Isandlwana three months after the
fight, they found that, although scavengers – vultures, domestic dogs,
jackals, even perhaps hyenas – had scattered some of the remains, other
bodies were still curiously intact. By opening up the stomach cavity, the
Zulus had facilitated a natural process of mummification, and despite
prolonged exposure to the elements, skin and hair remained on many of the
corpses, so that some were still recognisable. Although the British made
only cursory attempts to bury Zulu dead left on battlefields where they were
victorious, they were particularly concerned to cover up all remains at
Isandlwana, where it soon became impossible to distinguish between British
and Zulu dead. They were, nevertheless, frequently exposed by the summer
rains. As recently as the 1960s, bones of Zulus buried in nearby dongas were
revealed by a particularly heavy storm. It was worse on battlefields where no
attempt had been made to cover them over; so many remains were visible
for years after along the bank of a little stream which runs through part of
the 'Ndondakusuka battlefield that it has been known as *mathambo* – 'bones'
– ever since. Skulls were clearly visible on the 1884 civil war battlefield of
eTshaneni well into the twentieth century. Photographs of the oNdini
battlefield, apparently taken in 1880, show it littered with scattered long
bones and skulls. The traveller Mitford, walking across it one night in 1882,
found 'at every step skulls, gleaming white amid the grass, grin to the moon
with upturned faces and eyeloss sockets'.[22] H.P. Braadvedt, whose father
was a missionary at Mahlabathini, recalled that when he was a lad in the
1880s, he was scouting along the banks of a stream, looking for a place to
go fishing, when 'I was considerably startled by the sight of two almost
complete skeletons behind a bush. Probably these men fell in the Ulundi
battle, as at one time numerous skeletons lay scattered over the Ulundi
plains.' So prolific were the remains around oNdini that a local trader hit

upon the idea of collecting them together and shipping them to Durban to be used as bonemeal fertiliser; fortunately, news of his plan leaked out, and the dead were at least spared that indignity.[23]

Post-combat cleansing rituals

For the living, those who had come closest to the action were considered polluted by the *umnyama* released by the violent shedding of blood. Those who had killed one or more of the enemy and those who had *hlomula*'d a corpse were known as *izinxweleha*, and together with those who had been wounded themselves, were considered contaminated; they were unable to rejoin normal society until they had undergone cleansing rituals at the hands of the *izinyanga*. Nathaniel Isaacs had the possibly unique experience, for a white man, of undergoing these rituals when he was wounded during one of Shaka's punitive raids, and has left a valuable – if sceptical – description of what it entailed:

> For this purpose, the inyanger, or doctor, has a young heifer killed as a sacrifice to the Spirit for the speedy recovery of the patient; or rather, as I conceived, for the purpose of having the beef to eat. The excrements are taken from the small entrails, which, with some of the gall and some roots, are parboiled and given to be drunk. The patient is told (quite uselessly, I think) not to drink too much, but to take three sips, and sprinkle the remainder over his body. I refused to drink the mixture; my olfactory organs were too much disturbed during the process of preparing it to render partaking of it practicable. The inyanger, from my refusal, broke out in an almost unappeasable rage, and said 'that unless I drank of the mixture, I could not be permitted to take milk, fearing the cows might die, and if I approached the king I should make him ill': expostulation was vain, and being too weak to resist, I took some of the abominable compound; he then directed me to take a stick in my hand, which he presented to me, told me to spit on it, point it three times at the enemy, say 'eezie' every time, and afterwards throw it towards them. This was done in all cases of the wounded as a charm against the power of the enemy. After this I was directed to drink of a decoction of roots for the purpose of a vomit, so that the infernal mixture might be ejected. The decoction was not unpleasant, but it had no effect in removing the nauseous draught, the pertinacity of which to remain baffled the doctor's skill. I, however, had his permission to take milk, the only thing in my situation the least palatable, the more so, as it indicated the doctor's foolish ceremony to be at an end, which gratified me, as I wanted repose. He brought me some powder, which he wished to apply to the wound, but I resisted, and he did not force it. . . .[24]

After Isandlwana, the *izinxweleha* were very numerous. It took up to five days for the army to return to the royal homesteads on the Mahlabathini plain, travelling slowly because of the wounded. Even then, many men were so exhausted that they went straight home, rather than reporting to the king for the customary appraisal of the *amabutho*'s performance. The *izinxweleha* and tht wounded were separated off for, as Mpatshana – who had been wounded in the hand – explained, 'not one of us was brought into the presence of the king on our arrival, on the ground that that would have been a source of evil influence on the king'.[25] The king appointed particular homesteads where the *izinxweleha* and the wounded were to live until they had been properly doctored, and provided them with cattle to eat and the necessary medicines. The *izinxweleha*, still wearing the clothes of the dead and carrying their spears encrusted with dried gore, were referred to with some awe as being 'wet with yesterday's blood'.

It is interesting that the Zulus required cleansing rituals from those who had been most involved in combat – those who had killed and those who had been injured themselves – exactly those, indeed, who were most likely to suffer from those conditions now recognised by western doctors as post-traumatic stress. Zulu culture had no recognition of such a condition, and identified its symptoms as manifestations of the evil influence of the *umnyama* unleashed by violent death. Mangwanana Mcunu of the uVe recalled a curious incident of psychological injury at Isandlwana, and its sequel:

> ... one of the soldiers was chased up the rocks by a member of the Nokenke Regiment, who was transferred to our regiment as an *induna*, called Muti Ntshangase. This soldier could speak Zulu and appealed to Muti saying, 'Do not kill me in the sun, kill me in the shadows'. I imagine he wanted to get a place to hide. Muti stabbed him to death. It was a funny thing that we all talked of that Muti went mad soon after. Cetewayo was told of this incident. Muti was taken down to Ulundi from Isandhlawana under control and Cetewayo, who thought a lot of him, sent for some Shangane Doctors, to try to make him right again, and they succeeded. ...[26]

The cleansing ceremonies provided a crucial framework of psychological support, which recognised the emotional damage caused by combat, and recast feelings of horror, shame and guilt into forms that were deeply rooted in Zulu culture, and thereby allowed warriors not only to externalise them, but also to exorcise them.

The *izinxweleha* were separated off for four or five days. Each day they were required to go down to a nearby river, carrying their blood-stained spears point-upright, and singing the chants they had sung on their way to battle. At a point downstream from where drinking water was drawn, they stripped off and bathed. Many of them still wore necklaces containing charms and powdered medicine, and this was sufficient for most of them to be able to observe the necessary rituals, without the assistance of an *inyanga*. This consisted of *ncinda*'ing, sucking medicines from the finger-tips and squirting it through the mouth. Mpatshana's account confirms both Isaacs's experience, and the essentially cathartic nature of the ceremony:

> The [pot]sherd is put on the fire-place and the fire lit; then the stomach-contents (umswani) of a beast are squeezed into it. When boiling occurs, the medicine for sucking from the fingertips is poured in; then the sucking of the medicine takes place with both hands, and squirting of the liquid from the mouth toward the foe, saying as this is done. 'Come out, evil spirit; come out, mtakati [evil spirit]; fall, mtakati.'
>
> A man will ... stick his assegais into the ground near him as he takes the medicine. He will jump [over] the sherd, this way and that, squirting the medicine as he does so, this way and that, in the direction of the foe.[27]

Apportioning the honours of war

When all had undergone this treatment, they were summoned to the king, but before they were allowed into his presence they underwent a further *ncinda*, and were sprinkled with protective medicines, this time under the supervision of a senior *inyanga*. The king himself was protected by powdered medicines smeared across his body, and, as at the time of the *umKhosi*, he was supposed to have entered a state of deep spiritual rage. The *izinxweleha* wore sprigs of wild asparagus in their hair to indicate their status. Mtshayankomo kaMagolwane of the uKhandempemvu described the return of the triumphant army after Isandlwana, presenting the weapons with which they had killed to Cetshwayo in a ceremony known as *uku-pumpatisa inkosi*, 'to hoodwink the king'.

> We went into the enclosure where the cattle from the open veld were kept ... the companies crossed one another's paths, one approaching from the east, another from the west. As we went we exclaimed, 'By us! [*ie* we did it!] By us! By us!' Others said, 'What did we leave them? What did we leave them? Others exclaimed, 'It is war! It is war!' 'By us! By us!' Each man shouted his own cry. The king was now standing in his own enclosure.... He was in a rage, his visage was awful; he could no longer be looked upon. He came out, and passed through us, coming down to the main enclosure. His chair was brought, and he sat down. We then stood up and saluted, calling 'Bayede! You of the elephant! ... You of the innermost circle! You who devour men! Black lion!' The king said, 'Speak now. Tell me what you have experienced.'[28]

The regimental *izinduna* then regaled the king – 'hoodwinked' him – with tales of their regiments' performance. Like the doctoring ceremonies, the review of the army after a successful campaign seems to have been spread over several days. After the king had heard the outline of the fighting from the *amabutho* themselves, they were summoned again for a different ceremony in which it was decided which of them had best excelled itself. All of those who had actually stabbed in battle – as individuals they were now referred to as *ingwazi*, 'one who stabs', or *iqawe*, 'hero' – were required to take with them a thin wand of willow wood, *umnyezane*, stripped of bark. The right to be recognised as the *ibutho* which first 'stabbed' the enemy, engaging him, was jealously guarded, and there were often fierce disputes among the regiments as to who should claim the honour. The king made his own enquiries from his *izinduna*, but once the *izinxweleha* were in a fit condition to be brought before him, the entire army was paraded. The old challenges from before the campaign were recalled, and individual warriors who had challenged their counterparts in a rival *ibutho* stepped out, demanding, 'What did you do, son of So-and-so? I did thus and thus. What did *you* do?'[29] Although there was some good-natured discussion to decide who had won the wager, nothing further was said about the property which had been staked, and no attempt was made by the victor to claim his winnings.

By this time, the king had already discussed the performance of individual *amabutho* with his generals, and had decided which deserved to be honoured most. After Isandlwana he called out Ntuzwa kaNhlaka Mdlalose, the commander of the uMbonambi; Ntuzwa took with him a willow stick, and handed it to the king. After a few moments' teasing, in which the king shook the stick like a spear but did not throw it, Cetshwayo hurled it in the direction of the uMbonambi. 'The king's so doing,' explained Mpatshana, 'is a public acknowledgement of the king accepting such men, headed by their induna, as having really been the first to come up to the enemy and begin stabbing.'[30] The *izinxweleha* of that regiment were then entitled to cut their willow sticks into small blocks, and have them threaded into necklaces known as *iziqu*.

These *iziqu* were highly priced symbols of bravery. Fynn had seen them in Shaka's time, and likened them to bravery medals worn by European troops, and one of Fynn's companions described them in detail:

[They] consisted of several rows of small pieces of wood about the same size and shape as those used in playing draughts, strung together and made into necklaces and bracelets. Some of these warriors had their necks and arms ornamented with several rows of this description, and those particularly about the neck seemed to be very inconvenient to the wearer, and certainly were not very ornamental. But on inquiry we found that the Zulu warriors set great value on these apparently useless trifles, and that they were orders of merit conferred by Shaka on those who had distinguished themselves by daring deeds of bravery on the field of battle. Each row, whether around the neck or arm, was the distinguishing mark of some heroic deed, and which the wearer received from Shaka's own hand.[31]

The last remark is particularly interesting, since it is often said – indeed, Fynn himself believed so – that each bead in the necklace was the token of a man slain. This is inherently implausible, since the willow sticks carried by the *izinxweleha* would make dozens of such beads, and an average necklace would therefore represent an improbable degree of wholesale slaughter. It is possible, however, that this idea has arisen because warriors were allowed to add to the *iziqu* if they were once again recognised by the king in a later campaign. Certainly, Mpatshana stated that it was never permissible to replace *iziqu* beads unless fresh honours had been granted:

One always wears these things and keeps iziqu belonging to the campaign in connection with which they were got. If one cuts fresh ones, one asks, 'Have you gone once more and killed others in a fresh battle?' Hence one always keeps the old iziqu, though it is permissible to restring them. . . .
    No man would dare put on willow-wood [*ie* to which he was not entitled], for he would be put to death. A man wearing iziqu would be taken aside, and other men who had killed in battle would interrogate him. 'Where did you kill, friend?' Others [*ie* who were not themselves heroes] would be afraid to question him; they would look at him askance, and remain silent.[32]

So prized, indeed, were these awards that warriors who won them at Isandlwana were still being photographed with them sixty years later.
    Another mark of royal favour was the gift of bronze armbands, shaped like the cuff of a gauntlet, and called *izingxotha*. Worn on the right arm only, above the wrist, these were presented by the king to the *izilomo*, the royal favourites. They were made from slabs of metal traded from the Portuguese, and worked up into the characteristic shape by Zulu smiths. According to Ndukwana, the king carefully controlled their manufacture.

The armbands always had to be made at the royal kraal. The smith, when the king wanted armbands, would be sent for by the king; on his arrival he would be put up at the king's kraal, live there until he had completed his job, and would be rewarded by the king for his services. The armbands were distributed by the king to men of high standing, but not as a reward for anything special.[33]

Each *ingxotha* was individually made, and the surface was decorated by variations on a theme of raised patterning. They were status symbols of the highest order, though it is not entirely clear whether they were awarded throughout the kingdom's history; some accounts suggest that they were introduced during King Dingane's reign. The number awarded by each king was apparently small, perhaps no more than a few dozen, and they differed from the *iziqu* in that they were not a specific reward for military excellence. They were simply tokens of the king's great favour, awarded to those whom he felt were serving him well. Many *izikhulu* wore them simply by right of their position.

The spoils

There were other, more practical, rewards, to be apportioned, too. Any cattle taken in battle were the property of the nation, and their disposal rested with the king. Most would become part of the national herd, but some were distributed among the *amabutho*. Again, those warriors who had particularly distinguished themselves would be singled out for reward, and the bravest of them might receive as many as ten head. Others received less according to their degree of heroism. Since there were limited opportunities for Zulu commoners, particularly young men, to accumulate cattle, such rewards had a definite effect on a man's social standing, and made him a desirable partner when he was allowed to marry.

The warriors were allowed to keep a good deal of any other loot they found on the battlefield. After Isandlwana, breech-loading firearms were particularly prized. According to Mpatshana:

> All guns captured were retained by the impi, for everyone who got a gun claimed that he had seized it from the European he had himself killed. The guns were not taken to the king, but the king directed that they were to be brought up, when he inspected them and then told those who had them to retain them.[34]

Other artefacts of military value had been taken, too, including the swords and revolvers of officers, though these were retained as prestige items rather than for their practical use. Indeed, the Zulus had been singularly unimpressed by the 'volvovol', the revolver, since they had noted that it was seldom accurate, even at close range.[35] Thousands of rounds of cartridges were either taken, or torn open and the powder extracted. All of the pathetic panoply of camp life fell into Zulu hands at Isandlwana: hats, greatcoats, blankets, tools, shovels, cutlery and all manner of trinkets, were taken by those who had a use for them. The British tents were cut into handy canvas strips, and the rest discarded. Anything which looked vaguely alcoholic had been consumed to slake the voracious thirst induced by adrenalin and exertion; several accounts recall that warriors drank medicine, ink and paraffin in ignorance, and were poisoned by it. Tins and sacks of food were broken open and ransacked, and coins, watches and religious tokens taken or discarded according to taste. Most of the transport wagons were left on the field, but a few were dragged off by the retainers of the more westernised chiefs, such as Sihayo. A few horses, too, were looted, but most were killed as the warriors regarded them as 'the feet of the white men'. The two 7-pounder guns overrun at Isandlwana were left on the field until the king sent men to collect them; they were dragged by hand to oNdini, where attempts were made to work them – without success.

Treatment of cowards

If the heroes were rewarded, however, those who had hung back in battle, and were therefore judged cowards, could expect an unpleasant reception. Shaka, apparently, was particularly stern, executing out of hand those accused of cowardice. Fynn and Isaacs suggested that this was merely a manifestation of his inherently cruel personality, but it seems probable that he could not afford to be lenient at a time when the future of the kingdom depended on the army. When trying to forge a spirit of unity and courage among the army, Shaka could not let examples of cowardice go unnoticed or unpunished. Isaacs recalled a nasty moment when Shaka demanded to see a wound he had sustained in action, and then remarked that since it was in the back, it was clearly a proof of cowardice.[36] On that occasion Shaka was joking, but others were undoubtedly less fortunate. The number of men executed was probably small, but the killings, carried out in full view of the assembled *amabutho*, had a salutary effect. There is a bush near the site of Shaka's kwaBulawayo homestead where such killings took place, and it is still known, more than 150 years later, as the *isihlala samagwala* – The Cowards' Bush. Mtshapi kaNoradu, whose father had been one of Shaka's warriors, recorded the prevailing opinion that 'Tshaka used to order that a person should be seized, and his arm lifted up; he would then say, "Give him a taste of the assegai, the thing that he fears so much." He would then be stabbed as if he were a goat, and killed.'[37]

Punishments seldom seem to have been so draconian under the rule of the later kings. Military activity was less frequent during the reigns of Dingane and Mpande, and from the 1840s the growing power of the regional *izikhulu* made it difficult for the king to kill off his subjects without their support. Indeed, the presence of Natal across the border offered a refuge for Zulu commoners should the regime in Zululand become too repressive, and it was therefore impractical for the king to use the death penalty too freely. Nonetheless, such was the emphasis placed on personal bravery that cowards were treated with the greatest contempt by their colleagues, particularly those who had performed well themselves. They were identified in front of the whole army, and made to sit apart from their regiments. Then they were publicly humiliated in front of the king himself, as Mtshapi – who had been present on such occasions with the uKhandempemvu – described:

> The regiment would be summoned, would form a semi-circle, and would sit down. Meat would be placed in a heap. The potsherd would be standing next to the roaring fire which the izinceku [king's attendants] had made. Those who had not yet gone to war would not have their meat soaked in water; this was done to those who had gone to war, had experienced it, but who had not stabbed anyone. They would then deserve the potsherd. The roasted meat would be taken off the fire, and put on meat-trays; the meat for the cowards would be put aside, and put into the water. This would be done with the king looking on. It was he himself who gave the order, 'Put the cowards' meat in the water!' He would order them to eat the cold meat, while the prime meat would go to the heroes alone.[38]

The serving of cold meat was a gesture of contempt; often a successful warrior would take the meat across himself, dashing the water in the coward's face, knowing that he dared not respond. Girls whose lovers were singled out as cowards abandoned them, since they were likely to be taunted and mocked: 'Is it so, then, that two girls go about together?'[39] There are suggestions that even a warrior who had distinguished himself in a previous campaign, and who wore the *iziqu*, might be humbled if his courage was seen to fail him, and the king could order the string of his *iziqu* to be cut.[40] The effect of such disgrace in a society which valued service to the state and encouraged physical bravery can readily be imagined. Mtshapi's comments, however, suggested that such behaviour reflected a deliberate policy, and that the stigma was not necessarily permanent:

> Then, when war broke out, those men who had had their meat soaked in water would fight fiercely; they would throw themselves recklessly into battle. A man would do this in the hope that he could avoid being given cold meat, the meat that had been soaked in water. When the report on the battle was made to the king, the coward's conduct would also be reported. It would be said, 'Baba! When the fighting started, So-and-so, son of So-and-so, simply threw himself into it. He has left the potsherd of the cowards. Nkosi!' 'What did he do?' They would describe further how he had fought. The king would then praise him, and say, 'He has now left the potsherd of the cowards. Do not again give him the meat of the cowards; let him eat the meat of the heroes.'[41]

Once the cleansing ceremonies and reviews were finally over, the king allowed the army to disperse to their homes. All of those who had killed in battle – not just those whom the king had granted the right to wear *iziqu* – cut amulets from willow or from cow-horns to wear around their necks, and, as Mtshayankomo explained, they repaired their weapons and costume. 'We threw away the imitsha [loin coverings] we had been wearing. We unhafted our assegais, and fixed hew hafts to them. We then washed our assegais, and sharpened them until they shone.'[42]

The army in defeat

Under normal circumstances, when an army had returned from a campaign outside the country's borders, that would be the end of the matter. The warriors dispersed to their civilian homesteads until the king had a fresh task for them to perform. In 1879, however, the circumstances were not ordinary. The battles of 22 January had checked the British threat, but by no means ended the war. There was a merciful lull, in which the warriors were able to recuperate from their wounds and exhaustion, and help with the ripening harvest; but as soon as the British had been reinforced by troops from home, they resumed the invasion. King Cetshwayo was forced to recall his army in the middle of March, for the second phase of the war, which culminated in the battles of Khambula and Gingindlovu. They then dispersed again, and were mustered for the final time to oppose the invaders at oNdini, in the very heart of the Zulu kingdom.

Indeed, as the Anglo-Zulu war progressed, victory in the field gave way more frequently to defeat, and the Zulu army suffered a series of body-blows which subjected its infrastructure to such stress that at last it collapsed completely. Isandlwana had been an astonishing victory, but the cost had been so heavy that, as one Zulu put it, 'The dead are not to be counted, there are so many. The whole Zulu nation is mourning and weeping.'[43] Of course, on the same day as the Isandlwana victory, the Zulus had been checked, both at Nyezane on the coast, and at Rorke's Drift. The latter was particularly telling, because the Zulus had enjoyed a greater numerical superiority there than at Isandlwana, but the British were barricaded behind secure breastworks which effectively negated the Zulus numerical advantage. The fatal flaw in Zulu fighting techniques was first exposed at Rorke's Drift; by failing to make the most of their firearms, the Zulus were forced to rely on their stabbing spears, and the British barricades effectively kept them out of reach. Indeed, Lieutenant Chard's improvised walls of biscuit boxes and mealie-bags served much the same purpose as barbed wire in the greater conflicts on the Western Front in the First World War; they delayed the Zulu advance at close range, where they were subject to an extremely effective killing zone, made possible by the vastly superior firearms carried by the British. Nearly 600 Zulus were killed at Rorke's Drift, over half of them slaughtered at the very foot of the barricades. The lesson was not lost on either side; asked to explain the Zulu defeat, a warrior of the uDloko *ibutho* who had been present said ruefully, 'The soldiers were behind a schaans [barricade], and ... they were in a corner.'[44] Learning from his mistakes, Lord Chelmsford abandoned the open-order formations he had advocated before Isandlwana, and instead revived the old Napoleonic device of the square. The later battles of the war were fought under just the conditions imagined by Shaka more than fifty years before, and the inadequacy of numbers as a counter to concentrated modern firepower became brutally apparent.

In truth, the Zulu had always been vulnerable to such tactics. In Dingane's war against the Voortrekkers, the Zulu army had shown itself more than equal to small groups of men mounted on horseback, and it was not so much the horse and the gun that outclassed them, nor, indeed, the gun on its own; it was the combination of the gun and barricade. Lunguza kaMpukane left a vivid account of the Zulu helplessness before the Boer laager at Blood River, which describes the defeat in strikingly similar terms to those of the later battles against the British:

> The successive rushes of the Zulus on the Boer fort failed and were repulsed. The fort was made of wagons closely drawn together, with branches of trees put in between, these branches having been pulled in from surrounding parts by means of oxen. After our troops had been repulsed there was a general flight in various directions. The Boers charged; four came in our direction riding red horses, five in another direction, six in another. They fired on the Zulus with their guns. Our men hid in ant-bear holes, under ant-heaps, stuffing their heads in even though otherwise exposed, whilst others hid themselves under the heaps of corpses to be found in every direction. Men were shot who were already dead. I found men shot dead in front as well as behind me as we fled.... There was no chance of the Zulus doing anything.[45]

Small wonder that King Cetshwayo urged his men time and again to avoid fortified posts; not to put their faces into the holes of the wild beasts.[46] Tragically for the kingdom, the young men of 1879 ignored the lessons history had taught their elders, and they got their faces clawed.

The Zulu military outlook was based on an assumption of victory, and it had little or no provision to cope with defeat. The warriors simply attacked until they were exhausted, and the casualties became too heavy to bear. Then they retired from the field. Initially they did so in good order – 'sullenly' was the phrase that occurred to a number of British observers – but they had no physical or psychological reserves to draw upon, and this made them acutely vulnerable to determined pursuit. The British realised

this and, spurred on by a desire for vengeance after their losses at Isandlwana, Ntombe and Hlobane, harried them mercilessly whenever they
could. Although senior *izinduna* stayed with their men and tried valiantly to
rally them, the Zulu were too spent to obey. After both Khambula and
Gingindlovu, the British rode among them almost with impunity, shooting
them at will, then, when that mode of slaughter proved too slow, they
seized the warriors' own weapons and rode them down. Now and then a
man would turn and fight, but most were too exhausted even to try to evade
their pursuers. In one or two cases there are even stories of warriors killing
themselves rather than fall to the enemy. It was quite common for more
casualties to be inflicted during the pursuit than in the attack, and under
such circumstances the army simply fell apart. The warriors drifted away as
best as they could, abandoning their officers, and making for their homes.
The wounded were left on the field, to the not-too-tender mercies of the
British and their African allies, and there was no time to cover over even the
bodies of the *izilomo*. It was just as well that the Zulu were accustomed to
giving no quarter, for they seldom received any. Mgelija Ngema left a stark
account of his experiences after he was wounded at Khambula:

> On my way back ... I was one day overtaken by English soldiers and they
> said 'What is your regiment?' I said uVe and they said 'Why does Cetewayo
> send such young boys?' They saw the gun I had with me which I had taken
> from the soldier I had killed at [Hlobane], and all I know is I was shot here
> by one of them in my head and left for dead. I came round in the evening and
> crawled to a kraal where I was looked after and my wound washed.... [47]

When individual Zulus were taken prisoner, their captors were often
surprised at the fatalistic way they accepted their situation. On a number of
occasions, British troops in 1879 noted that captives seemed resigned, even
nonchalant, displaying little bitterness, and answering questions put to
them with apparent honesty, even when wounded. Guy Dawnay, a
volunteer officer with the Natal Native Contingent, 'found a wounded
prisoner shot through the stomach and side' after Gingindlovu, and mar-
velled that 'he walked along quite jauntily, and replied freely to all our
questions'. [48] No doubt such coolness had much to do with the fact that the
Zulus realised that, if they survived the initial horrors of the pursuit, they
were likely to be well treated by the British when captured.

After Khambula, Mnyamana Buthelezi tried to persuade the survivors to
return with him to report to the king, but the majority would not. Only the
most senior commanders dared face the king to report their failure. King
Cetshwayo bitterly reproached them for ignoring his advice but, despite
stories in the Natal press to the contrary, unsuccessful commanders were

seldom punished by the king. He occasionally threatened to kill those whose errors had been particularly glaring, but it was all bluster; senior generals – men like Mnyamana and Ntshingwayo – were far too powerful as *izikhulu* to be touched, and the worst that seems to have befallen their subordinates is that they were ordered out of the king's presence in disgrace. Prince Dabulamanzi hedged his defeat at Rorke's Drift in the manner of unsuccessful generals the world over: '[He] reported that he had successfully stormed and taken "the house"; he attacked and then retired, but admitted he had suffered heavily. . . .'[49] He then retreated under the cloud of his brother's disapproval to his eZulwini homestead near the coast. By the beginning of April, however, he was once again holding a command at the battle of Gingindlovu.

It is difficult not to feel admiration for the way the ordinary warriors responded to the king's summons time and again, once they had recovered from the initial shock of defeat.[50] Despite Khambula and Gingindlovu, which came within days of each other at opposite ends of the country and cost the Zulu as many as 3000 dead altogether, the army still responded to the king's call-up in late June 1879. By then the juggernaut of the British advance had reached the heartland of the Zulu kingdom, and the king required of his warriors nothing less than a last-ditch effort to save the nation. King Cetshwayo himself had come to realise that ultimate military victory was unlikely, but the army clung stubbornly to the belief that it was more than a match for the British provided it could catch them in the open, as they had at Isandlwana. When the king tried to send some of the nation's cattle to the British as a peace offering – part of his famous herd of all-white beasts – an exchange took place before the assembled regiments, which suggests both the suffering already endured by the Zulu, and the persistent defiance of the *amabutho*:

'O Zulu people [said Cetshwayo], I see that the white people have indeed come. I see that though you blunted them at Sandlwana, the next day they came on again. Though you blunted them at the stronghold of Rawane [Khambula], the next day they came on again. Then you came and told me that their army had driven you back and had done you harm. I say now that these oxen must go as a peace offering to the white people.' Then Matatshile ka Masipula of the Emgazini said, 'No, Nkosi. Is the king beginning to speak thus even though we Kandempemvu are far from finished?' The king replied, 'Matatshile, what do you mean by "far from finished"? Where is Zikode kaMasipula? Where is Mhlazana kaNgoza kaLudaba of the place of the Buthelezi people? Where is Mtshodo kaNtshingwayo kaMarole? Where is Mahu? Where is Somcuba kaMapitha? So you are far from finished? How is it that you can say that? Where is Gininda ka Masipula?'

When he had finished speaking, Matatshile answered, 'Is the king afraid? Does he think he will be defeated because those who sit around the eating mat {ie the izilomo} have been killed?' Again the king spoke. 'Yeh! Matatshile, if you look up, the sky will be far off; if you prod the ground with your stick, the earth will be hard. If the white men keep advancing when so many of them have been killed, and when so many of us have been killed, what is there to stop them?'[51]

The king sent his cattle, but on the way to the British camp the uKhandempemvu intercepted them and refused to let them pass. Then, on 4 July 1879, after a night of doctoring which could be heard in the British camp several miles away, the Zulu army went into battle for the last time. On the plain before oNdini the British met them in the open at last, and the inadequacies of the 'chest and horns' tactics were woefully and finally laid bare. The British formed a square, with soldiers four rows deep on all sides, and the lines broken here and there with artillery and Gatling guns. The Zulus surrounded the square but to no avail; despite several determined assaults, many warriors lost heart soon after the attack began. Mangwanana Mcunu of the uVe recalled the shock with which the amabutho realised that they had succeeded in surrounding the enemy, but still could not win:

We saw the soldiers marching across country. They stopped and we attacked. Men of every regiment I spoke to after who had attacked on other sides to where we had attacked said that the soldiers were facing them. We said the soldiers were facing us and yet others said they were facing them. As we broke and ran the cavalry came out after us....[52]

Sofikasho Zungu recalled that 'there was such a roar of guns we were utterly bewildered'.[53] The feeling of hopelessness shared by many warriors was summed up by one anonymous veteran who asked, 'What could we do against you English? You stand still, and only by turning something round {ie the handle of a Gatling} make the bodies of our warriors fly to pieces; legs here, arms there, heads, everything. Whouw! What can we do against that?'[54] Although several rushes were made with great determination, the majority of the warriors did not fight with quite the same spirit at oNdini as they had before, and several of the older amabutho retired before coming into action. As Mehlokazulu kaSihayo put it: 'At the Ondine battle, the last, we did not fight with the same spirit, because we were then frightened. We had had a severe lesson, and did not fight with the same zeal.'[55]

The Zulu kingdom had been defeated only once before by outsiders. In 1838 the Boers had broken the army at Blood River, and in the face of their advance King Dingane had set fire to his favourite homestead, eMgungundlovu, and fled. Yet, although the Boers had confiscated huge quantities of Zulu cattle and taken a large number of Zulu civilians into captivity, they had not occupied the Zulu kingdom. Most of the country had been untouched by the fighting, many of the *amakhanda* remained intact, and indeed those *amabutho* defeated at Blood River had survived the ordeal. The king had not been deposed; he simply moved the focus of the kingdom further north, and built a new eMgungundlovu north of the Mfolozi, near Nongoma. The apparatus of the state had therefore been shaken, but had by no means collapsed. Even when Dingane was defeated two years later, it was largely through the intervention of his brother Prince Mpande; instead of the state being broken up, Mpande – with Boer support – merely replaced Dingane on the throne. Although the consequences of this civil war were serious, the kingdom itself survived; Mpande not only continued with the *amabutho* system, he had some success in using it as a means of restoring royal authority.

In 1879, however, the defeat was absolute. The army dispersed after oNdini, and individual warriors admitted quite freely that they felt themselves beaten. British observers noted that within a few days their messengers could travel about the country with impunity, for the Zulu will to resist had collapsed. Cetshwayo was in hiding; when he sent orders for the *amabutho* to reform to build him a new royal homestead, following Dingane's example, they refused.[56] The majority of ordinary Zulu remained loyal to the king's person, but they knew his authority had been broken, and many of the *izikhulu* then made what terms with the British they could. All of the obvious signs of royal power had been broken. On 26 June British forces had systematically ravaged the emaKhosini valley, and nine *amakhanda* were destroyed, either by the British themselves, or by Zulus retreating before their advance. Among them had been esiKlebheni, and the sacred *eNkatheni* hut; and with it the *inkatha yezwe yakwaZulu* was burnt with the rest. After the battle of oNdini, the British systematically shelled or set fire to all the great *amakhanda* on the Mahlabathini plain, including oNdini itself. The coastal columns had been similarly destructive, and only a few royal homesteads in the more remote parts of the country had escaped their attention. At the end of August, King Cetshwayo himself, a tired and dispirited fugitive, was captured by British dragoons and taken to the coast, where he was put on a ship destined for exile in Cape Town.

The destruction of the Zulu army

The battle of oNdini undoubtedly marked the end of the old Zulu military system.[57] There may have been no hordes of unemployed and disillusioned ex-soldiers roaming the countryside as happened in the aftermath of European wars, but the army was gone, nonetheless. The Zulu warrior had never been a professional soldier, living outside the bounds of civilian society. He had been at best a citizen-soldier, a part-time warrior, and the extinction of the military system meant that he simply returned home and resumed the ordinary civilian aspects of his life. Zululand was, in any case, exhausted by war; even the most cursory of counts suggests that between six and ten thousand Zulu men had died defending their country, and there was scarcely a homestead in the country which did not mourn for someone. The British had looted thousands of head of cattle, and hundreds of ordinary civilian homesteads had been burnt in the later stages of the war, in an attempt to erode civilian support for resistance. Initially, this exhaustion seems to have been expressed by many Zulus as a relief that they were able to pursue their daily lives untroubled by the king's demands for service. A number of British commentators noted that almost immediately Zulu men began to marry freely, and at a much younger age; it was no longer necessary to wait for the king's sanction, and the habit of wearing the *isicoco*, 'the king's ring', began to die out as a result.[58]

Yet the *amabutho* system remained firmly rooted in the minds of the Zulu people. In the political settlement which followed the war, the British deliberately attempted to destroy the central role of the royal house by giving power instead to the regional *izikhulu*. With the king himself in exile, Zululand was broken up among thirteen chieftains, many of whom had either demonstrated overt sympathy for the British cause in 1879, or were thought to be simply pro-European and anti-monarchist. They represented, in effect, an attempt to establish a class of client chiefs through whom a level of indirect rule could be exerted. In fact, the settlement merely unleashed the decentralising forces that had always existed within the old kingdom, whilst at the same time arousing the anger of the pro-royalist faction. Zibhebhu kaMapitha, who had fought loyally for the king in 1879, was made one of the thirteen chiefs partly because he was involved in the colonial economy. Prince Hamu kaNzibe, who had defected to the British, was also given an appointment. Such men earned the distrust of the king's supporters, and violence broke out to such an extent that in 1882 the British agreed to allow Cetshwayo to return to Zululand in the hope of restoring order.

Military failure in the 1880s
Yet the king's position was impossible. He had been given only part of his former territory, and many anti-royalist leaders, such as Zibhebhu, refused to acknowledge him. Cetshwayo was forbidden by the British from reviving the military system, and was therefore effectively denied not only a means to defend himself, but to exercise control over his own followers. Some attempt was made to revitalise the *amabutho* system – a regiment apparently raised before the Zulu war, possibly as cadets, was renamed the uFalaza at this

time[59] – but it bore little relation to the sophisticated body of old. The king built a new oNdini homestead, only a few hundred yards from the complex burnt in 1879, but it was a much smaller affair, and no attempt was made to revive other *amakhanda*. With no *amakhanda* to house them, and no means of supporting them, any new *amabutho* were bound therefore to exist in little more than name only. Indeed, unlike the *amabutho* of old, who were raised from young men across the country regardless of local loyalties, the *amabutho* of the 1880s were formed only from the king's supporters, thereby denying one of the system's most important functions as a unifying agent of monarchical power.

Yet, when open civil war finally broke out, the *amabutho* did muster as fighting units, despite the British prohibition. Those Zulus who remained loyal to the royal house still recognised their old allegiance to their original *amabutho*, and some attempt was made to call up the pre-1879 units in the 1880s. They were, however, drastically reduced in numbers, not only through their casualties in 1879, but also because many of them no longer acknowledged the king's authority. A few might have mustered wearing something of their regalia, but the king's war-shields were long gone, and for the most part they offered no appearance of uniformity. They were no longer the Zulu army, merely the forces of the royalist faction, a fact they unintentionally acknowledged when they revived the name uSuthu, after Cetshwayo's party in the civil war of 1856. The uSuthu struck at Zibhebhu, but after some initial successes were caught off-guard and massacred in a skilfully planned ambush in the Msebe valley. Zibhebhu followed up with a strike at the king's new homestead at oNdini. He advanced to within a few miles of it without being spotted, and in the ensuing battle the uSuthu were scattered. The names of several of the old *amabutho* are mentioned in accounts of the fight – the uThulwana, the uMxapho, the uKhandempemvu and iNgobamakhosi – but their showing was poor, and Zibhebhu's vengeful forces chased them from the field. The new oNdini was burnt to the ground, and over sixty of the most important of the king's pre-war advisers were killed, including Ntshingwayo, who had commanded at Isandlwana, and Sihayo, whose sons' rashness had provoked the British invasion. The king himself was wounded, but escaped; he threw himself on British protection, but died within a few months, a broken man. With his defeat at oNdini, Zibhebhu's followers had completed the job begun by the British, and finished the old Zulu kingdom.

The story of the Zulu royal house in the last twenty years of the nineteenth century is essentially one of a refusal to adapt to changed times. After the second battle of oNdini, there was never any real chance that the royalists would unite the whole country behind them. Cetshwayo's heir, Dinuzulu, was recognised by the uSuthu as king, but had to resort to appealing for Boer support in order finally to defeat Zibhebhu. After Zibhebhu was scattered at eTshaneni in June 1884, the Boers claimed so much land in reward that the British finally intervened and annexed Zululand. The British continued to refuse to acknowledge the role of the uSuthu, however, and in 1888 they revolted, led, significantly, by Dinuzulu and several of Cetshwayo's brothers. British red-coats once again marched into Zululand, and the uSuthu were defeated in a series of short, sharp battles. Dinuzulu and his uncles were, like Cetshwayo before them, arrested and sent into exile.

Throughout the 1880s, the military outlook of the uSuthu had been essentially conservative. They had retained lip-service to the *amabutho* system – Dinuzulu raised up to five regiments[60] – but in effect the practical organisation in the field had been at company level. Looking back to the days before the 1879 war, they had made little attempt to adapt the traditional 'chest and horns' formation. On occasion – such as the battle of Ndunu Hill in June 1888, when Dinuzulu had personally led the uSuthu against a combined force of Zibhebhu's followers and colonial troops – it had still been successful. Yet, despite all lessons to the contrary, the uSuthu had continued to rely too heavily on the mass-attack by men on foot armed with shields and spears. They made no great concession either to the gun or the horse, and it is no coincidence that the one Zulu commander who emerged from this period with an enhanced reputation was not an uSuthu; he was their arch-enemy Zibhebhu. Zibhebhu proved himself a dynamic and innovative leader, a master of the ambush, well able to deal with the predictable tactics employed by his opponents; at Msebe he had routed a force of 5000 men, according to some accounts killing as many as 2000 for the loss of just ten of his own. When Zibhebhu was finally defeated at eTshaneni, it was by Boers on horseback, armed with breech-loading rifles. Both his successes and his ultimate defeat, therefore, were an effective demonstration of just how outmoded Zulu fighting techniques had by then become.[61]

The legacy of the *amabutho*

The defeat of the uSuthu in 1888 paved the way for the imposition of colonial rule in Zululand, based on the system of administration through local chiefs which prevailed in Natal. Although the British had been keen to break the power of the royal house, they did not attack the institution of regional chiefs; indeed, they used them as agents of exploitation and control. Ironically, the ethos of service through the *amabutho*, once the source of greatest resistance to European interventionism, was effectively subverted to serve the needs of the conquerors.[62] Where once they had worked to serve the king, young Zulu men now found themselves compelled to travel outside Zululand to work for wages, in order to pay to their chiefs the taxes levied on them by the colonial administration. The system of migrant labour, which had already come to other parts of South Africa and was to dominate the region's economy for generations to come, laying the economic seeds of apartheid, was born at last in Zululand.

There was one last, desperate attempt in Natal and Zululand to resist the juggernaut of white rule using traditional methods of violence. In 1906 there was a brief uprising, provoked by successive natural hardships and by the imposition of a poll tax. Its origins lay not in Zululand proper but in Natal, and its leader was Bambatha kaMancinza, chieftain of the Zondi people who lived in the Mpanza valley, south of the Thukela. Bambatha refused to pay the poll tax and promptly attacked colonial troops before taking to the bush with his armed followers. Bambatha and his supporters made a conscious effort to associate themselves with the heroic tradition of the Zulu kings, even to the point of adopting the old royalist war-cry, *uSuthu*. Bambatha crossed the Thukela and tried to persuade the Zulu to join him. Dinuzulu, not long back from exile, publicly refused to commit himself, although the rebels claimed his secret support. Only a few Zulu chiefs jointed the rebellion, but they were men of some note in the old kingdom: the ancient Sigananda of the Cube, whose father Zokufa had been a friend and ally of Shaka's, and Mehlokazulu kaSihayo, the veteran of Isandlwana. A series of skirmishes played out against the dramatic backdrop of the Thukela valley, however, proved that the rebels were no more adept at dealing with European firearms than the generation before them had been. In a few minor skirmishes Bambatha's men fought from the bush, and their limited successes suggested that more might have been made of such tactics, but in the major battles they reverted to the 'chest and horns' formation. Since the colonial forces were armed with quick-firing artillery, Maxim machine-guns and magazine rifles, the rebels suffered appalling casualties. Eventually the rebel forces concentrated at the mouth of the remote Mome gorge, only to find themselves trapped by colonial troops who executed a remarkable cross-country march at night. In the ensuing battle the rebels were shot down almost without fear of reply; both Mehlokazulu and Bambatha were killed, and the back of the rebellion was broken. Although fighting flared up elsewhere in Natal, it lacked the intensity of that in Zululand, and was easily suppressed.

Yet if the Bambatha rebellion demonstrated that the old Zulu military system was no longer valid, the heroic tradition embodied by that system continued to exercise a hold on the imagination of the Zulu people. In 1913 Dinuzulu died, and was succeeded by his son Solomon. The position of the Zulu kings in the twentieth century has not been enviable;

deprived of real power, they have been at the mercy of colonial and apartheid governments who have sought to subvert the emotional authority the royal house continues to exert over its followers. King Solomon's career was characterised by a struggle to find a framework within the context of a rapidly industrialising economy in which the Zulu monarchy could function.[63] To that end, he formed a number of *amabutho*. Although their numbers and functions were strictly limited, by exerting his right to *buta* them Solomon asserted his claim to the traditional mechanics of the independent past. The gesture was not lost on the colonial authorities, who regarded it with deep distrust. Indeed, the struggle to control the symbols of the old Zulu monarchy has been a major theme of the politics of Natal and Zululand right up to the present day. They have been used across the great philosophical divide, by both conservative elements, for whom the monarchy offered a vision of an ordered, élitist society innately opposed to twentieth-century concepts of socialism, and radical groups, for whom it represented an age of black supremacy. It was King Solomon who founded the original *Inkatha ya ka Zulu*, a loose grouping of Zulu royalists, black middle-class Christians and influential white farmers who found common ground in an attempt to restore the influence of the royal house. The movement was revived by Chief Mangosuthu Buthelezi in the 1970s, and transformed into the Inkatha Freedom Party. Chief Buthelezi, the most significant and controversial Zulu political leader of the apartheid and post-apartheid era, has always stressed the importance of the traditions of the Zulu royal house as a crucial element in Zulu cultural identity. The image of the *amabutho*, of the warrior tradition, pervades the rhetoric of much of the struggle for freedom in Natal, and has been evoked to varying effect by a wide range of contrasting groups. In 1930, black workers in Durban, protesting about issues varying from the government suppression of the illegal brewing business to poor pay and living conditions, called upon the spirit of Shaka to support them, burnt their passes to shouts of '*uSuthu!*', and held a meeting in the menacing formation 'of Zulu warfare – the formation of the horns of an ox'[64] In the terrible violence which marked the last days of apartheid, Zulus supporting the IFP carried 'traditional weapons' – home-made spears and shields – and referred to themselves as *amabutho*. Traditionalist Zulus still gather in ceremonial regalia to honour the heroic individuals and incidents of the nineteenth century.

Yet the true economic basis of the *amabutho* system collapsed rapidly in the face of growing industrialisation. The move to urban centres and the practice of migrant labour systems broke down the web of tradition within families. The last veterans of the 1879 war had passed to join their ancestral spirits by the 1940s, and even the sons and grandsons who listened to their stories are now thin on the ground. But ironically, as the physical links with the past have steadily snapped and fallen away, the Zulu kingdom has been recast in a new form. Following South Africa's first free elections in April 1994, the role of the Zulu royal house within the country was recognised in a new constitution. For the first time since the British deposed King Cetshwayo in 1879, the Zulu monarchy has been officially recognised. Whether there is any place in the military forces of the new South Africa for the ideology of the old Zulu military tradition remains to be seen.

NOTES

1. Major General W.C.F. Molyneux, *Campaigning in South Africa and Egypt*, London, 1896.
2. Fynn, *Diary*.
3. Mitford, *Through the Zulu Country*.
4. Cetshwayo's story in Webb and Wright, *A Zulu King Speaks*.
5. Lieutenant Robarts's letters in family possession, quoted in Castle and Knight, *Fearful Hard Times*.
6. Guy C. Dawnay, *Campaigns: Zulu 1879, Egypt 1882, Suakin 1885*, private publication *c.* 1886, reprinted London, 1989.
7. Account of Mgelija Ngema in Knight (ed.) *Kill Me in the Shadows, SOTQ* 74.
8. Leslie, *Among the Zulus and Amatongas*.
9. Harford in Child (ed.) *The Zulu War Diary of Colonel Henry Harford*.
10. H.C. Lugg, *A Natal Family Looks Back*, Durban, 1970.
11. Account of Mtshapi kaNoradu, Webb and Wright, *JSA* 4.
12. Account of Mkehlengana kaZulu in Webb and Wright, *JSA* 3.
13. Account of Mtshayankomo kaMagolwane, Webb and Wright, *JSA* 4.
14. Isaacs, *Travels and Adventure*.
15. Dr Blair Browne, *Surgical Experiences in the Zulu and Transvaal Wars, 1879 and 1881*, Edinburgh, 1883.
16. Letter from John Gill, dated Utrecht, 6 July 1879, published in *The Lancet*, 16 August 1879.
17. Hutton's account, included in Frank Emery, *The Red Soldier*.
18. Mitford, *Through the Zulu Country*.
19. Account of Mpatshana kaSodondo, Webb and Wright, *JSA* 3.
20. Account of Mgelija Ngema in Knight (ed.) *Kill Me in the Shadows, SOTQ* 74.
21. Samuelson, *LLA*.
22. Mitford, *Through the Zulu Country*.
23. H.P. Braadvedt, *Roaming Zululand with a Native Commissioner*, Pietermaritzburg, 1949.
24. Isaacs, *Travels and Adventure*.
25. Account of Mpatshana kaSodondo, Webb and Wright, *JSA* 3.
26. Account of Mangwanana Mcunu in Knight (ed.) *Kill Me in the Shadows, SOTQ* 74. The name 'Muti' is highly suggestive (*umuthi* = medicine) and may have been given to the individual concerned after the incident.
27. Account of Mpatshana kaSodondo, Webb and Wright, *JSA* 3.
28. Account of Mtshayankomo kaMagolwana, Webb and Wright, *JSA* 4.
29. Account of Mpatshana kaSodondo, Webb and Wright, *JSA* 3.

30. Ibid.
31. Account of Charles Rawden Maclean in Stephen Grey (ed.) *The Natal Papers of John Ross*, Pietermaritzburg, 1992.
32. Account of Mpatshana kaSodondo in Webb and Wright, *JSA* 3.
33. Account of Ndukwana kaMbengwana, Webb and Wright, *JSA* 4.
34. Ibid.
35. See, for example, the comments of the *induna* Vumandaba kaNtati to Mitford that 'for every man they [*ie* revolvers] killed, they fired a great many shots without hitting anybody.' Mitford, *Through the Zulu Country*.
36. Isaacs, *Travels and Adventure*.
37. Accounts of Mtshapi kaNoradu, Webb and Wright, *JSA* 4.
38. Ibid.
39. Account of Mpatshana kaSodondo, Webb and Wright, *JSA* 3.
40. Note in Bowden papers, Natal Museum, Pietermaritzburg.
41. Account of Mtshapi kaNoradu in Webb and Wright, *JSA* 4.
42. Account of Mtshayankomo kaMagolwana, Webb and Wright, *JSA* 4.
43. Statement of Cajana kaMathendeka, February 1879, *BBP* C2260.
44. Mitford, *Through the Zulu Country*.
45. Account of Lunguza kaMpukane, Webb and Wright, *JSA* 1.
46. 'Wild beasts' seems to have been a common Zulu term for whites; on Cetshwayo's advice, see Mgelija Ngema in Knight (ed.), *Kill Me in the Shadows, SOTQ* 74.
47. Ibid.
48. Dawnay, *Campaigns*.
49. Cetshwayo's Story, in Webb and Wright, *A Zulu King Speaks*.
50. Many were undoubtedly demoralised by their severe losses and the fact that the British advance seemed inexorable – see, for example, the comments of Cajana kaMathendeka in *BBP* C2260 – but this seems to have been an initial response which passed once the warriors had recovered from their exhaustion. Certainly, the Zulu king was able to field large forces until the very end of the war.
51. Account of Mtshapi kaNoradu, Webb and Wright, *JSA* 4.
52. Account of Mangwanana Mcunu in Knight (ed.) *Kill Me in the Shadows, SOTQ* 74.
53. Account of Sofikasho Zungu, ibid.
54. Mitford, *Through the Zulu Country*.
55. Account of Mehlokazulu kaSihayo, in Norris-Newman, *In Zululand*.
56. Vijn, *Cetshwayo's Dutchman*.
57. Jeff Guy, in *Destruction of the Zulu Kingdom*, argues that the military significance of the battle of Ulundi/oNdini has been overstated. John Laband disagrees, and provides convincing evidence of the decisive nature of the defeat – see *Kingdom in Crisis*. In either case, the battle was the last fought by the national army of an independent Zulu kingdom.
58. It is interesting to note that many Zulu who fought at Isandlwana with the younger *amabutho*, and who survived to be photographed at the fiftieth anniversary in 1929, had not donned the headring, though they were by then old men. If these men, who had grown up in pre-colonial society and fought to preserve it, many of whom were in their twenties at the time of the war and who probably married soon after it, did not bother to adopt the ring, the custom must have died out very quickly once the *amabutho* were disbanded.
59. Samuelson, *LLA*. The name uFalaza has been translated 'The Rubbish Talkers', because the king considered the Zulus had lost the ability to talk sense during his exile, or, more

convincingly, 'The Clouds', because the nation was tossed about on the winds of ill fortune.

60. Samuelson, *LLA*.
61. For a resumé of the fighting techniques of the 1880s, see Paul Thompson, *Isandlwana to Mome; Zulu experience of overt resistance to colonial rule* in *Soldiers of the Queen*, Issue 77, June 1994.
62. On this subject see Jeff Guy, *The destruction and reconstruction of Zulu society* in Shula Marks and Richard Rathbone (eds) *Industrialisation and change in South Africa*, London, 1982.
63. The most detailed treatment of King Solomon's reign is Nicholas Cope's *To Bind the Nation*, Pietermaritzburg, 1993.
64. See Paul La Hausse, *The Dispersal of the Regiments; African Popular Protest in Durban in 1930*, in the *Journal of Natal and Zulu History*, Vol. X, 1987.

Glossary of Zulu Military Terms

Note: in accordance with current orthographic practice, Zulu words are listed alphabetically according to their stem, rather than prefix.

isangoma (pl. *izangoma*): diviner or individual in touch with the spirit world, an intermediary able to intervene with the spirits on behalf of the living, and to detect witchcraft.

umbumbulozo: smaller size of war-shield, introduced among King Cetshwayo's followers in the 1850s, and popular thereafter.

ibutho (pl. *amabutho*): group formed according to the common age of its members; a male or female 'regiment', or a member thereof.

isicoco: a ring of fibre and gum worn bound into the hair on top of the head as the mark of a mature married man.

udibi (pl. *izindibi*): mat-carrier not yet old enough to join the *amabutho*.

induna (pl. *izinduna*): state official appointed to civil or military authority by the king or chief.

isigaba (pl. *izigaba*): division within an *ibutho*, usually consisting of companies who had enrolled at the same place.

ukugiya: to dance a solitary war-dance involving shadow-fighting.

isigodlo (pl. *izigodlo*): that part of a royal homestead set aside for the king's use, or members of the king's household, including girls presented to him as 'tribute', who served him, and whom he could dispose of in marriage.

isihlangu (pl. *izihlangu*): the largest size of regimental war-shield.

ikhanda (pl. *amakhanda*): royal homestead of the king which served as a barracks for the *amabutho*.

ikhehla (pl. *amakhehla*): a mature married man who has donned the headring.

umKhosi: annual festival of 'first-fruits', at which the king and nation are ritually strengthened.

inkosi (pl. *amakhosi*): king or hereditary chief.

ukukleza: to drink milk direct from the udders of a cow, as practised by youths newly enrolled in an *ibutho* – therefore to enlist, or undergo the period of cadetship.

umkhonto: a general name for a spear.

isikhulu (pl. *izikhulu*): a great man of the nation, usually implying one of the hereditary chiefs of the clans who made up the Zulu kingdom.

ilobolo: a gift of cattle handed to the family of the bride by the groom and his family prior to marriage.

isilomo (pl. *izilomo*): a royal favourite of the king, singled out for his patronage; often a great warrior.

impi: a military force of any size; a battle, war or warfare.

inceku (pl. *izinceku*): personal attendant or servant of a king or chief.

insizwa (pl. *izinsizwa*): a young man, not yet married, who has not put on the headring.

umnumzana (pl. *abanumzana*): family head, the head of a household.

umnyama: literally 'blackness', a time of potential spiritual pollution and psychic ill-omen.

intanga: an informal grouping comprising either males or females born within a specific span of four or five years, and who were considered linked because of their common age.

intelezi (pl. *izintelezi*): protective medicines, usually applied by sprinkling.

iviyo (pl. *amaviyo*): company within an *ibutho*.

inyanga (pl. *izinyanga*): a doctor or herbalist.

ukusoma: limited (external) sexual intercourse permitted before marriage (also known as *ukuhlobonga*).

umuthi (pl. *imithi*): medicines, both herbal and substances believed to have the spiritual power to heal or protect.

umuzi (pl. *imizi*): civilian homestead.

Zulu *Amabutho*
From King Shaka to the
Anglo-Zulu War

Any attempt to compile a definitive list of Zulu *amabutho* is fraught with difficulties. Although there is a wealth of source material, it can only be relied upon for the later period: European descriptions of the Zulu kings' armies become more plentiful with increased contact from the 1840s, while the British attempted to compile a list of regiments active in 1879 at the time of the Anglo-Zulu War. Although various scholars – Bryant, Samuelson, Faye – attempted to draw up a list of regiments later in the nineteenth century, working directly with Zulu informants, their sources' memory span at best dimly recalled the events of King Dingane's reign. The rapid expansion of the army, which went hand-in-hand with the state creation process in the 1820s, ensured that a plethora of *amabutho* names are associated with King Shaka; however, it is almost impossible, now, to disentangle the names of *amabutho* proper from the names of *izigaba*, or even the *amakhanda* with which they were associated. Nor does a degree of repetition help; both King Shaka and King Mpande raised regiments called uMbonambi, for example, while Mpande followed Dingane's precedent of naming a (different) regiment uDlambedlu. Similarly, no two sources agree on the exact order in which Shaka's regiments were enrolled.

The following list is therefore a synthesis, based on evidence given by James Stuart's Zulu informants and compared against lists compiled by Bryant, Samuelson, etc. It has been possible to find a considerable measure of agreement between sources for the period from 1828 onward, but that for the Shakan period is offered no more than tentatively. Although dates of formation of the early regiments have been included along with the rest, these should also be treated with caution.

Details of ceremonial costume and shield colours have been included, where known. Since all *amabutho* wore broadly similar costumes, differing usually only in details of headdress, those items common to all have not been listed – earflaps, cowtail body, leg and arm ornaments, and so on. Where shield colours are given, these should also be treated with caution, since it is probable that a regiment may have changed its shields up to three times during its period of active service. Colours for those regiments who fought in 1879 are generally those correct for the Anglo-Zulu War period. Where previous attempts have been made to translate the names of *amabutho* – notably by Samuelson, Faye and Fynney – a synthesis is included here, although it has not been possible to suggest the full subtlety of references implied by the more complex names.

King Shaka's *amabutho*

emBelebeleni Although there are references to an *emBelebele* ('a persistent worry') *ibutho*, this was apparently the name of an *ikhanda*, where a number of senior *amabutho* were quartered, including men 'inherited' from Shaka's father, Senzangakhona. These may have included the **amaWombe** ('a clash of arms') *ibutho* (formed *c.* 1816 from men born 1775–85) and, according to Bryant, the **uNomdayana, amaPhela** ('the cockroaches', 'taken over' from King Zwide kaLanga of the Ndwandwe after Shaka defeated him), the **amaKwenkwe, iziKwembu,** who carried duncoloured shields (Lunguza *JSA* 1) and **iziZimazana** *amabutho*. Lunguza adds a section called **uMpondozobekwapi,** who carried red shields with brown patches (*JSA* 1). Bryant suggests that all of these latter were formed in the period 1821–7, of men born *c.* 1801–7, but Stuart's sources suggest they may have been older.

isiKlebhe Possibly a senior *ibutho* or grouping based at the **isiKlebheni** *ikhanda*, and formed by Senzangakhona. Bryant says formed 1816 of youths born 1790–5. Carried grey shields (Lunguza *JSA* 1).

uFasimba 'The distant blue haze', formed *c.* 1818 from youths born *c.* 1795–8. Carried white shields (Lunguza, *JSA* 1).

isiPhezi 'To stop or hold up', also known as/incorporated with **uMgumanqa** (from a verb meaning to spoil and make stale) and **iNtontela** ('a tear') *amabutho*. The uDlangubo *ibutho* was apparently also added to the iNontela, and the amaGovu to the uDlangubo (Jantshi, *JSA* 1). Bryant says formed 1820–1, from men born *c.* 1789–99, although this may refer to the incorporated regiments, as some sources suggest the original **isiPhezi** were older. According to Lunguza (*JSA* 1) they carried white shields with markings; Mkehlengana (*JSA* 3), whose father Zulu was a member of the **uMgumanqa,** adds that they were white speckled with red or black hairs.

iziYendane Formed following Shaka's raids on the Drakensberg foothills, *c.* 1819, apparently consisting largely of Hlubi men, incorporated after that campaign. Carried red shields (Lunguza, *JSA* 1). Hlubi men wore their hair long, in a style known as *iziyendane*.

uZibolela Also known as uMbonambi, 'those who see or experience sorrow', formed in the period 1821–7, from youths born *c.* 1801–7.

uDlangezwa From *dla*, 'to eat up (as in destroy an enemy)', and *ngezwa*, 'I heard', thereby implying the glorious tales that will be heard of this *ibutho*. Formed *c.* 1823 from youths born *c.* 1802. Carried black shields with 'many' white spots (Lunguza, *JSA* 1).

uHlotane No dates given, but apparently followed uDlangezwa, and therefore must have been formed *c.* 1825.

izimPohlo The following *amabutho* were raised by Shaka, and were brigaded together under the name izimPohlo, 'those who smash'; there are suggestions, however, that this brigading took place later, in Dingane's reign, when the regiments were brought together and based at the *Mgungundlovu* homestead. Bryant says these regiments were formed in the period 1821–6, from youths born 1801–7.

> uGibabanye 'Those who oust', (also known as the uPhoko, millet). Carried black shields with white marks on the side. May have included sections called the uMpofu, who carried dun-coloured shields, and uMnyama, who carried black shields (Lunguza, *JSA* 1).
> uFojisa Carried black shields with white patches 'on the stomach' (Lunguza, *JSA* 1). This regiment included a section called uShoyisa, who carried shields from red cattle with large white markings on the upper legs (Lunguza, *JSA* 1).
> uNgqobolondo Carried black shields speckled with white (Lunguza, *JSA* 1).
> uMfolozi
> uDubinhlangu ('a throwing together of Riet Bucks').

uBhenkenya Also known as iNdabankhulu, 'the big affair'. Carried 'shields of black cattle with white markings on the stomach' (Lunguza, *JSA* 1). No dates given; apparently formed *c.* 1827, and may have been incorporated with iNgcobinga.

iNgcobinga (uJubingqwanga) Formed *c.* 1828 from youths born 1808. There is some confusion regarding the translation of the name uJubingqwanga, which is sometimes said to have derived from *ukujuba*, a royal directive, and *ingqwanga*, the base of a headring. A number of traditions suggest that Shaka ordered a regiment who had donned the headring at too early an age to cut it off. If so, the term in this context almost certainly applied to an earlier regiment, since the iNgcobinga was apparently a regiment of young men. One of Stuart's informants (Magidigidi, *JSA* 2) translates uJubingqwanga in this instance as a species of locust, to whom the **iNgcobinga** were likened. It is therefore interesting to note that the regiment was later called **iziNyosi** – 'the bees'. Carried speckled grey shields (Lunguza, *JSA* 1).

King Dingane's *amabutho*

iziNyosi Formerly Shaka's iNgcobinga.

uDlambedlu 'Those who worry at a thing and eat it up', formed *c.* 1829 from youths born *c.* 1809.

imVokwe 'Those who subjugate others', formed in the mid-1830s from youths born *c.* 1815.

imiKhulutshane 'The stumbling blocks', formed *c.*1833 from youths born *c.* 1813.

iHlaba 'The stabbers', also known as/included sections called **iziNgulut-shane**, and **izinDabakadengizbona** ('I see the affair'), who carried black shields with white spots (Lunguza, *JSA* 1). Formed *c.* 1837 from youths born *c.* 1817.

uKhokothi The name of a snake, formed 1837–8 from youths born *c.* 1817–18.

iNsewane 'The sharp youths', probably formed at the end of Dingane's reign, 1838–40.

Note: although Bryant lists the **Hlomendlini mhlope** ('the white troops armed at home') and **Hlomendlini mnyama** ('the black troops armed at home') as *amabutho*, these were in fact the names of two of King Dingane's *amakhanda*, where a variety of regiments were quartered.

King Mpande's *amabutho*

iNdabakawombe 'The affair (*indaba*) of the ambush, or clash of arms (*wombe*)', formed *c.* 1841 of youths born *c.* 1821. Was incorporated with Dingane's uKhokothi. Two descriptions of its costume survive: G.F. Angas sketched a member of the regiment in the 1840s carrying a white shield, and wearing a headdress consisting of a pad of fur over the crown, with ostrich feathers on top, and a bunch of crane feathers at the back of the head. A clipped ball of dark feathers is attached to the back of the head-band, and there are two large unidentified (eagle?) feathers at the side of the head. Small bunches of lourie feathers are attached to the leopardskin earflaps. By 1879 Fynney (*TZA*) described the uniform as that of a typical married *ibutho*, *ie* otter-skin headband, one or two crane feathers, white shield.

uDlambedlu 'Those who worry at a thing and eat it up', formed *c.* 1843 from youths born 1823, incorporated with Dingane's iNsewane. The uMdlenevu ('the burnt sides') and iNgwegwe ('the hooked stick') *amabutho* were also added to it. In 1879 said to have worn otter-skin headband, one or two crane feathers in otter-skin headband, white shields with black or red spots (Fynney, *TZA*).

izinGulube 'The wild pigs' (also iNkone, 'the black and white pigs'); formed *c.* 1845 from youths born *c.* 1825. Seems to have been linked to the uDlambedlu; may have been incorporated with it to keep up the numbers. Fynney gives the same uniform (*TZA*).

iSangqu 'The hunters' (also known as amaShishi, from their war-cry 'Shi! Shi! Shi! Shi-shi-shi!' which was derived from the sound made when setting a dog on the chase). Formed *c.* 1848 from youths born *c.* 1828. Sketched as a young regiment by Angas in the 1840s, they are wearing the *amaphovela* headdress and bunches of *sakabuli* feathers on either side of the head. Shields probably black. By 1879 Fynney (*TZA*) gives otter-skin headband, *amaphovela*, white shields.

uThulwana Named after a BaSotho chief, Thulare. Also known as ama-Boza from *amaboza 'nkomo ngotuli*, 'those who covered cattle with dust (*ie* looted and drove them off)' One section was known as iNhlambamasoka, after the emLambongwenya *ikhanda*, where it *kleza*'d, and which included a number of royal princes, Cetshwayo among them. Formed *c.* 1850, from youths born *c.* 1830. Incorporated with it were iNkonkoni ('the wildebeest', formed *c.* 1852), and iNdlondlo ('the adult crested mamba', formed *c.* 1853). At 'Ndondakusuka in 1856 the uThulwana are said to have carried black shields with white spots on lower side; by 1879 carried white shields with small red marks. Ceremonial uniform in 1879 consisted of otter-skin headband, *sakabuli* feathers on either side of head, white ostrich feathers on top of head, surmounted by crane feather (Fynney, *TZA*). Samuelson (*LLA*) adds that the ostrich feathers were at the side of the head, pointing back. Mpatshana (*JSA* 3) does not mention ostrich feathers, but confirms other items He adds that this regiment also wore a number of brass rings on the right forearm. Regimental war-cry was 'Mina! Mina! Mina! Hhahe!'

uDlokwe (or uDloko) 'The young crested mamba', formed *c.* 1855 from youths born *c.* 1835. According to Maxibana (*JSA* 2), carried red shields at 'Ndondakusuka in 1856, and wore a headdress consisting of a row of mixed black and white ostrich feathers. By 1879 Fynney describes their headdress as consisting of an otter-skin headband with one crane feather at front, and their shields as red with white patches, or plain white. Chant: '!Hogo! Hogo! Hogo!'

Note: it is not entirely clear which *amabutho* had married and donned the *isicoco* by 1879, although the above regiments appear to have done so and – with the possible exception of the **iNdluyengwe** – the following *amabutho* do not.

uDududu From the sound '*du! du! du!*' made by troops rushing forward. Formed c. 1857 from youths born c. 1837. The **iMbube** ('lion') were apparently incorporated with them. According to Fynney (*TZA*), wore otter-skin headband with *sakabuli* feathers on either side, and carried black shields with white spots.

iQwa 'The Frost', formed c. 1860 from youths born c. 1840. Possibly incorporated into **uDududu**. According to Fynney (*TZA*), wore leopardskin headbands with large bunch of black ostrich feathers surmounted by white ostrich feathers. May have incorporated **iNsukamngeni** (named as a reference to the Mgeni river in Natal, where Mpande halted during 'the breaking of the rope') who were of a similar age-group and, according to Fynney (*TZA*), wore the same uniform but with black shields with white markings low down.

uMxapho 'The mongrels or lapping dogs', also known as the **iMpunga**, from *umpung'ongafiyo*, which Faye translates as 'the greyheads that die not' but, since the men were not old in 1879, probably refers rather to the colour of their shields. This was a praise-name won at Nyezane in 1879. Incorporated with the **uHlawyi**, 'a shower of shot'. Formed c. 1860 from youths born c. 1840. Samuelson suggests that the **uMxapho** were incorporated into the **uDududu**, but in fact the two regiments functioned separately (the **uDududu** fighting at Isandlwana, for example, whilst the majority of the **uMxapho** were at Nyezane on the same day) and were probably *uphalane* (i.e. distinct units who were nonetheless considered closely related). Fynney (*TZA*) thought they wore leopardskin headbands, *sakabuli* feathers on either side of the head, black and white ostrich feathers at front of head and carried black shields, occasionally spotted. Mpatshana (*JSA* 3) thought they carried shields of any colour, but confirms the ostrich-feather headdress. In fact Fynney's information regarding the shield colours was out of date, and presumably referred to an earlier issue – the *impunga* title, linked by Faye to this *ibutho*, refers to a pattern of cattle hide, a pale off-white ground flecked lightly all over with brown or black hairs to give an overall grey impression. The **uMxapho** were heavily engaged in the skirmish at oNdini of 3 July 1879, and seem to have used the nearby kwaNodwengu *ikhanda* as their base for that operation. After the battle of Ulundi the following day the British extensively looted kwaNodwengu, and numbers of these *impunga* shields were taken as trophies, confirming the connection. Zibhebhu kaMapitha was a member of the *uMxapho* and commanded them on 3 July. The *uMxapho* had also fought at Gingindlovu, after which they adopted the cry 'ha, ha, ha, ha! It dug! It dug! We buried it (i.e. the British) in the ground at Gingindlovu!' (Mpatshana).

uMbonambi 'Those who behold or experience sorrow'. Incorporated with the **iNkonyanebomvu**, 'the red calf'. Formed c. 1862 from youths born c. 1842. According to Fynney (*TZA*), wore leopardskin headbands, with one plume of *sakabuli* feathers on top of the head. Samuelson (*LLA*) adds ostrich feathers upright on the head, and bunches of lourie feathers at the side; this latter may, however, have been a distinction granted after Isandlwana, where this *ibutho* was recognised as having been first to penetrate the British line. Fynney gives the shields as black or black with white spots; others also remember their shields as being spotted but the balance of colours – whether white or black predominated - is not clear. In fact the two colours seem to have been equally matched, a heavy mottling of small spots and blotches over a contrasting colour (rather than a pattern with larger, more distinct spots). One surviving shield which may be associated with the **uMbonambi** and which perhaps confirms this impression is white speckled with a large number of small dark spots which run together in places.

uNokhenke 'A battle formation running out of control' (various rendered 'the dividers' or 'the skirmishers'). Formed c. 1865 from youths born c. 1845. According to Fynney (*TZA*), wore leopardskin headbands, *sakabuli* feathers on either side of the head, and carried black shields with white spots. The battlefield visitors' centre at Isandlwana includes an *umbumbuluzo* shield recovered from the field during the building of the St. Vincent's mission in 1880; since this was built on ground covered by either the **uNokhenke** or **uKhandempemvu** *amabutho* during the battle it may reflect the shield colours of one or the other. This surviving shield is dark brown with a large white patch on the centre of the left face. At least two other shields, apparently dating to 1879, have survived elsewhere which display remarkably similar patterning, and strongly suggest a regimental uniformity.

iNdluyengwe 'The leopard's fine reddish markings', formed c. 1867 from youths born c. 1847. Incorporated by King Cetshwayo into the **uThulwana** c. 1877. According to Fynney (*TZA*) wore leopardskin headbands with black ostrich feathers at the front, surmounted by several long white ostrich feathers. Samuelson (*LLA*) adds that the ostrich feathers were on either side of the head pointing back. Fynney notes that their shields were black with large white spots on the lower half, although this information may have been out of date and related to the period before they were incorporated into the **uThulwana** (with whom they were deployed in 1879). It is possible that they were allowed to marry upon incorporation, and therefore had adopted the head-ring after

Fynney had made his notes and before the outbreak of war in 1879. Certainly the assumption of a social status, which was otherwise ahead of their years, was a factor in the resentment of the younger *amabutho,* which led to the clash at the First Fruits ceremony in late 1877. If the **iNdluyengwe** were newly married it is highly likely they were carrying similar shields to the **uThulwana** in 1879 and it is perhaps significant that after the battle of Rorke's Drift British observers noted that the Zulu dead all seemed to be married men carrying white shields.

uKhandempemvu 'Head with black and white markings', also known as **uMcijo**, 'the red needle pointed at both ends'. A large *ibutho*, which incorporated sections known as the **uMtulisazwe** ('to cause the land to be at peace') and **iNgqakamatshe** ('the catchers of stones'). Formed c. 1868 from youths born c. 1848. According to Mtshapi (*JSA* 4), who served with the regiment, the ceremonial headdress consisted of a leopardskin headband and *amaphovela*, with bunches of *sakabuli* feathers fixed in the headband. This is confirmed by Fynney (*TZA*) who says that the *sakabuli* feathers were at the side of the head. Mpatshana (*JSA* 3) adds that the **uMtulisazwe** had black cowtails attached to the tips of the *amaphovela* (confirmed by Mtshapi) and wore wide belts of white cow-hide. Mtshapi says that the shields were either black or dark brown with white markings (large spots, or patches down one side) – see also the comment on the **uNokhenke** above – although black shields with a large white patch across the centre and even white shields were added by Cetshwayo. It is possible these different shields were grouped together among companies formed from men living in particular districts so that companies had a degree of uniformity even if the *ibutho* as a whole did not. Regimental war-cry, '*Izulu!*' According to Mpatshana (*JSA* 3), one man of the **uKhandempemvu** would lead a chant with 'It is not to be seen; the hornbill is not to be seen. Do you burn the whiskers from the buffalo? Do you burn them? We catch the rocks of the sky!' The rest would respond with 'Catch! At the place of Hisi!'. The exact meaning is obscure, but apparently relates to a campaign against the Xhosa paramount, Hintsa. The reference to 'rocks of the sky' is apparently an allusion to treating bullets fired against them as if they were nothing more than hailstones. The **uMtulisazwe**'s chant was 'You were beaten down by the axe that strikes down! *Nhla! Nhla! Nhla!*'

iNgobamakhosi 'The humblers of kings', formed c. 1872 from youths born c. 1853. Leopardskin headband with white, black or red *amaphovela*, according to Fynney (*TZA*). Mpatshana (*JSA* 3), who served with this *ibutho*, adds a single bunch of *sakabuli* feathers on top of the head. Samuelson adds white ostrich feathers upright on head. Shields are variously described as black, red or spotted – they may indeed have been mixed but surviving examples which may relate to this *ibutho* are usually brown in colour, varying from almost black to a golden dun-colour. Regimental war-cry was '*Hohho! Hohho! Hohho!*' After Isandlwana they apparently adopted the chant '*Iya! Iya! Iya! O ho, ho, ho*, the lightening of the sky. *Tshitshilizi, tshitshilizi!* The sky is dangerous!'. The 'lightening of the sky' – *imbane wezulu* – was a reference to British rockets; the **iNgobamakhosi** had apparently over-run the Royal Artillery rocket battery at Isandlwana, and were later on the receiving end of rocket fire at both Khambula and Ulundi.

Note: both Bryant and Samuelson list an **amaPhela** *ibutho*, formed between 1846-51, although this does not appear on other lists. Bryant provides a possible solution to the mystery as he suggests it was broken up and sections added to the **iNdabakawombe** and **uDlambedlu**.

King Cetshwayo's *amabutho*

uVe 'The fly-catcher bird' (an allusion to their energy and youth) or **oLandandlovu**, 'the fetcher of the elephant'. Formed c. 1875–8 from youths born c. 1855–8. Incorporated on the eve of the Anglo-Zulu War with the **iNgobamakhosi**; Mangwanana Mchunu (*SOTQ* 74) who served with the regiment recalled that he carried a red shield with white markings in 1879; probably their shields were various shades of brown, after the manner of the **iNgobamakhosi**.

Note: a cadet *ibutho* was *kleza*'ing at the time of the Anglo-Zulu War; this regiment was *buta*'d by Cetshwayo on his return from exile as the **uFalaza**, 'the clouds of heaven', implying the Zulus were being tossed about hither and thither. One section was known as **uMsizi**, 'the smell of gunpowder', a reference to the conflict of 1879. These cadets were carrying mats for their elders during the Anglo-Zulu War and were therefore on the periphery of the fighting. *Amabutho* enrolled post-1879 have not been included in this list; although subsequent Zulu kings continued to enrol *amabutho* their recruitment – particularly in the troubled post-war years – was limited to royalist supporters and was not universal as it had been prior to 1879. Although some were notionally attached to royal homesteads there were no longer the great *amakhanda* to serve them as barracks, nor royal herds large enough to supply them with shields. Indeed, any attempt to marshal them as military forces in the manner of the days of independence were regarded with suspicion by the colonial authorities. Nevertheless, King Dinuzulu fielded some of the later *amabutho* as military units during the Zulu Civil War and 1888 Rebellion.

Most of King Mpande's *amabutho* were still functioning in 1879, although the older ones were of limited military value. Elements of the **iNdabakawombe** and **uDlambedlu** were kept back at oNdini by King Cetshwayo as a reserve, probably with other elderly men who had answered the muster; most of the *amabutho* younger than these were fully engaged in the fighting, however.

Principal Zulu Campaigns from King Shaka to the Anglo-Zulu War

The exact chronology of the campaigns fought in the early days of the Zulu kingdom is uncertain due to an almost total absence of written records. For this reason only those major campaigns of King Shaka's reign, whose dates can be given with a degree of confidence, have been listed. It should be noted that conflict in the Zululand area began at the end of the eighteenth or beginning of the nineteenth century, preceding the rise of Shaka by at least a decade. A number of small campaigns were fought by the Zulu over the period *c.* 1817–22, which resulted in the incorporation of their immediate neighbours in Shaka's kingdom; the major campaigns listed below were fought against the background of such continuing conflict.

c. **1816–18** Shaka assumes control of the Zulu chiefdom and begins to emerge as a significant political and military figure in his own right.

1818–19 At least two major campaigns were fought between the Zulu and the Ndwandwe chiefdom of Zwide kaLanga, whose heartland lay in northern Zululand, south of the Phongolo river. Tradition has it that the first campaign involved heavy fighting around KwaGqokli hill, south of the White Mfolozi river. This campaign was apparently indecisive, and led to a greater clash, which was resolved on the headwaters of the Mhlatuze river. The Ndwandwe were defeated and Zwide fled Zululand.

1824 The Zulu mount a raid into southern Natal, directed against the amaMpondo people.

1826 Elements of the Ndwandwe return to Zululand under Zwide's son Sikhunyana. They are defeated by Shaka at eNdolowane hill, in northern Zululand.

1827 Campaign to subjugate Chief Bheje of the Khumalo in central Zululand.

1828 Second campaign against the amaMpondo; the *ihlambo* campaign, the ritual 'washing of the spears' following the end of the mourning ceremonies for the death of Shaka's mother, Nandi, in August 1827.

1828 The oBhalule campaign, against the followers of Soshangane living along the Oliphants river in southern Mozambique. While the army was away on this campaign, King Shaka was assassinated, and succeeded by King Dingane.

1832 First expedition against the Ndebele kingdom of Mzilikazi ka-Mashobane in the eastern Transvaal.

1837 Second expedition against the Ndebele (note: there is some confusion regarding the number and exact dates of Dingane's campaigns against Mzilikazi).

1838 6 February: Massacre of Boer-leader Piet Retief and his followers at eMgungundlovu.

17 February: Zulu attacks on Trekker encampments in Drakensberg foothills.

10 April: Boer force routed at eThaleni in central Zululand.

17 April: Natal settlers and their African allies routed at 'battle of the Thukela', near Thukela mouth.

13 August: Second Zulu attack on encampments in Drakensberg foothills repulsed.

16 December: Zulus defeated at Ncome (Blood) River.

27 December: Boer force narrowly avoids entrapment at White Mfolozi.

1839 'The breaking of the Rope' – Prince Mpande abandons King Dingane and appeals for Boer help to defeat him.

1840 30 January: battle of amaQongqo – Mpande defeats Dingane.

c. **1852** Zulu raid into Swaziland.

1856 Civil war between followers of Prince Mbuyazi kaMpande (iziQoza) and Prince Cetshwayo kaMpande (uSuthu). Decisive battle at 'Ndonda-kusuka, near Thukela mouth, on 2 December, leaves uSuthu victorious.

1879 11 January: Outbreak of Anglo-Zulu War.

22 February: Zulu forces defending coastal area are defeated by Colonel Pearson's column at Nyezane. Main Zulu army defeats Centre Column at Isandlwana, but part of the reserve is repulsed during the mopping-up operation at Rorke's Drift.

February: Low intensity fighting around Eshowe in the south and Hlobane in the north.

12 March: British supply convoy overrun at Ntombe River.

28 March: British attack at Hlobane Mountain repulsed.

29 March: Main army defeated at Khambula.

2 April: Zulus defending coastal sector defeated at Gingindlovu.

June: Fresh British invasion of Zululand begins in the face of low-intensity resistance.

4 July: Zulu army defeated and dispersed at Ondini (Ulundi).

August/September: King Cetshwayo captured and exiled; British suppress remaining resistance within Zululand.

Senior Zulu Commanders 1818–79

King Shaka kaSenzangakhona Most traditions agree that Shaka was a talented general who frequently commanded the Zulu army in the field, particularly during major campaigns, such as those against the Ndwandwe in 1818–19 and 1826.

Mdlaka kaNcidi Head of the emGazini, a collateral lineage to the Zulu royal house, Shaka's most trusted commander, who acted as second-in-command when the king accompanied his forces, but commanded a number of distant expeditions himself, notably towards the end of Shaka's reign.

Ndlela kaSompisi Rose to a position of rank under Shaka, was appointed *induna* of the Ntuli people, and became the Zulu army's senior general when Mdlaka was killed in the coup following Shaka's assassination. Ndlela was one of the most powerful *izinduna* within Zululand during King Dingane's reign, and is thought to have commanded the Zulu army in the attacks on Mzilikazi and the war with the Boers. He commanded Dingane's forces in the battle at amaQongqo, and was apparently killed by Dingane following the defeat.

Nongalaza kaNondela Chief of the Nyandweni section of the amaQwabe, a senior commander under Dingane who was present at the battle of the Thukela, and subsequently became Mpande's commander-in-chief.

Ntshingwayo kaMahole Chief of the Khoza, an important adviser of King Cetshwayo, who was entrusted with the command of the main army during the early stages of the Anglo-Zulu War. He commanded at Isandlwana and Khambula, and may have been present at oNdini (Ulundi).

Mnyamana kaNgqengelele Chief of the Buthelezi, and one of the most powerful *izikhulu* in the kingdom, Mnyamana was King Cetshwayo's senior adviser. He accompanied the army during the Khambula campaign as the king's representative, an indication of the importance the Zulu placed on that expedition.

Mavumengwana kaNdlela Joint commander with Ntshingwayo during the Isandlwana campaign, a son of Ndlela kaSompisi. Also present at Gingindlovu.

274

Godide kaNdlela Chief of the Ntuli, commanded the coastal forces in early 1879, defeated by Colonel Pearson at Nyezane. An elder brother of Mavumengwana and son of Ndlela.

Somopho kaZikhala Thembu lineage head and senior commander on the coast during the Eshowe relief expedition; defeated by Lord Chelmsford at Gingindlovu.

Zibhebhu kaMapitha Young but powerful *isikhulu*, head of the Mandlakazi section of the Zulu royal house. Widely thought to have been one of the most original and dynamic commanders in the Anglo-Zulu War; commanded the scouts during the Isandlwana campaign, and was responsible for almost trapping Buller's horsemen on 3 July.

Prince Dabulamanzi kaMpande Younger brother of Cetshwayo who, through circumstance, found himself in command of the reserve at Isandlwana, and led them to attack Rorke's Drift. Also present at Gingindlovu.

Prince Ziwedu kaMpande Brother of Cetshwayo, who acted as his representative at the battle of oNdini (Ulundi).

Prince Mbilini waMswati Exiled member of Swazi royal house who gave allegiance to King Cetshwayo, and proved a daring guerrilla leader in the northern theatre during the 1879 war. Killed in action.

Bibliography

Baldwin, W.C., *African Hunting and Adventure*, London, 1894.

Ballard, C. *John Dunn: The White Chief of Zululand*, Craighall, 1985.

Barter, C. (under the pseudonym A Plain Woman) *Alone Among the Zulus*, London, *c.* 1879.

Bennett, Lt.-Col. I.H.W., *Eyewitness in Zululand: The Campaign Reminiscences of Col. W.A. Dunne, 1877–1881*, London, 1989.

Binns, C.T., *The Last Zulu King*, London, 1963.

Binns, C.T., *Dinuzulu*, 1968.

Binns, C.T., *The Warrior People*, London, 1975.

Bourquin, S., and Filter, H., (eds), *Paulina Dlamini: Servant of Two Kings*, Pietermaritzburg and Durban, 1986.

Braadvedt, H.P., *Roaming Zululand With a Native Commissioner*, Pietermaritzburg, 1949.

Browne, Dr D. Blair, *Surgical Experiences in the Zulu and Transvaal Wars, 1879 and 1881*, Edinburgh, 1883.

Bryant, A.T. *Zulu–English Dictionary*, Pietermaritzburg, 1905.

Bryant, A.T., *The Zulu People: As They Were Before the White Man Came*, Pietermaritzburg, 1929.

Bryant, A.T., *Zulu Medicine and Medicine-men*, Cape Town, 1966.

Bryant, A.T., *Olden Times in Zululand and Natal*, London, 1929.

Castle, I., and Knight, I., *Fearful Hard Times: The Siege and Relief of Eshowe*, London, 1994.

Child, D. (ed.), *The Zulu War Journal of Colonel Henry Harford, CB*, Pietermaritzburg, 1978.

Clarke, S. (ed.), *Invasion of Zululand, 1879*, Houghton, 1979.

Clarke, S. (ed), *Zululand at War 1879*, Houghton, 1984.

Cope, N., *To Bind the Nation*, Pietermaritzburg, 1993.

Dawnay, G.C., *Campaigns: Zulu 1879, Egypt 1882, Suakin 1885*, London (?), *c.* 1886.

Du Buisson, L., *The White Man Cometh*, Johannesburg, 1987.

Duminy, A., and Ballard, C., *The Anglo-Zulu War; New Perspectives*, Pietermaritzburg, 1981.

Dunn, J., (edited by Moodie, D.C.F.), *Cetywayo and the Three Generals*, Pietermaritzburg, 1886.

Emery, F., *The Red Soldier*, London, 1979.

Fuze, M., (edited and translated by H.C. Lugg and A.T. Cope), *The Black People and Whence They Came: A Zulu View*, Pietermaritzburg and Durban, 1979.
Fynney, F.B., *The Zulu Army and Zulu Headmen; Published by Direction of the Lieutenant-General Commanding*, Pietermaritzburg, 1878.

Gardiner, A., *Narrative of a Journey to the Zoolu Country*, London, 1836.
Gibson, J.Y., *The Story of the Zulus*, London, 1911.
Guy, J., *The Destruction of the Zulu Kingdom*, London, 1979.

Holme, N., *The Silver Wreath*, London, 1979.

Isaacs, N., *Travels and Adventure in Eastern Africa (Natal)*, London, 1836.

Knight, I., *Brave Men's Blood: The Epic of the Zulu War*, London, 1990.
Knight, I., *British Forces in Zululand 1879*, London, 1991.
Knight, I., *Nothing Remains but to Fight: The Defence of Rorke's Drift*, London, 1993.
Knight, I., *The Zulus*, London, 1989.
Knight, I., *Zulu: The Battles of Isandlwana and Rorke's Drift*, London, 1992.
Knight, I. (ed.) *By the Orders of the Great White Queen: Campaigning in Zululand through the Eyes of the British Soldier, 1879*, London, 1992.
Knight, I. (ed.), *There Will Be An Awful Row At Home About This*, Shoreham-By-Sea, 1987.
Knight, I., and Castle, I., *The Zulu War: Then and Now*, London, 1993.

Laband, J., *Kingdom in Crisis: The Zulu Response to the British Invasion of 1879*, Manchester and New York, 1992.
Laband, J., *Fight Us in the Open*, Pietermaritzburg and Ulundi, 1985.
Laband, J., *The Battle of Ulundi*, Pietermaritzburg and Ulundi, 1988.
Laband, J., and Thompson, P.S., *War Comes to Umvoti: The Natal–Zululand Border, 1878–79*, Durban, 1980.
Laband, J., and Thompson, P.S., with Henderson, S., *The Buffalo Border 1879: The Anglo-Zulu War in Northern Natal*, Durban, 1983.
Laband, J., and Thompson, P.S., *Field Guide to the War in Zululand and the Defence of Natal, 1879* (revised edition), Pietermaritzburg, 1987.

Laband, J., and Thompson, P.S., *Kingdom and Colony at War*, Pietermaritzburg and Constantia, 1990.

Laband, J., and Wright, J., *King Cetshwayo kaMpande*, Pietermaritzburg and Ulundi, 1983.

Laband, J., and Matthews, J., *The Battle of Isandlwana*, Pietermaritzburg and Ulundi, 1992.

Leslie, D., *Among the Zulus and Amatongas*, Edinburgh, 1875.

Ludlow, W.R., *Zululand and Cetewayo*, London, 1882.

Lugg, H.C., *Historic Natal and Zululand*, Pietermaritzburg, 1979.

Lugg, H.C., *A Natal Family Looks Back*, Durban, 1970.

Maclean, C.R., (edited by Stephen Grey), *The Natal Papers of John Ross*, Pietermaritzburg, 1992.

Marks, S., and Atmore, A. (eds), *Economy and Society in Pre-Industrial South Africa*, London, 1980.

Marks, S., and Rathbone, R. (eds), *Industrialisation and Change in South Africa*, London, 1982.

Mitford, B., *Through the Zulu Country: Its Battlefields and Its People*, London, 1883; and with an Introduction by Ian Knight, London, 1992.

Molyneux, W.C.F., *Campaigning in South Africa and Egypt*, London, 1896.

Moodie, D.C.F., (edited by John Laband), *Moodie's Zulu War*, Cape Town, 1988.

Morris, D.R., *The Washing of the Spears, The Rise and Fall of the Zulu Nation*, London, 1966.

Mynors, A.C.B., *Letters and Diary*, Margate, 1879.

Norris-Newman, C., *In Zululand with the British throughout the War of 1879*, London, 1880; and London, 1988.

Pieres, J.B. (ed.), *Before and After Shaka*, Grahamstown, 1981.

Pieres, J.B., *The House of Phalo*, Johannesburg, 1981.

Samuelson, R.C., *Long, Long Ago*, Durban, 1929.

Schreuder, D.M., *Gladstone and Kruger: Liberal Government and Colonial 'Home Rule', 1880–1885*, London and Toronto, 1969.

Smail, J.L., *From the Land of the Zulu Kings*, Durban, 1979.

Stuart, J., and Malcolm, D. (eds), *The Diary of Henry Francis Fynn*, Pietermaritzburg, 1950.

Summers, R., and Pagden, L.W., *The Warriors*, Cape Town, 1970.

Vijn, Cornelius (edited and translated by Rev. J.W. Colenso), *Cetshwayo's*

Dutchman: Being the Private Journal of a White Trader in Zululand during the British Invasion, 1879, London, 1880; and London, 1988.

War Office, *Narrative of Operations Connected With The Zulu War of 1879*, London, 1881; and London, 1989.

War Office, *Precis of Information concerning Zululand with a map prepared by the Intelligence Division*, London, 1895.

Webb, C. de B., and Wright, J.B. (eds), *A Zulu King Speaks: Statements Made by Cetshwayo kaMpande on the History and Customs of his People*, Pietermaritzburg and Durban, 1978.

Webb, C. de B., and Wright, J.B. (eds), *The James Stuart Archive of Recorded Oral Evidence Relating To The History of the Zulu and Neighbouring Peoples*, Pietermaritzburg and Durban, Vols 1–4, 1976, 1979, 1982, 1986.

Webb, C. de B. (ed.), 'A Zulu Boy's Recollections of the Zulu War', *Natalia* VIII, December 1978.

Wood, Sir E., *From Midshipman to Field Marshal*, London, 1906. 'E and H.W.', *Soldiers of the Cross in Zululand*, London, 1906.

Contemporary Newspapers and Magazines

Blackwoods Magazine (1879)
The Graphic (1879)
Illustrated London News (1879)
The Lancet (1879)
Natal Magazine (1879)
Natal Mercury (1879 and 1929)
Natal Witness (1879 and 1929)
North Devon Herald (1879)
The Standard (1879)
The Times (1879)
The Times of Natal (1879)
United Services Magazine (1894)

Modern Journals

Journal of African History
Journal of Natal and Zulu History
Journal of the Society for Army Historical Research
Natalia
Natal Museum Journal of Humanities
Soldiers of the Queen (Journal of the Victorian Military Society)
South African Military History Society Journal

Official Documents

British Parliamentary Papers

Private or Unpublished Papers

Carroll, G., Zulu War diary (private collection).

Chelmsford, Lord F., Papers, National Army Museum, London.

Notes on shield colours compiled by the department of Bantu Administration, 1961, possession of Mr S. Bourquin.

Robarts, W., Letters, 1879, family possession.

Sparks, Col. H., *Chelmsford's Ultimatum to King Cetewayo*, Killie Campbell Library, Durban.

Stafford, W., Accounts of Isandlwana in Talana Museum.

Symons, F., Papers, Killie Campbell Africana Library.

War Office files, 1879.

Index

Books on the Anglo-Zulu War
BY IAN KNIGHT

BRAVE MEN'S BLOOD
The Epic of the Zulu War, 1879
282 x 222mm, 200 pages, 270 contemporary
photographs and engravings
ISBN 0-947898-95-6

'BY THE ORDERS OF THE GREAT WHITE QUEEN'
Campaigning in Zululand Through the Eyes of
the British Soldier, 1879
222 x 141mm, 272 pages, 16 pages of illustrations
ISBN 1-85367-122-3

NOTHING REMAINS BUT TO FIGHT
The Defence of Rorke's Drift, 1879
282 x 222mm, 168 pages, illustrated throughout,
with 8 pages in colour
ISBN 1-85367-137-1

FEARFUL HARD TIMES
The Siege and Relief of Eshowe, 1879
by Ian Castle and Ian Knight
240 x 159mm, 256 pages, 67 halftones,
18 drawings, 8 maps
ISBN 1-85367-180-0

Books on the Anglo-Zulu War published by Greenhill Books

BLOOD ON THE PAINTED MOUNTAIN
Zulu Victory and Defeat, Hlobane and Kambula, 1879
by Ron Lock
240 x 159mm, 224 pages, 80 halftones, 13 maps. ISBN 1-85367-201-7

CETSHWAYO'S DUTCHMAN
by Cornelius Vijn
203 x 130mm, 216 pages, with 8 contemporary engravings.
ISBN 1-85367-007-3

NARRATIVE OF THE FIELD OPERATIONS
CONNECTED WITH THE ZULU WAR OF 1879
240 x 159mm, 192 pages plus 2 fold-outs, 14 maps and plans.
ISBN 1-85367-041-3

THE ROAD TO ISANDHLWANA
Colonel Anthony Durnford in Natal and Zululand, 1873–1879
by R.W.F. Droogleever
222 x 141mm, 192 pages, 57 illustrations, 17 maps. ISBN 1-85367-118-5

SHAKA ZULU
The Rise of the Zulu Empire
by E. A. Ritter
222 x 141mm, 412 pages, 12 pages of plates. ISBN 0-947898-99-9

THE SOUTH AFRICAN CAMPAIGN, 1879
by J. P. Mackinnon and S. H. Shadbolt
NEW INDEX BY JOHN YOUNG
272 x 201mm, 384 pages, 62 portrait photographs, 2 maps.
ISBN 1-85367-203-3

THEY FELL LIKE STONES
Battles and Casualties of the Zulu War, 1879
by John Young
INTRODUCTION BY KENNETH GRIFFITH
222 x 141mm, 224 pages, 120 illustrations. ISBN 1-85367-096-0

THROUGH THE ZULU COUNTRY
Its Battlefields and People
by Bertram Mitford
INTRODUCTION BY IAN KNIGHT
222 x 141mm, 288 pages, 19 illustrations. ISBN 1-85367-116-9